CLASSICAL EVANGELICAL
ESSAYS IN
OLD TESTAMENT INTERPRETATION

CLASSICAL EVANGELICAL ESSAYS IN OLD TESTAMENT INTERPRETATION

edited by

Walter C. Kaiser, Jr.
Associate Professor of Old Testament
Trinity Evangelical Divinity School

BAKER BOOK HOUSE
Grand Rapids, Michigan

ISBN: 0-8010-5314-5

First printing, June 1972
Second printing, September 1973
Third printing, May 1976
Fourth printing, May 1979

PHOTOLITHOPRINTED BY CUSHING - MALLOY, INC.
ANN ARBOR, MICHIGAN, UNITED STATES OF AMERICA
1979

IN APPRECIATION

FOR

THE LABORS OF ALL THE SAINTS
who wrote such articles as contained here

AND FOR

THE HERITAGE OF CHRISTIAN PARENTS
who first directed me to the Scriptures.

CONTENTS

INTRODUCTION

It is truly amazing to notice how many Old Testament issues currently being raised by Biblical scholarship, whether it be evangelical or not, are stated as if they were totally unaware of some of the finest moments in Old Testament scholarship. This collection of readings attempts to recapture a few samples of these classical essays. They all share in common an evangelical theological stance, a feature which enhanced their ability to probe more deeply and openly into the issues contained herein. Insofar as they were able to penetrate to the truth of the matter, their essays remain permanently useful and instructive.

With the publication of these essays, we lay down two challenges. The first is a challenge for all non-evangelicals and teachers of religion to renew their dialog with evangelical literature. Evangelical voices and positions ought to be represented in at least some of the collateral readings of the religion courses in all true liberally educated men, otherwise the risk of provincialism and indoctrination of students to those views favored by the teacher is extremely high. For decades on end, evangelicals have been requiring their students and readers to consult and digest a wide spectrum of theological positions only to be disappointed by the all too frequent provincialism of non-evangelicals. No other field of study has demonstrated this point more dramatically than the field of Biblical studies. May this convenient assembly of the fourteen best evangelical essays in the field of Old Testament studies prove helpful in remedying that situation. Even though these essays do not form a consolidated case or a single hypothesis, they do allow fair-minded men to examine a methodology and assess the results on some selected key issues.

Our second challenge is to the emerging group of young evangelical laymen and scholars. While there has been a truly revolutionary assault of entrenched positions founded on less than assured results and shattered philosophical bases, nevertheless it is extremely profitable to retrace the methods and results of that evangelical heritage. If evangelicals continue to work in isolation or ignorance of this heritage, they shall waste much of their time solving problems already completed by another generation and a situation will obtain which will be similar to that of the days of the last world war when scholars working on opposite sides of the battle lines often reduplicated each other's efforts in total ignorance of what other men were doing because of the conditions of those days.

Naturally, this is not a call to a blind acceptance of all that has been written simply because this editor labels the writers as evangelical. They too must be critically evaluated. Their style is vigorous, their freedom exhilarating and their conclusions are refreshing.

The three essays selected for the Pentateuch take up the vexing questions of the meaning of the genealogies of Genesis 5 and 11, the disclaimer of the patriarch's use of the divine name Yahweh (Jehovah) and the law-grace question particularly as it centers around the Christian's use of the ten commandments.

Robert Dick Wilson calls our attention to a possible meaning of the author's words in the Joshua 10:12-14 passage, and Patrick Fairbairn evaluates the permanent meaning of the words which obviously are conditioned by temporal, historical, and cultural references.

Four essays on the poetical books set forth options in interpretation which deserve greater visibility in our day, e.g., the shepherd-hypothesis of the Song of Songs; the theology of the Psalms of cursing, and the integrating key to an interpretation of life as set forth so effectively in J. Stafford Wright's article on Ecclesiastes.

In the prophetical books, we limited ourselves to two issues: the Isaiah 7 prediction, and the servant problem. The new covenant theme with its key problem of the relationship of the Old Testament to the New Testament is developed in the final section of Old Testament Biblical Theology. These essays do not obtain the predictive element at the expense of the historical or vice versa; neither do they lay claim to that most impossible hermeneutic of "double meaning" or "double fulfillment." Their single historical meaning continues by means of a corporate identity into the future. Even the problem of continuity/discontinuity between the Old Testament and the New Testament receives a bold advance under the careful inspection of E. W. Hengstenberg. How did we ever lose the answers he gave here?

Finally, two of the greatest hindrances to a free use of the Old Testament by students and laymen interested in religion are included here to facilitate this last hurdle: viz., Old Testament Ethics and Immortality. These two essays are landmark decisions in an area filled with great pitfalls.

The editor's indebtedness to these writers is enormous. They, though personally unknown to him, and often having long since departed this world, yet continue to speak to him as they point to the single authoritative meaning of the Biblical text. May he share his indebtness by inviting many other students and teachers to join with him in studying one of the richest series of lectures he has yet found on Old Testament interpretation as represented by these fourteen essays.

Special thanks are hereby tendered to Cornelius Zylstra, editor of Baker Book House for his ready assistance and to F. F. Bruce, editor of *Evangelical Quarterly,* who along with J. Stafford Wright have kindly granted their permission to reprint the article on Ecclesiastes.

W. C. Kaiser, Jr.

Part I
PENTATEUCH

Was Adam born in 4004 B.C. as Bishops Usher and Lightfoot contended? (Bishop Lightfoot actually refined the date and found that Adam was created on October 23, at nine A.M. forty-fifth meridian time! This led Brewster to quip, "Closer than this, as a cautious scholar, the Vice-Chancellor of Cambridge University did not venture to commit himself.") Lightfoot, Usher and many moderns sorely need the type of evidence William Henry Green first published in 1890.

I

PRIMEVAL CHRONOLOGY
by William Henry Green

The question of the possible reconciliation of the results of scientific inquiry respecting the antiquity of man and the age of the world with the Scripture chronology has been long and earnestly debated. On the one hand, scientists, deeming them irreconcilable, have been led to distrust the divine authority of the Scriptures; and, on the other hand, believers in the divine word have been led to look upon the investigations of science with an unfriendly eye, as though they were antagonistic to religious faith. In 1863, I had occasion to examine the method and structure of the biblical genealogies, and incidentally ventured the remark that herein lay the solution of the whole matter. I said: "There is an element of uncertainty in a computation of time which rests upon genealogies, as the sacred chronology so largely does. Who is to certify us that the antediluvian and ante-Abrahamic genealogies have not been condensed in the same manner as the post-Abrahamic? ... Our current chronology is based upon the *prima facie* impression of these genealogies. ... But if these recently discovered indications of the antiquity of man, over which scientific circles are now so excited, shall, when carefully inspected and thoroughly weighed, demonstrate all that any have imagined they might demonstrate, what then? They will simply show that the popular chronology is based upon a wrong interpretation, and that a select and partial register of ante-Abrahamic names has been mistaken for a complete one."

I here repeat, the discussion of the biblical genealogies above referred to, and add some further considerations which seem to me to justify the belief that the genealogies in Genesis 5 and 11 were not intended to be used, and cannot properly be used, for the construction of a chronology.

It can scarcely be necessary to adduce proof to one who has even a superficial acquaintance with the genealogies of the Bible, that these are frequently abbreviated by the omission of unimportant names. In fact, abridgment is the general rule, induced by the indisposition of the sacred writers to encumber their pages with more names than were necessary for their immediate purpose. This is so constantly the case, and the reason for it so obvious, that the occurrence of it need create no surprise anywhere, and we are at liberty to suppose it whenever anything in the circumstances of the case favors that belief.

The omissions in the genealogy of our Lord as given in Matthew 1 are familiar to all. Thus in verse 8 three names are dropped between Joram and Ozias (Uzziah), viz., Ahaziah (2 Kings 8:25), Joash (2 Kings 12:1), and Amaziah (2 Kings 14:1); and in verse 11 Jehoiakim is omitted after Josiah (2 Kings 23:34; 1 Chron. 3:16); and in verse 1 the entire genealogy is summed up in two steps, "Jesus Christ, the son of David, the son of Abraham."

Other instances abound elsewhere; we mention only a few of the most striking. In 1 Chronicles 26:24 we read in a list of appointments made by King David (see 1 Chron. 24:3; 25:1; 26:26), that Shebuel,[1] the son of Gershom, the son of Moses, was ruler of the treasures; and again in 1 Chronicles 23:15, 16, we find it written, "The sons of Moses were Gershom and Eliezer. Of the sons of Gershom Shebuel was the chief." Now it is absurd to suppose that the author of Chronicles was so grossly ignorant as to suppose that the grandson of Moses could be living in the reign of David, and appointed by him to a responsible office. Again, in the same connection (1 Chron. 26:31), we read that "among the Hebronites was Jerijah the chief;" and this Jerijah, or Jeriah (for the names are identical), was, according to 23:19, the first of the sons of Hebron, and Hebron was (v. 12) the son of Kohath, the son of Levi (v. 6). So that if no contraction in the genealogical lists is allowed, we have the great-grandson of Levi holding a prominent office in the reign of David.

The genealogy of Ezra is recorded in the book which bears his name; but we learn from another passage, in which the same line of

---

[1] He is called in 1 Chron. 24:20 a son of Amram, the ancestor of Moses; for Shubael and Shebuel are in all probability mere orthographic variations of the same name.

descent is given, that it has been abridged by the omission of six
consecutive names. This will appear from the following comparison,
viz.:

	1 Chronicles 6:3-14	Ezra 7:1-5
1.	Aaron	Aaron
2.	Eleazar	Eleazar
3.	Phinehas	Phinehas
4.	Abishua	Abishua
5.	Bukki	Bukki
6.	Uzzi	Uzzi
7.	Zerahiah	Zerahiah
8.	Meraioth	Meraioth
9.	Amariah	
10.	Ahitub	
11.	Zadok	
12.	Ahimaaz	
13.	Azariah	
14.	Johanan	
15.	Azariah	Azariah
16.	Amariah	Amariah
17.	Ahitub	Ahitub
18.	Zadok	Zadok
19.	Shallum	Shallum
20.	Hilkiah	Hilkiah
21.	Azariah	Azariah
22.	Seraiah	Seraiah
	Ezra	

Still further, Ezra relates (8:1, 2):

"These are now the chief of their fathers, and this is the genealogy of them that went up with me from Babylon, in the reign of
Artaxerxes the king. Of the sons of Phinehas, Gershom. Of the sons
of Ithamar, Daniel. Of the sons of David, Hattush."

Here, if no abridgment of the genealogy is allowed, we should
have a great-grandson and a grandson of Aaron, and a son of David
coming up with Ezra from Babylon after the captivity.

This disposition to abbreviate genealogies by the omission of whatever is unessential to the immediate purpose of the writer is shown by still more remarkable reductions than those which we have been considering. Persons of different degrees of relationship are sometimes thrown together under a common title descriptive of the majority, and all words of explanation, even those which seem essential to the sense, are rigorously excluded, the supplying of these chasms being left to the independent knowledge of the reader. Hence several passages in the genealogies of Chronicles have now become hopelessly obscure. They may have been intelligible enough to contemporaries: but for those who have no extraneous sources of information, the key to their explanation is wanting. In other cases we are able to understand them, because the information necessary to make them intelligible is supplied from parallel passages of Scripture. Thus the opening verses of Chronicles contain the following bald list of names without a word of explanation, viz.: Adam, Seth, Enosh; Kenan, Mahalalel, Jared; Enoch, Methuselah, Lamech; Noah, Shem, Ham, and Japheth.

We are not told who these persons are, how they were related to each other, or whether they were related. The writer presumes that his readers have the book of Genesis in their hands, and that the simple mention of these names in their order will be sufficient to remind them that the first ten trace the line of descent from father to son from the first to the second great progenitor of mankind; and that the last three are brothers, although nothing is said to indicate that their relationship is different from the preceding.

Again the family of Eliphaz, the son of Esau, is spoken of in the following terms in 1 Chronicles 1:36: "The sons of Eliphaz: Teman and Omar, Zephi and Gatam, Kenaz and Timna, and Amalek."

Now, by turning to Genesis 36:11, 12, we shall see that the first five are sons of Eliphaz, and the sixth his concubine, who was the mother of the seventh. This is so plainly written in Genesis that the author of the Chronicles, were he the most inveterate blunderer, could not have mistaken it. But trusting to the knowledge of his readers to supply the omission, he leaves out the statement respecting Eliphaz's concubine, but at the same time connects her name and that of her son with the family to which they belong, and this though he was professedly giving a statement of the sons of Eliphaz.

So, likewise, in the pedigree of Samuel (or Shemuel, v. 33, the difference in orthography is due to our translators, and is not in the original), which is given in 1 Chronicles 6 in both an ascending and descending series. Thus in verses 22-24: "The sons of Kohath; Amminadab his son, Korah his son, Assir his son; Elkanah his son, and Ebiasaph his son, and Assir his son; Tahath his son. . . ."

The extent to which the framer of this list has studied comprehensiveness and conciseness will appear from the fact, which no one would suspect unless informed from other sources, that while the general law which prevails in it is that of descent from father to son, the third, fourth, and fifth names represent brothers. This is shown by a comparison of Exodus 6:24, and the parallel genealogy, 1 Chronicles 6:36, 37. So that the true line of descent is the following, viz.:

In verses 22-24—	Kohath	In verses 37-38—	Kohath
	Amminadab		Izhar
	Korah		Korah
Assir, Elkanah,	Ebiasaph		Ebiasaph
	Assir		Assir
	Tahath, etc.		Tahath, etc.

The circumstance that the son of Kohath is called in one list Amminadab, and in the other Izhar, is no real discrepancy and can create no embarrasment, since it is no unusual thing for the same person to have two names. Witness Abram and Abraham; Jacob and Israel; Joseph and Zaphenath-paneah (Gen. 41:45), Hoshea, Jehoshua (Num. 13:16) (or Joshua) and Jeshua (Neh. 8:17), Gideon and Jerubbaal (Judg. 6:32), Solomon and Jedidiah (2 Sam. 12:24, 25), Azariah and Uzziah (2 Kings 15:1, 13), Daniel and Belteshazzar, Hananiah, Mishael, Azariah and Shadrach, Meshach, Abednego (Dan. 1:7); Saul and Paul, Thomas and Didymus, Cephas and Peter, and in profane history Cyaxares and Darius, Octavianus and Augustus, Napoleon and Bonaparte, Ferretti and Pius IX.

The genealogy of Moses and Aaron is thus stated in Exodus 6:

V. 16. "And these are the names of the sons of Levi, according to their generations; Gershon, and Kohath, and Merari: and the years of the life of Levi were an hundred and thirty and seven years."

17. "The sons of Gershon . . . ."

18. "And the sons of Kohath; Amram, and Izhar, and Hebron, and Uzziel; and the years of the life of Kohath were an hundred and thirty and three years."

19. "And the sons of Merari . . . ."

20. "And Amram took him Jochebed his father's sister to wife; and she bare him Aaron and Moses: and the years of the life of Amram were an hundred and thirty and seven years."

21. "And the sons of Izhar . . . ."

22. "And the sons of Uzziel . . . ."

There is abundant proof that this genealogy has been condensed, as we have already seen that so many others have been, by the dropping of some of the less important names.

This is afforded, in the first place, by parallel genealogies of the same period; as that of Bezaleel (1 Chron. 2:18-20), which records seven generations from Jacob; and that of Joshua (1 Chron. 7:23-27), which records eleven. Now it is scarcely conceivable that there should be eleven links in the line of descent from Jacob to Joshua, and only four from Jacob to Moses.

A still more convincing proof is yielded by Numbers 3:19, 27, 28, from which it appears that the four sons of Kohath severally gave rise to the families of the Amramites, the Izharites, the Hebronites, and the Uzzielites; and that the number of the male members of these families of a month old and upward was 8600 one year after the Exodus. So that, if no abridgment has taken place in the genealogy, the grandfather of Moses had, in the lifetime of the latter, 8600 descendants of the male sex alone, 2,750 of them being between the ages of thirty and fifty (Num. 4:36).

Another proof equally convincing is to be found in the fact that Levi's son Kohath was born before the descent into Egypt (Gen. 46:11); and the abode of the children of Israel in Egypt continued 430 years (Exod. 12:40, 41). Now as Moses was eighty years old at the Exodus (Exod. 7:7) he must have been born more than 350 years after Kohath, who consequently could not have been his own grandfather.

This genealogy, whose abbreviated character is so clearly established, is of special importance for the immediate purpose of this paper, because it might appear, at first sight, as though such an assumption was precluded in the present instance, and as though the letter of Scripture shut us up to the inevitable conclusion that there were four links, and no more, from Jacob to Moses. The names which are found without deviation in all the genealogies are Jacob, Levi, Kohath, Amram, Moses (Exod. 6:16-20; Num. 3:17-19; 26:57-59; 1 Chron. 6:1-3, 16-18; 23:6, 12, 13). Now unquestionably Levi was Jacob's own son. So likewise Kohath was the son of Levi (Gen. 46:11) and born before the descent into Egypt. Amram also was the immediate descendant of Kohath. It does not seem possible, as Kurtz proposed, to insert the missing links between them. For, in the first place, according to Numbers 26:59, "The name of Amram's wife was Jochebed, the daughter of Levi, whom her mother bare to Levi in Egypt," this Jochebed being (Exod. 6:20) Amram's aunt, or his father's sister. Now, it is true, that "a daughter of Levi" might have the general sense of a descendant of Levi, as the woman healed by our Lord (Luke 13:16) is called "a daughter of Abraham;" and her being born to Levi might simply mean that she sprang from him (comp. Gen. 46:25). But these expressions must here be taken in a strict sense, and Jochebed accordingly must have been Levi's own daughter and the sister of Kohath, who must in consequence have been Amram's own father. This appears from a second consideration, viz., that Amram was (Num. 3:27) the father of one of the subdivisions of the Kohathites, these subdivisions springing from Kohath's own children and comprising together 8600 male descendants. Moses' father surely could not have been the ancestor of one-fourth of this number in Moses' own days.

To avoid this difficulty Tiele and Keil assume that there were two Amrams, one the son of Kohath, another the father of Moses, who was a more remote descendant but bore the same name with his ancestor. This relieves the embarrassment created by the Am-

ramites (Num. 3:27) but is still liable to that which arises from
making Jochebed the mother of Moses. And further, the structure
of the genealogy in Exodus 6 is such as to make this hypothesis
unnatural and improbable. Verse 16 names the three sons of Levi,
Gershom, Kohath, and Merari; verses 17-19, the sons of each in
their order; verses 20-22, the children of Kohath's sons; verses 23,
24, contain descendants of the next generation, and verse 25 the
generation next following. Now, according to the view of Tiele and
Keil, we must either suppose that the Amram, Izhar, and Uzziel of
verses 20-22 are all different from the Amram, Izhar, and Uzziel of
verse 18, or else that Amram, though belonging to a later generation
than Izhar and Uzziel, is introduced before them, which the regular
structure of the genealogy forbids; and besides, the sons of Izhar
and the sons of Uzziel, who are here named, were the contemporaries of Moses and Aaron the sons of Amram (Num. 16:1; Lev.
10:4).

This subject may be relieved from all perplexity, however, by
observing that Amram and Jochebed were not the immediate
parents, but the ancestors of Aaron and Moses. How many generations may have intervened, we cannot tell. It is indeed said (Exod.
6:20; Num. 26:59), that Jochebed bare them to Amram. But in the
language of the genealogies this simply means that they were
descended from her and from Amram. Thus, in Genesis 46:18, after
recording the sons of Zilpah, her grandsons, and her great-
grandsons, the writer adds, "These are the sons of Zilpah . . . and
these she bare unto Jacob, even sixteen souls." The same thing
recurs in the case of Bilhah (v. 25): "She bare these unto Jacob; all
the souls were seven," (comp. also vv. 15, 22). No one can pretend
here that the author of this register did not use the terms under-
standingly of descendants beyond the first generation. In like manner, according to Matthew 1:11, Josias begat his grandson Jecho-
nias, and verse 8, Joram begat his great-great-grandson Ozias. And in
Genesis 10:15-18 Canaan, the grandson of Noah, is said to have
begotten several whole nations, the Jebusite, the Amorite, the
Girgasite, the Hivite, etc. (Comp. also Gen. 25:23; Deut. 4:25; 2
Kings 20:18; Isa. 51:2.) Nothing can be plainer, therefore, than
that, in the usage of the Bible, "to bear" and "to beget" are used in

a wide sense to indicate descent, without restriction to the immediate offspring.[2]

It is no serious objection to this view of the case that in Leviticus 10:4 Uzziel, Amram's brother, is called "the uncle of Aaron." The Hebrew word here rendered "uncle," though often specifically applied to a definite degree of relationship, has, both from etymology and usage, a much wider sense. A great-great-grand-uncle is still an uncle, and would properly be described by the term here used.

It may also be observed that in the actual history of the birth of Moses his parents are not called Amram and Jochebed. It is simply said (Exod. 2:1), "and there went a man of the house of Levi, and took a wife a daughter of Levi."

After these preliminary observations, which were originally drawn up for another purpose, I come to the more immediate design of the present paper, by proceeding to inquire, whether the genealogies of Genesis 5 and 11 are necessarily to be considered as complete, and embracing all the links in the line of descent from Adam to Noah and from Shem to Abraham. And upon this I remark—

1. That the analogy of Scripture genealogies is decidedly against such a supposition. In numerous other instances there is incontrovertible evidence of more or less abridgment. This may even be the case where various circumstances combine to produce a different impression at the outset. Nevertheless, we have seen that this first impression may be dissipated by a more careful examination and a comparison of collateral data. The result of our investigations thus far is sufficient to show that it is precarious to assume that any biblical genealogy is designed to be strictly continuous, unless it can be subjected to some external tests which prove it to be so. And it is to be observed that the Scriptures furnish no collateral information whatever respecting the period covered by the genealogies now

---

[2] In Ruth 4:17 Ruth's child is called "a son born to Naomi," who was Ruth's mother-in-law and not even an ancestor of the child in the strict sense. Zerubbabel is called familiarly the son of Shealtiel (Ezra 3:2; Hag. 1:1), and is so stated to be in the genealogies of both Matt. 1:12 and Luke 3:27, though in reality he was his nephew (2 Chron. 3:17-19). That descent as reckoned in genealogies is not always that of actual parentage appears from the comparison of the ancestry of our Lord as given by Matthew and by Luke.

in question. The creation, the Flood, the call of Abraham, are great facts, which stand out distinctly in primeval sacred history. A few incidents respecting our first parents and their sons Cain and Abel are recorded. Then there is an almost total blank until the Flood, with nothing whatever to fill the gap, and nothing to suggest the length of time intervening but what is found in the genealogy stretching between these two points. And the case is substantially the same from the Flood to Abraham. So far as the biblical records go, we are left not only without adequate data, but without any data whatever, which can be brought into comparison with these genealogies for the sake of testing their continuity and completeness.

If, therefore, any really trustworthy data can be gathered from any source whatever, from any realm of scientific or antiquarian research, which can be brought into comparison with these genealogies for the sake of determining the question, whether they have noted every link in the chain of descent, or whether, as in other manifest instances, links have been omitted, such data should be welcomed and the comparison fearlessly made. Science would simply perform the office, in this instance, which information gathered from other parts of Scripture is unhesitatingly allowed to do in regard to those genealogies previously examined.

And it may be worth noting here that a single particular in which a comparison may be instituted between the primeval history of man and Genesis 5, suggests especial caution before affirming the absolute completeness of the latter. The letter of the genealogical record (5:3) if we were dependent on it alone, might naturally lead us to infer that Seth was Adam's first child. But we know from Chapter 4 that he had already had two sons, Cain and Abel, and from 4:17 that he must have had a daughter, and from 4:14 that he had probably had several sons and daughters, whose families had swollen to a considerable number before Adam's one hundred and thirtieth year, in which Seth was born. Yet of all this the genealogy gives us no inkling.

2. Is there not, however, a peculiarity in the construction of these genealogies which forbids our applying to them an inference drawn from others not so constructed? The fact that each member

of the series is said to have begotten the one next succeeding, is, in the light of the wide use of this term which we have discovered in other cases, no evidence of itself that links have not been omitted. But do not the chronological statements introduced into these genealogies oblige us to regard them as necessarily continuous? Why should the author be so particular to state, in every case, with unfailing regularity, the age of each patriarch at the birth of his son, unless it was his design thus to construct a chronology of this entire period, and to afford his readers the necessary elements for a computation of the interval from the creation to the deluge and from the deluge to Abraham? And if this was his design, he must, of course, have aimed to make his list complete. The omission of even a single name would create an error.

But are we really justified in supposing that the author of these genealogies entertained such a purpose? It is a noticeable fact that he never puts them to such a use himself. He nowhere sums these numbers, nor suggests their summation. No chronological statement is deduced from these genealogies, either by him or by any inspired writer. There is no computation anywhere in Scripture of the time that elapsed from the creation or from the deluge, as there is from the descent into Egypt to the Exodus (Exod. 12:40), or from the Exodus to the building of the temple (1 Kings 6:1). And if the numbers in these genealogies are for the sake of constructing a chronology, why are numbers introduced which have no possible relation to such a purpose? Why are we told how long each patriarch lived after the birth of his son, and what was the entire length of his life? These numbers are given with the same regularity as the age of each at the birth of his son; and they are of no use in making up a chronology of the period. They merely afford us a conspectus of individual lives. And for this reason doubtless they are recorded. They exhibit in these selected examples the original term of human life. They show what it was in the ages before the Flood. They show how it was afterwards gradually narrowed down. But in order to do this it was not necessary that every individual should be named in the line from Adam to Noah and from Noah to Abraham, nor anything approaching it. A series of specimen lives, with the appropriate numbers attached, this is all that has been furnished us. And if this be the case, the notion of basing a chronological computation upon these genealogies is a fundamental mistake. It is putting them to a purpose that they were not designed to subserve, and to which from the method of their construction they are not adapted. When it is said, for example, that "Enosh lived ninety years and begat Kenan," the well-established usage of the word "begat" makes this statement equally true and equally accordant with analogy, whether Kenan was an immediate or a remote descendant of Enosh; whether Kenan was himself born, when Enosh was ninety years of age or one was born from whom Kenan sprang. These genealogies may yield us the minimum length of time that it is possible to accept for the period that they cover; but they can make no account of the duration represented by the names that have been dropped from the register, as needless for the author's particular purpose.

3. The abode of the children of Israel in Egypt affords for our present purpose the best Scripture parallel to the periods now under consideration. The greater part of this term of 430 years is left blank in the sacred history. A few incidents are mentioned at the beginning connected with the descent of Jacob and his family into Egypt and their settlement there. And at its close mention is made of some incidents in the life of Moses and the events leading to the Exodus. But with these exceptions no account is given of this long period. The interval is only bridged by a genealogy extending from Levi to Moses and Aaron and their contemporaries among their immediate relatives (Exod. 6:16-26). This genealogy records the length of each man's life in the principal line of descent, viz., Levi (v. 16), Kohath (v. 18), Amram (v. 20). The correspondence in the points just indicated with the genealogies of Genesis 5 and 11, and the periods which they cover, is certainly remarkable. And as they proceeded from the same pen, we may fairly infer from the similarity of construction a similarity of design. Now it has been shown already that the genealogy from Levi to Moses cannot have recorded all the links in that line of descent, and that it could not, therefore, have been intended to be used as a basis of chronological computation. This is rendered absolutely certain by the explicit statement in Exodus 12:40. It further appears from the fact that

the numbers given in this genealogy exhibit the longevity of the patriarchs named, but cannot be so concatenated as to sum up the entire period; thus suggesting the inference that the numbers in the other genealogies, with which we are now concerned, were given with a like design, and not with the view of enabling the reader to construct the chronology.

4. As is well known, the texts of the Septuagint and of the Samaritan Pentateuch vary systematically from the Hebrew in both the genealogies of Genesis 5 and 11. According to the chronologies based on these texts respectively, the interval between the Flood and the birth of Abraham was 292 (Hebrew), 942 (Samaritan), or 1172 years (Septuagint). Some have been disposed in this state of the case to adopt the chronology drawn from the Septuagint, as affording here the needed relief. But the superior accuracy of the Hebrew text in this instance, as well as generally elsewhere, can be incontrovertibly established. This resource, then, is a broken reed.

Thus in the Hebrew text of Genesis 5, the ages of different patriarchs at the birth of the son named are quite irregular, and vary from sixty-five to one hundred and eighty-seven. But the versions seek to bring them into closer conformity, and to introduce something like a regular gradation. The Septuagint proceeds on the assumption that patriarchs of such enormous longevity should be nearly two centuries old at the birth of their son. Accordingly, when, in the Hebrew, they fall much below this standard, one hundred years are added to the number preceding the birth of the son and the same amount deducted from the number following his birth; the total length of each life is thus preserved without change, the proportion of its different parts alone being altered. The Samaritan, on the other hand, assumes a gradual diminution in the ages of successive patriarchs prior to the birth of their son, none rising to a century after the first two. When, therefore, the number in the Hebrew text exceeds one hundred, one hundred is deducted and the same amount added to the years after the son was born. In the case of Lamech the reduction is greater still, in order to effect the necessary diminution. Accordingly the years assigned to the several antediluvian patriarchs before the birth of their son in these several texts is as follows:—

	Hebrew	Septragint	Samaritan
Adam	130	230	130
Seth	105	205	105
Enosh	90	190	90
Kenan	70	170	70
Mahalalel	65	165	65
Jared	162	162	62
Enoch	65	165	65
Methuselah	187	$\begin{cases} 167^3 \\ 187 \end{cases}$	67
Lamech	182	188	53
Noah	600	600	600

A simple glance at these numbers is sufficient to show that the Hebrew is the original, from which the others diverge on the one side or the other, according to the principle which they have severally adopted. It likewise creates a strong presumption that the object contemplated in these changes was to make the lives more symmetrical, rather than to effect an alteration in the chronology.

5. The structure of the genealogies in Genesis 5 and 11 also favors the belief that they do not register all the names in these respective lines of descent. Their regularity seems to indicate intentional arrangement. Each genealogy includes ten names, Noah being the tenth from Adam, and Terah the tenth from Noah. And each ends with a father having three sons, as is likewise the case with the Cainite genealogy (4:17-22). The Sethite genealogy (chap. 5) culminates in its seventh member, Enoch, who "walked with God, and he was not, for God took him." The Cainite genealogy also culminates in its seventh member, Lamech, with his polygamy, bloody revenge, and boastful arrogance. The genealogy descending from Shem divides evenly at its fifth member, Peleg; and "in his days was the earth divided." Now as the adjustment of the genealogy in Matthew 1 into three periods of fourteen generations each is brought about by dropping the requisite number of names, it seems

---

[3] The number varies in different manuscripts.

in the highest degree probable that the symmetry of these primitive genealogies is artificial rather than natural. It is much more likely that this definite number of names fitting into a regular scheme has been selected as sufficiently representing the periods to which they belong, than that all these striking numerical coincidences should have happened to occur in these successive instances.

It may further be added that if the genealogy in Chapter 11 is complete, Peleg, who marks the entrance of a new period, died while all his ancestors from Noah onward were still living. Indeed Shem, Arphaxad, Selah, and Eber must all have outlived not only Peleg, but all the generations following as far as and including Terah. The whole impression of the narrative in Abraham's days is that the Flood was an event long since past, and that the actors in it had passed away ages before. And yet if a chronology is to be constructed out of this genealogy, Noah was for fifty-eight years the contemporary of Abraham, and Shem actually survived him thirty-five years, provided 11:26 is to be taken in its natural sense, that Abraham was born in Terah's seventieth year. This conclusion is well-nigh incredible. The calculation which leads to such a result, must proceed upon a wrong assumption.

On these various grounds we conclude that the Scriptures furnish no data for a chronological computation prior to the life of Abraham; and that the Mosaic records do not fix and were not intended to fix the precise date either of the Flood or of the creation of the world.

BIBLIOGRAPHY

Kaiser, Walter C. Jr. "The Literary Form of Genesis 1-11," in *New Perspectives on the Old Testament*. (ed. J. Barton Payne), Waco, Texas: Word Books, 1970, 48-65.

Malamat, Abraham, "King Lists of the Old Babylonian Period and Biblical Genealogies," *Journal of American Oriental Society*. 88 (1968), 163-73.

Warfield, Benj. B., "On the Antiquity and Unity of the Human Race," *Princeton Theological Review,* 9(1911), 1-25.

Whitcomb, John, and Morris, Henry M. *The Genesis Flood.* Philadelphia: Presbyterian and Reformed Publishing Co., 1966, Appendix II, 474-89.

II

YAHWEH (JEHOVAH) AND EXODUS 6:3

by Robert Dick Wilson

Editor's Introduction

One text all non-evangelical Biblical scholars take literally to the last English syllable is Exodus 6:3. On this platform has been erected the monumental documentary theory with its famous J,E,D,P documents (representing 850, 750, 621, and 450 B.C. dates respectively for commiting to writing each of the alleged divisions of the Pentateuch until it was finally completed with all editorial reworkings in 400 B.C.)!

The whole theory was artificial from the start, as Wilson pointed out years ago. Nevertheless, the scholarly community remained intransigent. Look again at the internal evidence, compare the external evidences now coming from the epigraphic materials of the Ancient Near East, and decide for yourself where the truth lies.

In criticising a document there are at least three fundamental principles upon which we should proceed: *First,* the document must be supposed to be in harmony with itself and interpreted accordingly. *Secondly,* it must be presumed to be in harmony with its sources of information. *Thirdly,* it should be in accordance with its supposed time, place, and circumstances.[1]

I. The Critical Theory Is Inconsistent

1. The critics hold that Exodus 6:3, which the RV renders, "And I appeared unto Abraham, unto Isaac, and unto Jacob as God Almighty (*El Shaddai*); but by my name Jehovah I was not known unto them," belongs to P and that P means to say that El Shaddai

---

[1] Briggs, *The Higher Criticism of the Hexateuch*, p. 4.

and not Jehovah was the name of God known to the patriarchs, Abraham, Isaac, and Jacob. Therefore they assign four passages, Genesis 17:1, 28:3, 35:11, and 48:3 to P., since El Shaddai is found in them. It is to be observed, however, regarding these passages that, in 17:1, it is said that *Jehovah* appeared to Abram, saying, I am El Shaddai; and in 35:11 that *Elohim* appeared to Jacob saying, I am El Shaddai. In 28:3 Isaac says to Jacob, El Shaddai bless thee; and in 48:3 Jacob says in the presence of Joseph and his two sons, El Shaddai appeared unto me. In a fifth passage, Genesis 43:14, Jacob uses this appellation in his prayer for his sons who are starting for Egypt. But this verse is assigned to E or J by the critics and the El Shaddai attributed to the Redactor. Is it not singular that if P thought El Shaddai was a proper name for God he should have used Elohim about seventy times before Exodus 6:3 and El Shaddai only four times? Is it not extraordinary that, if the writer of Exodus 6:3 meant that God "appeared" to the patriarchs under the name of El Shaddai, only once in P should it be said that El Shaddai "appeared," just the same number of times that P says that Jehovah "appeared" and that Elohim "appeared"? Jehovah alone (or Jehovah Elohim) is alleged to have occured in J, and Elohim alone in E; but El Shaddai is found but four times in P and Elohim seventy times.

If P alone thought that El Shaddai was the only name of God known in the time of the patriarchs, how about Genesis 43:14, which the critics assign to E or J? We have seen that they escape the consequences of this assignment simply by asserting that El Shaddai is an interpolation of the Redactor. But did the Redactor also think that the patriarchs used El Shaddai rather than Jehovah? Why, then did he not cut out Jehovah and put El Shaddai into the text of J? Besides, if P alone thought that Shaddai was a specifically patriarchal designation, how about its use in Genesis 49:25 and Numbers 24:4, 16, which are assigned to J or JE? All of these questions will be appropriately answered if we take Shaddai and El Shaddai as appellations, "the Almighty" or "a mighty God," and not as proper names.

2. A historical or ostensibly historical document should, if possible, be interpreted in harmony with its sources and with earlier

histories supposedly known to the author. What then were the sources of P? According to datings advocated by the critics they could have been only J, E, D, H, and Judges, Samuel, Kings, Jeremiah, Ezekiel, Hosea, Amos, Obadiah, Nahum, Zephaniah, and parts of other books. Now the only one of these sources or earlier works in which El Shaddai occurs is Ezekiel 10:5, "And the sound of the cherubim's wings was heard unto the outer court as the voice of Almighty God (El Shaddai) when he speaketh." Shaddai alone occurs in the Pentateuch only in Genesis 49:25 (J) and in Numbers 24:4, 16 (JE). In Genesis 49:24, 25, we read in the Blessing of Joseph that "the arms of his hands were made strong by the hands of the Almighty One of Jacob (from thence is the Shepherd, the stone of Israel) even by the God of thy fathers, who shall help thee, and by the Almighty (Shaddai) who shall bless thee." The Samaritan Hebrew text and version of this verse both read El Shaddai instead of Shaddai, a reading supported by the Syriac and apparently by the Septuagint. If we take the latter reading we would find God Almighty to be parallel with the Almighty One of Jacob who is also called the God of thy fathers (i.e., of Jacob). This psalm of Jacob refers in verse 18 to Jehovah in the words, "I have waited for Thee, O Jehovah"; so that if P got his information about El Shaddai in this psalm he would have known that Jehovah was used by the patriarch Jacob at least. Nothing is said in this psalm about either Jehovah or El Shaddai having "appeared." In Numbers 24:4, 16 Balaam uses the phrase: "which saw the vision of the Almighty (Shaddai)."[2] Since this chapter is assigned to JE, P must have known, if he got his information here, that Shaddai was supposed by his sources to have been used after the declaration made in Exodus 6:3; for JE certainly places the episode of Balaam about forty years after the event recorded in Exodus 6:3.

These being the only places in the Old Testament where Shaddai occurs in the portions assigned by the critics to a date before 550 B.C., it follows that the critics' interpretation of Exodus 6:3 makes P to be out of harmony with all its known sources.

---

[2] Shaddai is rendered in Greek and Syriac by "God," in Arabic by "the sufficient one"; and in the Samaritan version by "field," they having read *sadai* for *shaddai*.

3. In documents which in their opinion were written after 550 B.C. we never find El Shaddai; but Shaddai alone occurs thirty times in Job, and in Ruth, 1:20, 21; Isaiah 13:14; Joel 1:15; Psalm 68:15; 91:1. Not one of these passages refers to the patriarchs or to God as "appearing" to them or to anyone else. In twenty-seven of them Shaddai is used as parallel to other names of God. There is no intimation that Shaddai was a more ancient designation than these other terms. It follows, therefore, that, as interpreted by the critics, P in its use of El Shaddai is not congruous with the usage of these other books which the critics allege to have been written in post-captivity times. To be sure, if Job was written in the time of the patriarchs we can see where the author of P got his idea that they had used Shaddai as a name for God. Or even if some of the other passages came from the time to which they have been assigned by tradition we might see how he got the idea; even though they say nothing of revelation or the patriarchs. But as the case stands for the critics we find that the author of P must have invented the whole conception. For neither Ezekiel, Job, J, E, H, D, Joel, Jonah, Deutero-Isaiah, Ruth, nor the Psalms, furnish any ground for supposing that the patriarchs used this appellation for God; and the certainly late writings such as Daniel, Haggai, Zechariah, Malachi, Esther, Chronicles, Ezra, and Nehemiah, never mention the name at all. Whether we take the traditional view of the post-captivity literature, or the radical, there would therefore be no contemporary evidence to show that the hypothetical writer of P, provided that he lived in post-captivity times, was in his use of Shaddai in harmony with contemporaneous usage and ideas.

II. Correct Exegisis Supports Unity of Pentateuch

Having shown that the interpretation of Exodus 6:3 advanced by the critics is out of harmony with the rest of P, that it does not agree with the rest of the Pentateuch, and that it does not fit into the time at which P is alleged to have been written, it remains to see whether this passage can be so interpreted as to be brought into agreement with the traditional view of the Pentateuch as the work of Moses. This we shall attempt to show by an examination of the text, grammar, and vocabulary of the verse, under the following heads: (1) "appeared," (2) "as," (3) "God" *El*, (4) "Almighty" *Shaddai*, (5) "but" *waw*, (6) "name," (7) "known," (8) the form of the last sentence—can it be interrogative?

1. The "appearing of God to men is described in several different ways in the Old Testament.

a. The most usual expression is that found here in Exodus 6:3, where the Niphal of the verb "to see" (*ra'ah*) is used. With the Deity as subject this verb occurs forty-three times as follows:

(1) Jehovah, Genesis 12:7 *bis* (J); 17:1 (J); 18:1 (J); 22:14 (J); 26:2, 24 (J); Exodus 3:14 (E); 4:1, 5 (J); 6:3 (P); Leviticus 9:4 (P); 16:2 (P); Numbers 14:14 (JE); Deuteronomy 31:15 (JE); 1 Kings 3:5; 9:2; 1 Chronicles 1:7; 3:1; 7:12; Jeremiah 3:13; Zechariah 9:14.

(2) The glory of Jehovah, Exodus 16:10 (P); Leviticus 9:6, 23 (P); Numbers 14:10 (P); 16:19 (P); 17:7 (P); 20:6 (P); Isaiah 60:2; Psalm 90:16.

(3) The angel of Jehovah, Exodus 3:2 (J); Judges 3:21 *bis;* 6:12; 13:3, 21.

(4) Jehovah of Hosts, Malachi 3:2.

(5) Jehovah, God of Israel, 1 Kings 11:2.

(6) Elohim, Genesis 35:9 (P).

(7) The man (i.e., the angel of Jehovah), Judges 13:10.

(8) El, Genesis 35:1 (E).

(9) El Shaddai, Genesis 48:3 (P).

b. Other expressions are the following:

(1) In the following cases it is said that man "saw" the Deity, the Kal of the verb (*ra'ah*) being used:

(a) Jehovah, 1 Kings 22:19; 2 Chronicles 18:18.

(b) The glory of Jehovah, Exodus 16:7 (P); Isaiah 35:2.

(c) The angel of Jehovah, Numbers 22:31 (E); 1 Chronicles 21:16, 20.

(d) The majesty of Jehovah, Isaiah 26:10.

(e) The Lord (*Yah*) Isaiah 38:11.

(f) The King, Jehovah of Hosts, Isaiah 6:5.

(g) Lord (*Adonai*), Isaiah 6:1; Amos 9:1.

(h) The Holy ONe of Israel, Isaiah 17:7.

(i) Elohim, Genesis 32:30 (J); 33:10 (J); Judges 13:32, 1 Samuel 28:13.

(2) The Hiphil of "to see" (ra'ah) with the Deity as subject, occurs in the Old Testament twenty-two times: Genesis 1; Exodus 2; Deuteronomy 3; Judges 1; 2 Kings 1; Psalm 4; Jeremiah 3; Ezekiel 1; Nahum 1; Habakkuk 1; Zechariah 2. In the Pentateuch it is found in J in Exodus 9:16; in E in Genesis 48:11; in P in Exodus 25:9; Numbers 8:4; in D in Deuteronomy 3:24; 4:36; 5:21.

(3) The verb hazah "to see" is used in Exodus 24:11 (J) with Elohim as object, in Job 19:26 with Eloah as object, and in Numbers 24:4, 16 (JE) with Shaddai as object.

(4) Of the words for "vision" mar'eh is used in Genesis 15:1 (E); in connection with Jehovah and mahazeh in Numbers 24:4, 16 with Shaddai.

(5) The verb "to reveal" (galah, Niphal form) is found in the Pentateuch only in Genesis 35:7 (E). Isaiah employs it in 40:5; 53:1; 54:1. It is found also in 1 Samuel 2:27; 3:7, 21.

It is clear from the above evidence that the Deity is said in all the documents J, E, D, H, and P to have "appeared" and that the Niphal of ra'ah, "to see," the most common expression used to describe it, is found in all of them.

2. The proposition b^e which occurs in Exodus 6:3 before El Shaddai is the so-called Beth essentiae and is to be translated ordinarily by "as," or "as being," or "in the character of." It is found in Genesis 21:12 (P); Exodus 18:4; 32:22 (both E); Deuteronomy 26:5; 28:62; 33:26; Leviticus 17:11 (H). It occurs also in Judges 11:35; Psalm 35:2; 37:20; 39:7; 54:6; 55:19; 68:5, 33; 118:7; 146:5; Proverbs 3:26; Ecclesiastes 7:14; Job 23:13; Isaiah 26:4; 40:10; 48:10; Hosea 13:9.

In Exodus 6:3 we should translate "as being El Shaddai," and "as being Shemi Jahweh" or "in the character of a mighty God" and "in the character of my name Jehovah," the force of the proposition being regarded as carried over to the second phrase.

3. El occurs about two hundred and twenty times in the Old Testament, in Genesis 9; Exodus 4; Numbers 11; Deuteronomy 10; Joshua 3 (or 35 times in the Hexateuch, J 2; E 5; D 10; P 5), 1 Samuel 1, 2 Samuel 2; Isaiah 25; Jeremiah 2; Ezekiel 7; Daniel 4;

Hosea 3; Jonah 1; Micah 2; Nahum 1; Zechariah 2; Malachi 2; Psalm 71; Job 55; Proverbs 1. It frequently takes after it an attributive adjective, or a noun in construction. Thus E represents El as jealous, D as great and terrible and merciful, JE as jealous, merciful, gracious and living; and J speaks of a seeing God (*El ro'i*) an eternal God (*El 'Olam*), Deut. 32, of a God of a stranger (or a strange God), a god of trustworthiness, and a God who begat us, 1 Samuel 2:3 of a God of knowledge. Genesis 14 four times calls El the Most High (*'Elyon*), and Deuteronomy 32:8 names him simply *'Elyon*. From this evidence it seems clear, that El was in use in all periods of Hebrew literature and also that the limiting adjectives and genitives did not denote names of different gods, but were generally at least nothing but appellations of attributes or characteristics.

4. As to the word Shaddai, there is uncertainty as to its root, form, and meaning. If it were from a root *Shadah*, it would be of the same form as *sadai* which is sometimes read in the Hebrew text instead of *sade* "field." In Babylonian the root *shadu* means "to be high," and derivatives mean "mountain," and "the summit of a mountain" and perhaps "majesty." In this case, we might take *shaddai* as a synonym of *'elyon* "Most High," as used in Genesis 14.

A second derivation is from the root *shadad* "to be strong." The Greek translator of Job apparently had this derivation before him when he rendered *shaddai* as "Almighty,"[3]—a translation which has been generally followed in the English version. In the Syriac an equivalent word *hassino* "strong" is found in Job 6:4; 8:3, 5; 11:7; 13:3; 15:25; 27:2, 13; 29:5; 37:23.

A third derivation is from the relative pronoun and the word "sufficiency."

Our ignorance of the real meaning of the word is further illustrated by the fact that the Greek translators of the Pentateuch invariably render both Shaddai and El Shaddai by *theos*, that the translation of Job renders it eight times by *kurios*, that the Syriac

---

[3] Fifteen times in all, to wit: 5:17; 8:5; 11:7; 15:25; 22:17, 25; 23:16; 27:2, 11, 13; 32:8; 33:4; 34:10, 35:13; 37:22.

version renders it twenty-two times by *Aloho* (God), and in the Pentateuch usually transliterates it.

In conclusion, the evidence clearly shows that the Hebrews who translated the Old Testament, or part of it, into Samaritan, Syriac, Greek, and Arabic, knew nothing of a god called Shaddai or of Shaddai as a name for God. Only in the Greek of Ezekiel 1:24 and in the Syriac of Genesis 17:1; 35:11; and Exodus 6:3 is there any indication that either El Shaddai or Shaddai was ever considered to be a proper name like Jehovah.

5. The particle *Waw* usually means "and." The meaning "but" is comparatively seldom the correct one.

6. *Shemi* has been taken by most interpreters and translators as meaning "my name."

As to the syntactical relation of the phrase "my name Jehovah" the ancient and modern versions vary. Some take it as the preposed object "my name Jehovah did I not make known" (so the Septuagint, Latin Vulgate, Syriac, and the Targum of Onkelos) and seem to have read the Niphal as a Hiphil. The Samaritan Targum gives a literal rendering. The AV puts "by" before "my name" and inserts "the name of" before El Shaddai. The RV puts "as" before El Shaddai and "by" before "my name." The RV margin suggests "as to" before "my name" and omits "the name of" before "El Shaddai." The Targum of Jonathan renders literally except that it explains "and my name Jehovah" as meaning "but as the face (or presence) of my Shekina." By this simple interpretation the Targum of Jonathan, without any change of text, brings the verse into agreement with the preceding history of the Pentateuch.

As to the meaning of "name" it can scarcely be held that any post-captivity writer really thought that the mere sound of the name itself had never been heard before the time of Moses. But if the writer of P did think so, it is preposterous to suppose that the Redactor who put J and P together should have accepted P's opinion and then allowed the Jehovah of J to remain in Genesis as the ordinary name of God. The Redactor at least, and the people who accepted his composite work as the work of Moses, must have interpreted this verse in a sense agreeing with what had gone before. Now such sentences as "my name is in him" (Exod. 23:21), "to put his name there" (Deut. 12:5), "for his name's sake" (Ps. 79:9), "according to thy name so is thy praise" (Ps. 48:11), show that the name meant the power, visible presence, honor, or repute, of the person named. The Targum of Jonathan explains "my name Jehovah" as "the face (or presence) of my Shekinah."

7. That "knowing" the name of Jehovah means more than merely knowing the word itself, is apparent from Isaiah 19:21, where we read: And Jehovah shall be known to Egypt and Egypt shall know Jehovah in that day.

The form used here in Exodus 6:3 may mean: I was known, I was made known, or I allowed myself to be known.

8. Questions in Hebrew and other Semitic languages may be asked either with or without an interrogative particle. The following evidence goes to show that the last clause of Exodus 6:3 might be read "was I not made known to them?" This interpretation would remove at one blow the whole foundation of the critical position, so far as it is based on this verse.

In *Arabic* "a question is sometimes indicated by the tone of the voice."

In *Syriac* there is no special syntactical or formal method of indicating direct questions. Such interrogative sentences can only be distinguished from sentences of affirmation by the emphasis.

In *Hebrew* "frequently the natural emphasis upon the words (especially when the most emphatic word is placed at the beginning of the sentence) is of itself sufficient to indicate an interrogative sentence."

As examples of this type of interrogative sentence, the following may be cited: Genesis 18:12, "After I am waxed old shall I have pleasure, my lord being old also?" Genesis 27:24, "Thou art my son Esau?" Exodus 8:22, "Should we sacrifice the abomination of the Egyptians before them, would they not stone us?" Exodus 9:11, "As yet exaltest thou thyself against my people, that thou wilt not let them go?" Exodus 33:14, "Shall my presence go, then I shall give thee rest?" Judges 11:23, "And shouldest thou possess it?" Judges 14:16, "Behold I have not told it my father nor my mother, and shall I tell it thee?" Samuel 11:12, "Shall Saul reign over us?" 20:9, "If I knew certainly that evil was determined by my father to come upon thee, then would not I tell it thee?" 22:7, "Will the son of Jesse give every one of you fields and vineyards?" 22:15, "Did I then begin to inquire of God for him?" 24:14, "If a man find his enemy, will he let him go well away?" 25:11, "Shall I then take my bread and my water?" 30:8, "Shall I pursue after this troop?" 2 Samuel 11:11, "Shall I then go into my house?" 16:17, "Is this thy kindness to thy friends?" 18:29, "Is the young man Absalom safe?" 19:23, "Shall there any man be put to death this day in Israel?" 23:5, "Verily will he not make it to grow?" 1 Kings, 1:24, "Hast thou said Adonijah shall reign after me?" 21:7, "Dost thou govern the kingdom of Israel?" 2 Kings 5:26, "Went not mine heart with thee?" Hosea 10:9, "Shall not the war against the unjust overtake them in Gibeah?" (Ewald, Henderson, *et al.*). Isaiah 37:11, "And shalt thou be delivered?" Jeremiah 25:29, "Like a hammer which breaketh the rock in pieces?" 45:5, "And seekest thou great things for thyself?" 49:12, "And art thou he that shall go altogether unpunished?" Ezekiel 11:3, "Is not the building of houses near?" (Ewald). 11:13. "Wilt thou make a full end of the remnant of Israel?" (Ewald). 29:13, "And shall I be inquired of by you?" 32:2, "Art thou like a young lion of the nations?" (Ewald). Jonah 4:11, "Should I not spare Nineveh?" Habakkuk 2:19, "Shall it teach?" Zechariah 8:6, "Should it also be marvelous in my eyes?" Malachi 2:15, "And did not he make one?" Job 2:9, "Dost thou still retain thy integrity?" 2:10, "Shall we receive good?" 10:9, "And wilt thou bring me into dust again?" 14:3, "Dost thou open thy eyes?" 37:18, "Hast thou with him spread out the sky?" 38:18, Hast thou perceived the breadth of the earth?" 39:2, "Canst thou number the months?" 41:1, "Canst thou draw out Leviathan?" Lamentations 1:12, "Is it nothing to you, all ye that pass by?" 3:38, "Out of the mouth of the most high proceedeth not evil and good?" Nehemiah 5:7, "Do ye exact usury every one of his brother?"

In view of the exegetical problems which are involved in the interpretation of this verse, the Versions, both ancient and modern are of unusual interest. The following may be cited:

1. The Greek Septuagint: And God (*ho theos*) spake to Moses and said to him: I am (the) Lord (*kurios*) and he appeared to

Abram and Isaac and Jacob, being their God, and my name *kurios* I manifested not to them.

2. The Latin Vulgate: And spake the Lord (*Dominus*) to Moses, saying: I am the Lord who appeared to Abraham, Isaac, and Jacob, as (*in*) omnipotent God, and my name Adonai I did not show (*indicavi*) to them.

3. The Targum of Onkelos: And spake Jehovah with Moses and said to him: I am Jehovah, and I was revealed to Abraham, to Isaac, and to Jacob as God Almighty and my name Jehovah I did not make known to them.

4. The Targum of Pseudo-Jonathan: And Jehovah spake with Moses and said to him: "I am Jehovah who revealed himself unto thee in the midst of the bush and said to thee, I am Jehovah, and I revealed myself to Abraham, to Isaac, and Jacob as an Almighty God, and my name Jehovah, but as the face of my Shekina I was not made known to them.

5. The Peshito: And spake the Lord (Moryo) with Moses and said to him: I am the Lord and I appeared to Abraham and to Isaac and to Jacob as the God El Shaddai and the name of the Lord I did not show to them.

6. The Samaritan Hebrew text agrees with the Hebrew, except that it has Jehovah instead of God in verse 2, and adds *waw* (and) after Abraham.

7. The Samaritan Targum is a literal rendering of the Hebrew.

8. The Arabic of Saadya: Then spake God to Moses and said to him: I am God who named myself to Abraham, Isaac and Jacob as the Mighty, the Sufficient, and my name is God.

9. The English version: And God spake unto Moses and said unto him: I am the Lord (RV, Jehovah) and I appeared unto Abraham and unto Isaac and unto Jacob by *the name of* (RV, as) God Almighty; but by (RV, or "as to") my name Jehovah was I (RV I was) not known (RV or *made known*) unto them.

10. The Dutch translation: Then spake God unto Moses and said unto him: I am the Lord and I appeared to Abraham, Isaac and Jacob as God the Almighty; but by my name Lord I was not known to them.

11. Luther's German version: And God spake with Moses and said unto him: I am the Lord and I appeared to Abraham, Isaac, and Jacob that I would be their Almighty God but my name Lord was not revealed to them.

On the basis of the investigation of the verse given above the writer would suggest the following renderings: And God spake unto Moses and said unto him; I am Jehovah and I appeared unto Abraham, unto Isaac, and unto Jacob in the character of the God of Might (or, mighty God) and in the character of my name Jehovah I did not make myself known unto them. Or, if the last part of the verse is to be regarded as a question, the rendering should be: And in the character of my name Jehovah did I not make myself known unto them? Either of these suggested translations will bring this verse into entire harmony with the rest of the Pentateuch. Consequently, it is unfair and illogical to use a forced translation of Exodus 6:3 in support of a theory that would destroy the unity of authorship and the Mosaic origin of the Pentateuch.

BIBLIOGRAPHY

Kitchen, Kenneth. *Ancient Orient and Old Testament.* Chicago: Inter-Varsity Press, 1966, 112-138.

Martin, W. J. *Stylistic Criteria and The Analysis of the Pentateuch.* London: Tyndale Press, 1955, 5-23. (Some fascinating alternatives to Wilson's interpretation.)

Motyer, J. A. *The Revelation of the Divine Name.* London: Tyndale Press, 1956, 3-31. (The best analysis of the passage.)

Yamauchi, Edwin. *Composition and Corroboration in Classical and Biblical Studies.* Philadelphia: Presbyterian and Reformed Publishing Co., 1966, 7-38.

III

UNDERSTANDING
THE TEN COMMANDMENTS

by Ezekiel Hopkins

Editor's Introduction

Nothing characterizes the essence of the Old Testament like the one word "Law"; and that is an atonymn for "grace." But is the separation that sharp? Is there no truth or grace in the Old Testament, much less in the Law itself? Are we free from God's moral law as we are from the civil and ceremonial aspects? What criteria does Scripture supply for such fine distinctions?

This old Puritan preacher had some insights needed in an age which now complains about its relativistic bind in the ethical realm. Could it be because even the evangelicals have denied the relevance of God's moral law for their present lives?

Two things in general are required to perfect a Christian; the one a clear and distinct knowledge of his duty, the other, a conscientious practice of it, correspondent to his knowledge; and both are equally necessary. For, as we can have no solid or well-grounded hope of eternal salvation, without obedience; so we can have no sure established rule for our obedience, without knowledge. Therefore, our work and office is, not only to exhort, but to instruct; not only to excite the affections, but to inform the judgment: we must as well illuminate as warm.

Knowledge, indeed, may be found without practice; and our age abounds with speculative Christians, whose religion is but like the rickets, that makes them grow large in the head, but narrow in the breast; whose brains are replenished with notions, but their hearts straitened towards God, and their lives black and deformed.

But, although knowledge may be without practice, yet the

practice of godliness cannot be without knowledge. For, if we know not the limits of sin and duty, what is required and what is forbidden, it cannot be supposed but that, in this corrupted state of our natures, we shall unavoidably run into many heinous miscarriages.

Therefore, that we might be informed what we ought to do and what to avoid, it hath pleased God, the great Governor and righteous Judge of all, to prescribe laws for the regulating of our actions; and, that we might not be ignorant what they are, he hath openly promulgated them in his word. For when we had miserably defaced the law of nature originally written in our hearts, so that many of its commands were no longer legible, it seemed good to his infinite wisdom and mercy to transcribe and copy out that law in the sacred tables of the Scriptures; and to superadd many positive precepts and injunctions not before imposed. Hence the Bible is the statute-book of God's kingdom, wherein is comprised the whole body of the heavenly law, the perfect rules of a holy life, and the sure promises of a glorious one.

And the Decalogue, or Ten Commandments, is a summary, or brief epitome of the law, written by the immediate finger of God, and contracted into an abridgment not only to ease our memories but to gain our veneration; for sententious commands best befit majesty. And, indeed, if we consider the paucity of the expressions, and yet the copiousness and variety of the matter contained in them, we must needs acknowledge not only their authority to be divine, but likewise the skill and art in reducing the *whole duty of man* to so brief a compendium. The words are but few, called therefore *the Words of the Covenant,* or *the Ten Words* (Exod. 34:28); but the sense and matter contained in them is vast and infinite: the rest of Scripture is but a commentary upon them, either exhorting us to obedience by arguments, or alluring us to it by promises; warning us against transgression by threatenings, or exciting us to the one, and restraining us from the other, by examples recorded in the historical part of it.

I. And now if any one ask, "What need all this long discourse about the law? Is it not fully *abrogated* by the coming of Christ?

Shall we again be brought under that heavy yoke of bondage, which neither we nor our fathers were able to bear? Doth not the Scripture frequently testify that we are not now under the law, but under grace? that Christ was made under the law, to free those who were under the law? and, therefore, to terrify and overawe men's consciences by the authority of the law; what is it but to make the gospel a legal dispensation, unworthy of that Christian liberty into which our Savior hath vindicated us, who has by his obedience fulfilled the law, and by his death abolished it?"

To this I answer: Far be it from every Christian to indulge himself in any licentiousness, from such a corrupt and rotten notion of the law's abrogation; for, so far is it from being abolished by the coming of Christ, that he himself expressly tells us, he came not *to destroy the law, but to fulfil* it (Matt. 5:17); that is, either to perform or else to perfect and fill up the law; and (v. 18), he avers that *"till heaven and earth pass, one jot or one tittle shall in no wise pass from the law till all be fulfilled,"* that is, till the consummation and fulfilling of all things; and then the law which was our rule on earth shall become our nature in heaven.

When therefore Paul speaks, as he frequently does, of the abrogation and disannulling of the law, we must carefully discern and distinguish both what is taught us respecting *the law,* and what is taught us respecting *the abrogation* of the law, or any part of it.

The law, which God delivered by Moses, was of three kinds: Ceremonial, Judicial, and Moral.

The *Ceremonial* Law was wholly taken up in enjoining those observances of sacrifices and offerings, and various methods of purification and cleansing, which were typical of Christ, and that sacrifice of his, which alone was able to take away sin.

The *Judicial* Law consisted of those constitutions which God prescribed the Jews for their civil government, and was the standing law of their nation. By this law were to be tried and determined all actions and suits between party and party: as in all other nations, there are particular laws and statutes for the decision of controversies that may arise among them.

But the *Moral* Law is a body of precepts, which carry a universal and natural equity in them; being so conformable to the light of reason and the dictates of every man's conscience, that as soon as ever they are declared and understood, they must needs be subscribed to as just and right.

These are the three sorts of laws which commonly go under the name of the Law of Moses: all of which had respect, either to those things which prefigured the Messiah to come, or to those which concerned their political and civil government as a distinct nation from others, or to such natural virtues and duties of piety towards God and righteousness towards men, as were common to them with all the rest of mankind.

And now as to the abrogation or continued obligation of these several laws, I desire you heedfully to attend to the following propositions.

1. The Ceremonial Law is, *as to the Jews, properly abrogated, and its obligation and authority utterly taken away and repealed;* for so the apostle is to be understood, when, in his epistles, he so often speaks of the abrogation and disannulling of the law: he speaks, I say, of the Ceremonial Law and Aaronical observances; which, indeed, were so fulfilled by Christ as to be abolished. So that, to maintain now a necessity of legal sacrifices, and purifyings, and sprinklings, is no less than to evacuate the death of Christ; and to deny the shedding of that blood that alone can purify us from all pollutions: which is but to catch at the shadow and lose the substance.

And as to us, who are the posterity and descendants of the Gentiles, it is more proper to affirm that *the Ceremonial Law was never in force,* than that it is truly abrogated; for the Ceremonial Law was national to the Jews, and, in a sort, peculiar to them only; neither did God intend that the observance of it should be imposed upon any other people, as a thing necessary for their future happiness, even though they should be proselyted.

And this appears, both because God expressly commands all those who were to be subject to the Ceremonial Law, that they should appear at Jerusalem, thrice in the year, before the Lord (Exod. 34:23, 24), which would have been impossible for those in countries far remote from Jerusalem; and because all their sacrifices and oblations, in which consisted the chiefest part of the ceremonial worship, were to be offered up only at Jerusalem; which would have been alike impossible, if this command of sacrificing had been intended by God to be obligatory on all the world. Therefore, doubtless, that command, even while it was in force, obliged none but the Jewish nation.

We find also that, even before Christ's coming, the Jews themselves did not impose the observance of the Ceremonial Law alike upon all proselytes; but their proselytes were of two sorts. Some, indeed, as the *Proselyti, Legis,* became perfect Jews in religion, lived among them, and engaged themselves to the full observance of the whole law; yet some, called *Proselyti Portae,* were only so far converted as to acknowledge and worship the only true God, but obliged not themselves to the performance of what the Levitical law required. These the Jews admitted into participation of the same common hope and salvation with themselves, when they professed their faith in God the Creator, and their obedience to the law of nature, together with the seven traditional precepts of Noah.

Hence we find Paul himself, who so earnestly in all his epistles opposes the observance of the Ceremonial Law, yet submits to the use of those rites (Acts 21:26; 16:3), by which he evidently declares that those believers who were of that nation, though they were freed from the necessity, yet they might lawfully, as yet, observe the Aaronical constitutions; especially, when, to avoid giving offense, it might be expedient so to do. So tender a thing is the peace of the church!

But then, concerning the Gentiles; although, before the coming of Christ, they might become perfect proselytes to the whole law of Moses, they should not subject themselves to the dogmatizing commands of false teachers, who required them to be circumcised and to keep the Ceremonial Law; but that they be required only to abstain "from meat offered to idols, and from blood, and from things strangled, and from fornication," that is, as judicious Mr. Hooker very probably interprets it, from incestuous marriages within prohibited degrees. And all those commands, laid upon them by the apostles, are the very precepts of Noah. But circumcision and other observances of the Ceremonial Law they were not obliged to: yea, they were obliged not to observe them, as being subversions of their souls (Acts 15:24). And therefore we find that the same holy apostle, who himself circumcised Timothy because he was the son of a Jewess, when he writes to the Gentiles, tells them expressly, that if they be circumcised Christ shall profit them nothing (Gal. 5:2).

Thus we see how far and in what sense the Ceremonial Law is abrogated.

2. As to the *Judicial Law,* and those precepts which were given to the Jews for the government of their civil state, that law is not at all abrogated.

Not to us, for it was never intended to oblige us. Neither, indeed, is it at all necessary that the laws of every nation should be conformed to the laws which the Jews lived under; for, doubtless, each state has its liberty to frame such constitutions as may best serve to obtain the ends of government.

Neither is the Judicial Law abrogated to the Jews: for though now, in their scattered state, the laws cease to be of force, because the Jews cease to be a body politic; yet, were their dispersion again collected into one republic, most probably the same national laws would bind them now, as did in former times, when they were a happy and flourishing kingdom.

3. Concerning the *Moral Law,* of which I am now to treat more especially, that is partly abrogated and partly not: abrogated, as to some of its circumstances; but not as to any thing of its substance, authority and obligation.

(1) To believers *The Moral Law is abrogated as to its condemning power.*

Though it sentences every sinner to death, and curses everyone who continues not in all things written therein to do them; yet, through the intervention of Christ's satisfaction and obedience, the sins of a believer are graciously pardoned, and the curse abolished, it being discharged wholly upon Christ, and received all into his body on the cross, "Christ hath redeemed us from the curse of the law, being made a curse for us" (Gal. 3:13); so that we may therefore triumphantly exult with the apostle, "There is now no condemnation to them that are in Christ Jesus" (Rom. 8:1).

(2) But, *as it has a power of obliging the conscience as a*

standing rule for our obedience, it remains still in its full vigor and authority.

It still directs us what we ought to do; binds the conscience to the performance of it; brings guilt upon the soul, if we transgress it; and reduces us to the necessity either of bitter repentance, or of eternal condemnation. For, in this sense, heaven and earth shall sooner pass away than one jot or tittle shall pass from the law.

Therefore Antinomianism is to be abominated, which derogates from the value and validity of the law, and contends that it is to all purposes extinct to believers, even as to its preceptive and regulating power; and that no other obligation to duty lies upon them who are in Christ Jesus, but only from the law of gratitude: that God requires not obedience from them upon so low and sordid an account as the fear of his wrath and dread severity; but all is to flow only from the principle of love and the sweet temper of a grateful and ingenuous spirit.

This is a most pestilent doctrine, which plucks down the fence of the law, and opens a gap for all manner of licentiousness and libertinism to rush in upon the Christian world; for, seeing that the Moral Law is no other than the Law of Nature written upon man's heart at the first, some positives only being superadded; upon the same account as we are men, upon the same we owe obedience to the dictates of it.

And, indeed, we may find every part of this law enforced in the gospel; charged upon us with the same threatenings, and recommended to us by the same promises; and all interpreted to us by our Savior himself, to the greatest advantage of strictness and severity. We find the same rules for our actions, the same duties required, the same sins forbidden in the gospel as in the law.

Yet, withal, a higher degree of obedience is now required from us under the dispensation of the gospel than was expected under the more obscure and shadowy exhibitions of gospel-grace by legal types and figures. We confess that the Israelites, before the coming of Christ, were no more under a Covenant of Works than we are now; but yet the Covenant of Grace was more darkly administered to them: and therefore, we having now received both a clearer light to discover what is our duty, and a more plentiful effusion of the

Holy Ghost to enable us to perform it, and better promises, more express and significant testimonies of God's acceptance, and more full assurance of our own reward, it lies upon us, and we are under obligation, having all these helps and advantages above them, to endeavor that our holiness and obedience should be much superior to theirs; and that we should serve God with more readiness and alacrity, since now by Jesus Christ our yoke is made easy and our burden light.

So that you see we are far from being released from our obligation to obedience; but rather, that obligation is made the stricter by Christ's coming into the world: and every transgression against the Moral Law is enhanced to an excess of sin and guilt, not only by the authority of God's injunction, which still continues inviolable; but likewise from the sanction of our Mediator and Redeemer who hath invigorated the precepts of the law by his express command, and promised us the assistance of his Spirit to observe and perform them.

II. I think it requisite to propound some *general rules for the right understanding and expounding of the Commandments,* which will be of great use to us for our right apprehending the full latitude and extent of them.

The Psalmist tells us, the commandments of God are *exceeding broad* (Ps. 119:96). And so indeed they are in the comprehensiveness of their injunctions, extending their authority over all the actions of our lives; but they are also exceeding strait, as to any toleration or indulgence given to the unruly lusts and appetites of men.

Now that we may conceive somewhat of this breadth and reach of the law of God, observe these following rules:

1. *All those precepts which are dispersed in the holy Scriptures, and which concern the regulating of our lives and actions, although not found expressly mentioned in the Decalogue, may yet very aptly be reduced under one of these ten commands.*

There is no duty required nor sin forbidden by God but it falls under one, at least, of these Ten Words, and sometimes under more than one; and therefore, to the right and genuine interpretation of this law we must take in whatsoever the prophets, apostles, or our Lord himself hath taught, as comments and expositions upon it; for the Decalogue is a compendium of all they have taught concerning moral worship and justice.

Yea, our Savior epitomizes this very epitome itself, and reduces these ten words to two: *love to God,* which comprehendeth all the duties of the first table; and *love to our neighbor,* which comprehendeth all the duties of the second table: and he tells us, that "upon these two hang all the law and the prophets" (Matt. 22:37-40). And certainly, a due love of God and of our neighbor will make us careful to perform all the duties of religion to the one, and of justice to the other; and keep us from attempting any violation to his honor, or violence to their right: therefore the Apostle tells us that "love is the fulfilling of the law" (Rom. 13:10); that "the end of the commandment is charity" (1 Tim. 1:5), or love: the end, that is the completion or the consummation of the commandment, is love, both to God and to one another.

2. Since most of the commandments are delivered in negative or prohibiting terms, and only the fourth and fifth in affirmative or enjoining, we may observe this rule: that *the affirmative commands include the prohibition of the contrary sin; and the negative commands include the injunction of the contrary duty.*

That the contrary to what is forbidden must be commanded, and the contrary to what is commanded be forbidden, is manifest. As, for instance, God in the third commandment forbids the taking of his name in vain: therefore, by consequence, the hallowing and sanctifying his name is therein commanded. The fourth requires the sanctifying of the Sabbath-day: therefore it surely follows that the profanation of it is thereby forbidden. The fifth commands us to honor our parents: therefore it forbids us to be disobedient or injurious to them. And so of the rest.

3. Observe, also, that *every negative command binds always, and to every moment of time; but the affirmative precepts, though they bind always, yet they do not bind to every moment;* that is, as to the habit of obedience, they do; but not as to the acts.

To make this plain by instance.

The first commandment, "Thou shalt have no other gods before me," bindeth always, and to every moment of time; so that he is guilty of idolatry whosoever shall at any time set up any other god to worship besides the Lord Jehovah. But the affirmative precept, which is included in this negative, namely, to worship, to love, to invoke, to depend on God, though it obligeth us always, (for we must never act contrary hereunto,) and likewise obliges us to every moment of time, in respect to the *habits* of divine love, and faith, and worship; yet it does not oblige us to every moment in respect of the *acts* of these habits; for it is impossible always to be actually praying, praising, and worshipping God, neither is it required, for this would make one duty shock and interfere with another.

So likewise, the fourth commandment, which is affirmative, "Remember that thou keep holy the Sabbath-day," always obliges; and whosoever at any time profanes the Sabbath, is guilty of the violation of this law but it does not, it cannot oblige to every moment of time, since this day only makes its weekly returns, and every parcel of time is not a Sabbath-day.

So, likewise, the fifth commandment is positive, "Honor thy father and thy mother," and binds always; so that we sin if at any time we are refractory and disobedient unto their lawful commands: but it does not oblige to the acts of honor and reverence in every moment of time, for that is impossible; or were it not, it would be but mimical and ridiculous.

But now the negative precepts oblige us to every moment of time; and whosoever ceases the observance of them for any one moment, is thereby involved in sin, and becomes guilty, and a transgressor before God: such are, "Thou shalt not take the name of the Lord thy God in vain; Thou shalt not kill; Thou shalt not steal; Thou shalt not commit adultery," etc. Now there is no moment of time whatsoever that can render the non-observance of these commands allowable, nor are there any circumstances that can excuse it from guilt. Whosoever profanes the name of God by rash swearing or trivial or impertinent uttering of it, whosoever sheds innocent blood, whosoever purloins from another what is rightly his, whosoever is guilty of any uncleanness; let it be at what time, in what place, after what manner soever, let it be done passionately or deliberately, whether he be tempted to it or not; yet he is a transgressor of the law, and liable to that curse and death which God hath threatened to inflict upon every soul of man that does evil. Whereas, in the affirmative precepts, there are some times and seasons to which we are not bound, so as actually to perform the duties enjoined us. This I suppose is clear, and without exception.

4. Observe this rule also: that *the same precept which forbids the external and outward acts of sin, forbids likewise the inward desires and motions of sin in the heart; and the same precept which requires the external acts of duty, requires likewise those holy affections of the soul that are suitable thereunto.*

As, for instance, the same command that requires me to worship God, exacts from me not only the outward service of the lip or of the knee, but much more the inward reverence and affection of my soul: that I should prostrate, not my body only, but my very heart as his feet; fearing him as the great God, and loving him as the greatest good, and with all the tenderness and dearness of a ravished soul cleaving to him and clasping about him as my only joy and happiness. Therefore, those are highly guilty of the violation of this command who worship God only with their bodies, when their hearts are far estranged from him; offering up only the shell and husk of a duty, when the pith and substance which should fill it is given either to the world or to their lusts: such as these are guilty of idolatry even in serving and worshipping the true God; for they set up their idols in their hearts when they come to inquire of him, as the prophet complains (Ezek. 14:7). So, likewise, that positive command, "Honor thy father and thy mother," not only requires from us the external acts of obedience to all the lawful commands of our parents and magistrates, and those whom God hath set in authority over us; but requires farther, an inward love, veneration and esteem for them in our hearts. For, though men can take no farther cognizance of us than by our overt-acts; and if those be regular, they are likewise satisfactory to all human laws: yet this is not sufficient satisfaction to the law of God, for God is the discerner and judge of the heart and soul; and *his* law hath this special prerogative above all others, that it can with authority prescribe to our very thoughts, desires and affections.

And then, as for *negative* commands, they forbid not only the external acts of sin but the inward motions of lust, sinful desires, and evil concupiscence. Thus we find it at large (Matt. 5), where our Savior makes it a great part of his object in his sermon on the mount, to clear and vindicate the Moral Law from the corrupt glosses and interpretations of the Scribes and Pharisees; and to show that the authority of the law reached to prohibit, not only sinful *actions,* as that corrupt generation thought, but sinful *affections* too, "Ye have heard that it was said by them of old time, Thou shalt not kill; and whosoever shall kill shall be in danger of the judgment" (v. 21). Here they stopped in the very bark and rind of the comand, and thought it no offense, though they suffered their hearts to burn with wrath, and malice, and revenge, so long as they pent it up there, and did not suffer it to break forth into bloody murder. But what saith our Savior, v. 22? "But I say unto you, that whosoever is angry with his brother without a cause, shall be in danger of the judgment; and whosoever shall say to his brother, Raca, shall be in danger of the council; but whosoever shall say, Thou fool, shall be in danger of hell fire" (v. 22). You see here, that not only the horrid sin of murder is forbidden by the law, but all the incentives to it and degrees of it; as anger conceived inwardly in the heart, or expressed outwardly in words.

So that the sense of our Savior in all this allusion seems to be this: that whereas the Scribes and Pharisees had restrained that command, *Thou shalt not kill,* only to actual murder, as if nothing else were forbidden besides open violence and blood; our Savior, contrariwise, teaches that not only that furious and barbarous sin of murder, but also rash and causeless anger, though it only boil in the heart, much more if it cast forth its foam at the mouth in reviling speeches, falls under that prohibition, "Thou shalt not kill." All these degrees deserve to be punished with eternal death; but, as among the Jews, some were punished with lighter, others with more grievous penalties, so shall it be at the Great Judgment: anger in our hearts shall be condemned with eternal punishment; but, if it break forth into reviling expressions the condemnation shall be more intolerable, and by so much more, by how much the reproaches are more bitter and sarcastical.

This, in brief, I take to be the true meaning of this difficult speech of our Savior: the whole scope whereof shows, that not only the gross acts of sin, but also the inward dispositions and corrupt affections unto sin, and every degree and tendency towards it, are forbidden and threatened by the holy law of God.

So, likewise, "Ye have heard that it was said by them of old time, Thou shalt not commit adultery; but I say unto you, that whosoever looketh on a woman to lust after her, hath committed adultery with her already in his heart" (5:27). Here our Savior brings inward concupiscence to the bar; and makes the heart and eye plead guilty, although shame or fear might restrain grosser acts.

Thus it appears that the same precept which forbids the outward acts of sin, forbids likewise the inward desires and motions of sin in the heart.

And, indeed, there is a great deal of reason for it. For God, who is our lawgiver, is a spirit. He sees and converses with our spirits. There is not the least thought that flits in our soul, not the least shadow of an imagination cast upon our fancy, not the stillest breathing of a desire in our heart but God is privy to it: he sees to the very bottom of that deep spring and source of thoughts that is in our heart: he beholds them in their causes and occasions; and *knows our thoughts,* as the Psalmist speaks, *afar off:* he beholds our souls more clearly and distinctly than we can behold one another's faces; and therefore it is but fit and rational that his laws should reach as far as his knowledge; and that he should prescribe rules to that, the irregularity of which he can observe and punish.

Hence it is that the apostle, considering what an energy the law has upon that part of man which seems most free and uncontrolled, his mind and spirit, calls it a *spiritual* law: "We know," saith he, "that the law is spiritual" (Rom. 7:14); and that, because the searching and convincing power of it enters into our spirits, cites our thoughts, accuses our desires, condemns our affections: which no other law in the world besides this can do. Therefore "the Word of God is" by the apostle said to be "quick and powerful, and sharper than any two-edged sword, piercing even to the dividing asunder of soul and spirit, and of the joints and marrow, and is a discerner of the thoughts and intents of the heart" (Heb. 4:12).

It is therefore a fourth rule for the right understanding of the extent and latitude of the commands, that the same precept which forbids the outward acts of sin, forbids also the inward desires and motions of sin in the heart.

5. *The command not only forbids the sin that is expressly mentioned, but all occasions and inducements leading to that sin.*

We may observe that there are many sins that are not expressly forbidden in any one commandment, but yet are reductively forbidden in every one towards the violation of which they may prove occasions. And as some one sin may be an occasion to all others, so it may be well said to be forbidden in every precept of the Decalogue.

I shall give only two of this kind: familiarity with evil persons, or keeping evil company; and the sin of drunkenness.

As for *evil company,* it is evident that though it be not expressly forbidden in any one commandment, yet, as it is a strong temptation and inducement to the violation of all of them, so it is a sin against them all. There are no such sure factors for the devil as wicked company, who will strive to rub their vice upon as many as they can infect. And therefore, you, who delight in the company either of atheists, or idolaters, or swearers, or sabbath-breakers, or disobedient rebels, or murderers, or whoremongers, or thieves, or perjured persons, or covetous muck-worms, you are guilty of the breach of each of these commandments; for you run yourself into the very snare of the devil, and take the same course to make yourself so which made them such. And therefore we are all forbidden to keep company with such profane and profligate wretches by the very same commandment which forbids their impieties, whatsoever they be.

And as for *drunkenness,* whereas in the apostle's days, even among the heathen themselves, shame so far prevailed upon vice and debauchery, that it left sobriety the day, and took only the night to itself (1 Thess. 5:7); yet now among us Christians wickedness is grown so profligate that we meet the drunkard reeling and staggering even at noon-day, ready to discharge his vomit in our faces or our bosoms.

Thus you see there are some sins which though not expressly

forbidden in the Decalogue, yet are virtually and reductively forbidden, as being the fomenters and occasions of others; and among these drunkenness especially, which strikes at every law that God hath enjoined us, the guilt whereof is universal as well as the sin epidemical.

6. *The commands of the first table are not to be kept for the sake of the second; but the commands of the second are to be kept for the sake of the first.*

The first table commands those duties which immediately respect the service and worship of God; the second, those which respect our demeanor towards men. Now the worship and service of God is not to be performed out of respect to men; but our duty towards men is to be observed out of respect to God. For he that worships God that he might thereby recommend himself to men, is but a hypocrite and formalist; and he that performs his duty towards men without respecting God in it, is but a mere civil moralist. The first table commands us not to worship idols, not to swear, not to profane the Sabbath. The laws of the magistrate command the very same; and those who are guilty of the breach of them are liable to human punishments. But if we abstain from these sins solely because they will expose us to shame or suffering among men; if we worship God merely that men may respect and venerate us, all the pomp and ostentation of our religion is but hypocrisy, and as such shall have its reward; for God requires to be served not for man's sake, but for his own.

The second table prescribes the right ordering of our conversation towards men; that we should be dutiful and obedient to our superiors, loving and kind to our equals, charitable and beneficial to our inferiors, and just and righteous towards all. These duties are not to be done only for man's sake, but for God's; and those who perform them without respecting him in them, lose both their acceptance and reward. And therefore our Savior condemns that love and beneficence which proceeds merely upon human and prudential accounts. "If ye love them which love you, what reward have ye? do not even the publicans the same?" (Matt. 5:46). And "If ye do good to them which do good to you, what thank have ye? for sinners also do even the same. And if ye lend to them of whom ye hope to receive, what thank have ye? for sinners also lend to sinners, to receive as much again" (Luke 6:33, 34).

7. *The commands of the first table, so far forth as they are purely moral, supersede our obedience to the commands of the second table, when they are not both consistent.*

As, for instance: we are in the second table required to obey our parents, and to maintain and preserve our own lives; yet, if we are brought into such circumstances as that we must necessarily disobey either God or them—either prostitute our souls to guilt, or our lives to execution—in such a case our Savior hath instructed us. "If any man come to me, and hate not his father, and mother, and wife, and children, yea, and his own life also, he cannot be my disciple" (Luke 14:26). Indeed, a positive hatred of these is unnatural and impious; but the hatred which our Savior here intends is *comparative;* that is, a *loving them less* than Christ, less than religion and piety. And if the commands of the one or the concerns of the other are at any time to be violated or neglected, it must only be when we are sure that they are incompatible with a good conscience and true godliness.

8. Again, whereas, in the first table, there is one command partly moral and natural, partly positive and instituted, and that is our observation of the Sabbath, we may observe that *our obligation to the duties of the second table often supersedes our obedience to that command of the first table.*

It frequently happens that works of necessity and mercy will not permit us to be employed in works of piety, nor to sanctify the Sabbath after such a manner as else we ought; for the Lord requires mercy rather than sacrifice (Hos. 6:6). And this our Savior alleges (Matt. 9:13). In which sense it holds true, that "The Sabbath was made for man, and not man for the Sabbath" (Mark 2:27). Whatsoever therefore is a work of necessity, or a work of charity and mercy, and that not only towards man, but even towards brute beasts themselves, may lawfully be done on the Sabbath-day, without bringing upon us the guilt of profanation; for that which is purely moral in the second table doth in a sort derogate from what is but positive and instituted in the first.

9. *Whatsoever is forbidden in any command, both all the signs*

and symptoms of it, and likewise all the effects and consequence of it, are forbidden in the same.

Thus, under the prohibition of idolatry, falls the prohibition of feasting in the idol-temples, and eating meats sacrificed to them, as being too evident a sign of our communion with them.

So, in the commands in which pride is forbidden (which are chiefly the first and second, for a proud man sets up himself for his god, is his own idol, and is his own idolater), in the same are forbidden all the signs and effects of pride; as a lofty look and a mincing gait, an affected behavior and vain fantastic apparel, against which the prophet largely declaims (Isa. 3:16-26); because, although pride does not formally consist in these things, yet they are signs and effects of pride, and contrary to that modesty and decency which God requires.

10. *The connection between the commands is so close and intimate, and they are so linked together, that whoever breaks one of them is guilty of all.*

Now that bond which runs through them and knits them thus together, is the authority and sovereignty of God enjoining their observance: so that whoever fails in his due obedience to any one, virtually and interpretatively does transgress them all.

Thus we find it expressly affirmed, "Whosoever shall keep the whole law, and yet offend in one point, he is guilty of all" (James 2:10). Not as though the violation of one precept were actually the violation of another; for many may steal, and yet not actually murder; many again may murder, and yet not actually commit adultery: but this place of the apostle must be understood of violating that authority which passes through them all, and by which all the commandments have their sanction. For since the authority of the great God is one and the same in all these laws, he that shall so far disrespect this authority as wilfully to break one of them, evidently declares that he owns it not in any. And although other considerations may restrain such a one from those crimes which are forbidden by some commandments, yet his observance of them is no part of obedience, nor can it be interpreted to be performed out of conscience and respect towards God; for were it so, the same authority which withheld him from murder, or theft, or adultery, would likewise restrain him from lying, or taking the name of God in vain; and he that is guilty of these offenses, is likewise guilty of all, because the same authority is stamped upon them all alike, and is alike violated in the transgression of each. And this very reason the apostle subjoins to his assertion, "He that said, Do not commit adultery, said also, Do not kill. Now, if thou commit no adultery, yet if thou kill, thou art become a transgressor of the law" (v. 11), yea, of the whole law, as breaking that fence which God had set about his law, even his sovereign and absolute authority.

These are the rules which may direct your understandings to a right knowledge of the latitude and comprehensiveness of the law.

BIBLIOGRAPHY

Calvin, John. *Institutes of the Christian Religion.* II,viii, "An Exposition of the Moral Law."

Fairbairn, Patrick. *The Revelation of Law in Scripture.* Grand Rapids: Zondervan Publishing House, 1957 (r.p. of 1869 edition). (This is the most definitive statement of the issues and solutions to be found.)

Henry, Carl F. H. "The Law and The Gospel" in *Christian Personal Ethics.* Grand Rapids: Wm. B. Eerdmans Publishing Co., 1957, 350-62.

Kaiser, Walter C. Jr., "Leviticus 18:5 and Paul: Do this and you Shall Live (Eternally?)," *Journal of Evangelical Theological Society.* XIV (1971). (Attempts to answer the question: "Was there a hypothetical offer of salvation in law observance?")

Kevan, Ernest F. *The Moral Law.* Jenkintown, Pa.: Sovereign Grace Publishers, 1963. (A broad coverage of the issues from the Puritan position).

_____. *Keep His Commandments.* London: Tyndale Press, 1964.

Part II
HISTORICAL BOOKS

IV

UNDERSTANDING
"THE SUN STOOD STILL"

by Robert Dick Wilson

Editor's Introduction

Does the Bible teach that the world stopped its rotation once in the days of Joshua and later on in the days of Ahaz? Some evangelical scholars believe that the writer of Joshua meant to indicate that God intervened for Joshua in such a way as to give extended relief from the heat of the sun and the aid of a violent hailstorm upon the heads of a fleeing enemy.

In spite of all the recent and old rumors concerning a "missing day" observed by astronomers and space scientists, not one shred of solid evidence has come forward. The Biblical facts and vocabulary still remain.

While reading through the lists of synonyms in a syllabary contained in the Cuneiform Texts, volume XIX, 19,[1] I found one in which the words *atalû, adiru,* and *da'amu,* are given. Now, it is well known that *atalû* is the ordinary word in the astronomical tablets for "eclipse" and that the verb *adâru* means "to be dark." Recalling that the radicals *dm* are the root of the verbs occurring in Joshua 10:12, 13, I immediately turned up the passage and at once recognized that it would make good sense to render the form *dōm* in Joshua's prayer by "become dark," or "be eclipsed." This led me to a further study of the works of Epping, Kugler, Thompson, Weidner, and Virolleaud, on the astronomy of the Babylonians, and I was delighted to find not only that the root *dm* is of not infrequent occurrence, but also that two other significant words of the Joshua

---

[1] Cf. p. 50, I, 1 (4).

passage are technical terms in the astronomical science of the Babylonians. The most important of these terms, next to *dm*, is the technical use of *'āmad* "to stand." It occurs frequently on the tablets to denote the point, or place, in the heavens at which a star ceases to go in one direction and begins its return journey to its starting-point. To the naked eye, a star seems to "stand still" for a time before starting on its return passage, just as a runner in a race up and down a land would stand still as he was turning to run back to the starting-point. In a second sense, the verb is used for the "staying" of a star in a constellation, or house, of the zodiac. The other technical word is the *ḥᵃṣî (Bab. iṣi) of verse 13, translated* "midst" in the English version. While not denying that this word may and often does mean "midst," in Hebrew, as, for example, in "midnight" (*ḥᵃṣî hallaylā*), it seems that in Babylonian in the two places where it is used in the astronomical tablets, it has the sense more usual in Hebrew of "half," being employed in the one case to denote the half of a cloud and in the other the half of the moon. According to this interpretation, it would mean in Joshua the period from midday to sunset, or ninety degrees.

I further found that in many places in Virolleaud's tablets treating especially of the sun and moon, both are said to be darkened together, the word for darkening being *dm*. Proceeding from these data, I translated the passage in Joshua and saw that the whole situation was cleared up, except where it states, according to the common version, that the sun did not go in for "about a whole day." Having long ago come to the conclusion that this phrase does not mean what the English version implies, I made a new investigation of all the places where the preposition *kaf* (here rendered "about") and the word *tāmîm*, "whole," as well as its root *tāmam*, are employed in the Old Testament. The result of the investigation[2] was to confirm my opinion that the phrase should be translated "as on a completed (or ordinary) day." It must be borne in mind by those who read my translation, that the verb *bô'* is used in Hebrew for the "going in" of the sun, in the evening, and the verb *yāṣā'* for its "coming out," in the morning. The Babylonian uses the same

---

2 Cf. p. 53. V.

word for the "coming out" of the sun, but uses *erēbu* (from which the Hebrew derives *'ereb*, its term for evening) to denote the "going in," at sunset. With this in mind, we can understand what Ben Sira means when he says that through Joshua the sun stood, one day becoming like two. He means apparently that the day of the battle had two *comings out* of the sun, one at sunrise and the other at midday, when it came out from behind the moon; and that it had two *goings-in*, one when it went in behind the moon and the other at sunset.

This translation shows us, moreover, how Jehovah fought for Israel. It was not merely with storm and hail that the enemy was discomfited, but his very gods were compelled to hide their faces at noonday. At the prayer of Israel's leader, both of their chief deities, the sun and the moon, were darkened, or eclipsed. So, as we can well imagine would be the case, they were terrified beyond measure, thinking that the end of all things had come; and they were discomfited and smitten and turned and fled.

Herodotus tells of an eclipse of the sun which occurred during a battle between the Lydians and the Medes, that scared both of the combatants so much that they stopped fighting and made an immediate peace.[3] Later, after Xerxes had assembled his army for the invasion of Greece, an eclipse took place while he was still at Sardis which terrified him to such an extent, that only after a favorable interpretation of the eclipse by the Magi, who affirmed that it meant the destruction of the Greeks, would he proceed with his undertaking.[4] So, also, our best modern observers tell us how all nature seems terrified by an eclipse, and how they, in spite of themselves, could not suppress a feeling of dread in the presence of this appalling phenomenon.

It will be perceived that the translation suggested does away with the miraculous character of the event in so far as it involves the solar system and the law of gravitation. It is true, also, that it runs counter to Jewish exegesis and to all the ancient versions, except perhaps the Greek, which is somewhat ambiguous and difficult of

---

[3] Bk. I. 74, 103.
[4] Bk. VII. 37.

explanation. Notwithstanding this, I confess to a feeling of relief, as far as I myself am concerned, that I shall no longer feel myself forced by a strict exegesis to believe that the Scriptures teach that there actually occurred a miracle involving so tremendous a reversal of all the laws of gravitation. It can readily be understood how the Jewish interpreters of later times, either through ignorance, or because of their overwhelming desire to magnify their own importance in the scheme of the universe, should have embraced the opportunity that the ambiguous terms of this purely scientific account afforded them to enhance the magnitude of the divine interference in their behalf. But for us today there lies in this passage the more useful lesson of faith in God as the answerer of prayer. How stupendous was the faith of Joshua as shown in his prayer! How immediate and complete was God's answer to that prayer! He who knew beforehand what Joshua would ask, had made all preparations to grant his request. For his are hearts and stars, and darkness and light, and faith and love and victory, excelling in their lasting glory all the transient miracles of standing suns. Lastly, mark that the inspired writer says that it was the extraordinary answer to the prayer of a man that made that day at Gibeon to be unlike every other day before or since. In following his interpretation of its significance, let us rest content.

I would suggest the following translation:

> Be eclipsed, O sun, in Gibeon,
> And thou moon in the valley of Ajalon!

And the sun was eclipsed and the moon turned back, while the nation was avenged on its enemies. Is it not written upon the book of Jashar?

> And the sun stayed in the half of the heavens,
> And set not hastily as when a day is done.

And there never was a day like that day before or since, in respect to Jehovah's hearing the voice of a man."

BIBLIOGRAPHY

Blair, Hugh. "Joshua," *The New Bible Commentary:* Revised (eds. D. Guthrie, and J. A. Motyer). Grand Rapids: Wm. B. Eerdmans Publishing Co., 1970 (first edition, 1953) pp. 243-45.

Maunder, E. W. "The Battle of Beth-Horon," *International Standard Bible Encyclopedia,* I. Grand Rapids: Wm. B. Eerdmans Publishing Co., 446-49.

Ramm, Bernard. *The Christian View of Science and Scripture.* Grand Rapids: Wm. B. Eerdmans Publishing Co., 1955, pp. 156-61.

V.

THE HISTORICAL ELEMENT
IN GOD'S REVELATION

by Patrick Fairbairn

Editor's Introduction

*What permanent value can the historical sections of the Scriptures
hold for modern man? Must we be reduced to that arbitrary process
of "spiritualizing" the text? Can those large sections of historical
text only be salvaged by cheap allegorizing? Fairbairn set the pace
for an issue which still troubles Old Testament Biblical theologians.*

The fact that a historical element enters deeply into God's
revelations of himself in Scripture is one of the most distinguishing
characteristics of Scripture as a Divine revelation, and as such is
prominently exhibited at the commencement of the Epistle to the
Hebrews, in the words, "God, who at sundry times, and in divers
manners, spake in time past unto the fathers by the prophets, hath
in these last days spoken unto us by His Son." The simple fact,
however, no longer satisfies; it comes at certain points into conflict
with the critical, individualizing spirit of the age. But, to have the
matter distinctly before us, we must first look at the consequences
necessarily growing out of the fact with regard to the character it
imparts to Divine revelation, and then consider the exceptions
taken against it in whole or in part.

I. First, in respect to the fact, we have to take into account the
extent to which the characteristic in question prevails. There is not
merely a historical element in Scripture, but this so as even to
impart to the revelation itself a history. Though supernatural in its
origin, it is yet perfectly natural and human in its mode of working
and its course of development. It stands associated with human
wants and emergencies, as the occasions which called it forth;

human agencies were employed to minister it; and, for transmission
to future times, it has been written in the common tongues and
dialects of men, and under the diversified forms of composition
with which they are otherwise familiar. So little does this revelation
of God affect a merely ideal or super-earthly style—so much does it
let itself down among the transactions and movements of history,
that it has ever been with outstanding and important facts that it
has associated its more fundamental ideas. In these, primarily, God
has made himself known to man. And hence, alike in the Old and
the New Testament Scriptures, the historical books stand first; the
foundation of all is there; the rest is but the structure built on it;
and just as is the reality and significance of the facts recorded in
them, such also is the truth of the doctrines, and the measure of the
obligations and hopes growing out of them.

But since revelation thus has a history, it necessarily has also a
progress; for all history, in the proper sense, has such. It is not a
purposeless moving to and fro, or a wearisome iteration, a turning
back again upon itself, but an advance—if at times halting, or
circuitous, still an advance—toward some specific end. So, in a
peculiar manner, is it with the book of God's revelation; there is an
end, because it is of him, who never can work but for some aim
worthy of himself, and with unerring wisdom subordinates everything to its accomplishment. That end may be variously described,
according to the point of view from which it is contemplated; but,
speaking generally, it may be said to include such an unfolding of
the character and purposes of God in grace, as shall secure for those
who accept its teachings, salvation from the ruin of sin, practical
conformity to the will of God, and the bringing in of the everlasting
kingdom of righteousness and peace, with which both the good of
his people and the glory of his own name are identified. This is the
grand theme pursued throughout; the different parts and stages of
revelation are but progressive developments of it, and, to be rightly
understood, must be viewed with reference to their place in the
great whole. So that the revelation of God in Scripture finds, in this
respect, its appropriate image in those temple-waters seen in vision
by the prophet—issuing at first like a little streamlet from the seat
of the Divine majesty, but growing apace, and growing, not by

supplies ministered from without, but as it were by self-production, and carrying with it the more—the more it increased in volume and approached its final resting-place—the vivifying influences which shed all around them the aspect of life and beauty.

Now, this characteristic of Divine revelation, as being historically developed, and thence subject to the law of progress, has undoubtedly its dark side to our view; there are points about it which seem mysterious, and which we have no means of satisfactorily explicating. In particular, the small measures of light which for ages it furnished respecting the more peculiar things of God, the imperfect form of administration under which the affairs of his kingdom were necessarily placed till the fulness of the time had come for the manifested Saviour, and still in a measure cleaving to it—such things undoubtedly appear strange to us, and are somewhat difficult to reconcile with our abstract notions of wisdom and benevolence. Why should the world have been kept so long in comparative darkness, when some further communications from the upper Sanctuary might have relieved it? Why delay so long the forthcoming of the great realities, on which all was mainly to depend for life and blessing? Or, since the realities have come, why not take more effective means for having them brought everywhere to bear on the understandings and consciences of men? Questions of this sort not unnaturally present themselves; and though, in regard at least to the first of them, we can point to a wide-reaching analogy in the natural course of providence, yet, in the general, we want materials for arriving at an intelligent view of the whole subject, such as might enable us to unravel the mysteries which hang around it. It behoves us to remember, that in things which touch so profoundly upon the purposes of God, and the plan of his universal government, we meanwhile know but in part; and instead of vainly agitating the questions, why it is thus and not otherwise, should rather apply our minds to the discovery of the practical aims, which we have reason to believe stand associated with the state of things as it actually exists, and as we have personally to do with it.

Looking at the matter in this spirit, and with such an object in view, we can readily perceive various advantages arising from such an introduction of the historical element as has been described into

the method of God's revelation of his mind and will to men. First
of all, it serves (if we may so speak) to *humanize* the revelation—
does, in a measure, for its teachings of truth and duty what, in a
still more peculiar manner, was done by the Incarnation. It is,
indeed, at bottom, merely a recognizing and acting on the truth,
that man was made in the image of God, and that only by laying
hold of what remains of this image, and sanctifying it for higher
uses, can the Spirit of God effectually disclose Divine things, and
obtain for them a proper lodgment in the soul: the rays of the
eternal Sun must reach it, not by direct effulgence, but "through
the luminous atmosphere of created minds." Then, as another
result, let it be considered how well this method accords with and
secures that fulness and variety, which is necessary to Scripture as
the book which, from its very design, was to provide the seed-corn
of spiritual thought and instruction for all times—a book for the
sanctification of humanity, and the developing in the soul of a
higher life than that of nature. An end like this could never have
been served by some general announcements, systematized exhibitions of doctrine, or stereotyped prescriptions of order and duty,
without respect to diversities of time, and the ever-varying evolu-
tions of the world's history. There was needed for its accomplishment precisely what we find in Scripture—a rich and various treas-
ury of knowledge, with ample materials for quiet meditation, the
incitement of active energy, and the soothing influences of consolation and hope—and so, resembling more the freedom and fulness of
nature than the formality and precision of art. Hence, as has been
well said, "Scripture cannot be mapped or its contents cataloged;
but, after all our diligence to the end of our lives, and to the end of
the church, it must be an unexplored and unsubdued land, with
heights and valleys, forests and streams, on the right and left of our
path, full of concealed wonders and choice treasures." One may
readily enough master a system of doctrine, or become conversant
with even a complicated scheme of religious observance; but a
history, a life, especially such lives and memorable transactions as
are found in Scripture, above all, what is written of our blessed
Lord, his marvellous career, his Divine works and not less Divine
discourses, his atoning death and glorious resurrection—who can

ever say he has exhausted these? Who does not rather feel—if he really makes himself at home with them—that there belongs to them a kind of infinite suggestiveness, such as is fitted to yield perpetually fresh life and instruction to thoughtful minds? And this, not as in the case of human works, for a certain class merely of mankind, but for all who will be at pains to search into its manifold and pregnant meaning. Hence the Word of God stands so closely associated with study, meditation, and prayer, without which it cannot accomplish its design—cannot even make its treasures properly known. And on this account, "the church and theology must, while they are in the flesh, eat their bread by the sweat of their brow; which is not only not a judgment, but, for our present state, a great blessing. If the highest were indeed so easy and simple, then the flesh would soon become indolent and satisfied. God gives us the truth in his word, but he takes care that we must all win it for ourselves ever afresh. He has therefore with great wisdom arranged the Bible as it is." Still further, in the actual structure of revelation, there is an interesting exhibition of the progressive character of the Divine plan, and of the organic connection between its several parts—in this a witness of the general organism of the human family, and, for individual members thereof, a type of the progress through which the divinely educated mind must ever pass, as from childhood to youth, and from youth to the ripeness and vigor of manhood. It thus has, as it could not otherwise have done, its milk for babes and its meat for strong men. And the scheme of God for the highest wellbeing of his people, is seen to be no transient or fitful conception, but a purpose lying deep in the eternal counsel of his will—thence gradually working itself into the history of the world—proceeding onwards from age to age, rising from one stage of development to another, the same grand principles maintained, the same moral aims pursued, through all external changes of position and varying forms of administration, till the scheme reached its consummation in the appearance and kingdom of Christ.

II. If the account now given of the matter, and the conclusion just drawn as to its practical bearing—drawn in the language of Scripture—be correct, then the historical and progressive character of revelation, the circumstance of God's mind and will being com-

municated, in the first instance, to particular individuals, and associated with specific times and places in the past, does not destroy
its application or impair its usefulness to men of other times: we,
too, are interested in the facts it records, we are bound by the law
of righteousness it reveals, we have to answer for all its calls and
invitations, its lessons of wisdom and its threatenings of judgment.
But here exception is taken by the representatives and advocates of
individualism, sometimes under a less, sometimes under a more
extreme form; in the one case denying any direct claim on our faith
and obedience, in respect to what is written in Old Testament
Scripture, but yielding it in respect to the New; in the other, placing
both substantially in the same category, and alleging, that because
of the remoteness of the period to which the gospel era belongs,
and the historical circumstances of the time no longer existing, the
things recorded and enjoined also in New Testament Scripture are
without any binding authority on the heart and conscience. It may
be the part of wisdom to accredit and observe them, but there can
be no moral blame if we should feel unable to do that, if we should
take up an unbelieving and independent position.

1. Persons of the former class, who claim only a partial exemp-
tion from the authoritative teaching of Scripture—from the binding
power of its earlier revelations—speak after this fashion: We were
not yet alive, nor did the economy under which we live exist, when
the things were spoken or done, through which God made revelation of himself to men of the olden time—when Abraham, for
example, at the Divine command, left his father's house, and was
taken into covenant with God, or when Israel, at a subsequent
period, were redeemed from the land of Egypt, that they might
occupy a certain position and calling; and however important the
transactions may have been in themselves, or however suitable for
the time being the commands given, they still can have no direct
authority over us; nor can we have to do with them as grounds of
moral obligation, except in so far as they have been resumed in the
teaching of Christ, or are responded to in our Christian consciousness. Of late years this form of objection has been so frequently
advanced, that it is unnecessary to produce quotations; and not
uncommonly the reasons attached especially to the fifth command

in the Decalogue, and also to the fourth as given in Deuteronomy 5:15, pointing, the one to Israel's heritage of Canaan, and the other to their redemption from Egypt, are regarded as conclusive evidences of the merely local and temporal nature in particular of the commands imposed in the Decalogue.

The mode of contemplation on which this line of objection proceeds is far from new; in principle it is as old as Christianity. For the view it adopts of Old Testament Scripture was firmly maintained by the unbelieving Jews of apostolic times, though applied by them rather to the blessings promised than to the duties enjoined. They imagined that, because they were the descendants of those to whom the word originally came, they alone were entitled to appropriate the privileges and hopes it secured to the faithful, or if others, yet only by becoming proselytes to Judaism, and joining themselves to the favored seed. Fierce conflicts sprung up on this very point in subsequent times. Tertullian mentions a disputation of great keenness and length, which took place in his neighborhood, between a Christian and a Jewish proselyte, and in which the latter sought "to claim the law of God for himself" (*sibi vindicare dei legem instituerit*). Conceiving the merits of the question to have been darkened, rather than otherwise, by words without knowledge, Tertullian took occasion from it to write his treatise against the Jews, in which he endeavored to show that God, as the Creator and Governor of all men, gave the law through Moses to one people, but in order that it might be imparted to all nations, and in a form which was destined, according to Old Testament Scripture itself, to undergo an important change for the better. Nearly two centuries later we find Augustine resuming the theme, and, after adducing various passages from Moses and the prophets about the redemption God had wrought for men, and the greater things still in prospect, the Jews are introduced as proudly erecting themselves and saying, "*We* are the persons; this is said of us; it was said *to* us; for *we* are Israel, God's people."[1] Thus the historical element in revelation,

---

[1] "Adv. Judaeos," sec. 9. Both Augustine and Tertullian have sharply exhibited, in their respective treatises, the substantial identity of the calling of believers in Christian and pre-Christian times. But in respect to the general principles of duty, they both except the

from the time it became peculiarly associated with the family of Abraham, was turned by them into an argument for claiming a kind of exclusive right to its provisions—as if Jehovah were the God of the Jews only; just as now it is applied to the purpose of fixing on the Jews an exclusive obligation to submit to its requirements of duty—except in so far as the matter therein contained may be coincident with the general principles of moral obligation. The ground of both applications is the same—namely, by reason of the historical accompaniments of certain parts of Divine revelation, to circumscribe its sphere, and confine its authoritative teaching within merely local and temporary channels.

Now, as this is a point which concerns the proper bearing and interpretation of Scripture, it is to Scripture itself that the appeal must be made. But on making such an appeal, the principle that emerges is very nearly the converse of that just mentioned: it is, that the *particular* features in revelation, derived from its historical accompaniments, were meant to be, not to the prejudice or the subversion, but rather for the sake, of its *general* interest and application. They but served to give more point to its meaning, and render more secure its preservation in the world. So that, instead of saying, in respect to one part or another of the sacred volume, I find therein a word of God to such a person, or at such a period in the past, therefore not strictly for me; I should rather, according to the method of Scripture, say, Here, at such a time and to such a party, was a revelation in the mind and will of Him who is Lord of heaven and earth, made to persons of like nature and calling with myself—made, indeed, *to* them, but only that it might *through*

---

law of the weekly Sabbath; with them, as with the Fathers generally, this was a prominent distinction between the believing Jew and the believing Christian—the Sabbath being viewed, in common with many of the later Jews, as a day of simple rest from work—a kind of sanctimonious idleness and repose—hence, no further related to the Christian than as a prefiguration of his cessation from sin, and spiritual rest in Christ. All the precepts of the Decalogue they regarded as strictly binding but this (so expressly Aug., 'De Spiritu et Lit.,' c. xiv.; also Tert., 'De Idolatria,' c. 14; 'Adv. Jud.,' c. 4); or this only in the sense now specified. It was a branch of the Patristic misconceptions respecting Old Testament subjects, and one of the most unfortunate of them. However, Tertullian in one place, 'Adv. Marcionem,' iv. 12, reasons with substantial correctness as to our Lord's treatment of the Sabbath, and His views regarding it, maintaining that it allowed certain kinds of work.

them be conveyed and certified to others; and coming, as it does to me, a component part of the Word, which reveals the character of the Most High, and which, as such, he delights most peculiarly to magnify, I also am bound to listen to it as the voice of God speaking to me through my brother-man, and should make conscience of observing it—in so far as it is not plainly of a local and temporary nature, and consequently unsuited to my position and circumstances.

There are, no doubt, things of this latter description in the Word of God—things which, in their direct and literal form, are inapplicable to any one now; for this is a necessary consequence of the play that has been given to the historical element in Scripture. But then it is in a measure common to *all* Scripture—not wanting even in its later communications. Our Lord himself spake words to His disciples, addressed to them both commands and promises, which are no longer applicable in the letter, as when he called some to leave their ordinary occupations and follow him, or gave them assurance of an infallible direction and supernatural gifts. And how many things are there in the epistles to the churches, which had special reference to the circumstances of the time, and called for services which partook of the local and temporary? But such things create no difficulty to the commonest understanding; nor, if honestly desirous to learn the mind of God, can any one fail to derive from such portions of Scripture the lessons they were designed to teach—on the supposition of the requisite care and pains being applied to them. It is, therefore, but a difference in degree which in this respect exists between the Scriptures of the New and those of the Old Testament; there is in the Old Testament merely a larger proportion of things which, if viewed superficially, are not, in point of form, applicable to the circumstances, or binding on the consciences of believers in Christian times; while yet they are all inwrought with lines of truth, and law, and promise, which give them a significance and a value for every age of the church. The *ultimate* aim and object of what was done was more important than its direct use.

From the time that God began to select a particular line as the channel of his revealed will to man, he made it clear that the good of all was intended. A special honor was in this respect to be conferred on the progeny of Shem, as compared with the other branches of Noah's posterity; but it was not doubtfully intimated that those other branches should participate in the benefit (Gen. 9:26, 27). When, however, the Divine purpose took effect, as it so early did, in the selection of Abraham and his seed, the end aimed at was from the first announced to be of the most comprehensive kind—namely, that in Abraham and his seed "all the families of the earth should be blessed." It was but giving expression in another form to this announcement, and breathing the spirit couched in it, when Moses, pointing to the destiny of Israel, exclaimed, "Rejoice, O ye nations, with his people" (Deut. 32:43); and when the Psalmist prayed, "God be merciful to us and bless us, that thy way may be known upon earth, thy saving health among all nations" (Ps. 67)—the true prosperity of Israel being thus expressly coupled with the general diffusion of God's knowledge and blessing, and the one sought with a view to the other. Hence also the temple, which was at once the symbol and the center of all that God was to Israel, was designated by the prophet "an house of prayer for all peoples" (Isa. 56:7). And hence, yet again, and as the proper issue of the whole, Jesus—the Israel by way of eminence, the impersonation of all that Israel should have been, but never more than most imperfectly was—the One in whom at once the calling of Israel and the grand purpose of God for the good of men found their true realization— he, while appearing only as a Jew among Jews, yet was not less the life and light of the world—revealing the Father for men of every age and country, and making reconciliation for iniquity on behalf of all who should believe on his name, to the farthest limits of the earth and to the very end of time.

Looking thus, in a general way, over the field of Divine revelation, we perceive that it bears respect to mankind at large; and that what is special in it as to person, or time, or place, was not designed to narrow the range of its application, or render it the less profitable to any one for "doctrine, for reproof, for correction, and for instruction in righteousness." And when we turn to particular passages of Scripture, and see how God-inspired men understood and used what came from Heaven, in other times and places than those in which they themselves lived, the same impression is yet more deepened on our minds—for we find them personally recognizing and acting on the principle in question.

In the Book of Psalms, for instance, how constantly do the sacred writers, when seeking to revive and strengthen a languishing faith, throw themselves back upon the earlier manifestations of God, and recall what He had said or done in former times, as having permanent value and abiding force even for them! "I will remember the works of the Lord, surely I will remember thy wonders of old. Thou art the God that doest wonders: Thou hast declared thy strength among the people. Thou hast with thine arm redeemed thy people, the sons of Jacob and Joseph." It was virtually saying, Thou didst it all, that we might know and believe what Thou canst, and what Thou wilt do still.

The principle is even more strikingly exhibited in Hosea 12:3-6, "He [namely, Jacob] took his brother by the heel in the womb, and by his strength he had power with God: yea, he had power over the angel, and prevailed; he wept, and made supplication unto him: he found him in Bethel, and there he [God] spake with us—even Jehovah, God of hosts, Jehovah is his name." That is, Jehovah, the I am, he who is the same yesterday, today, and for ever, in speaking ages ago with Jacob at Bethel, and at Peniel giving him strength over the angel, did in effect do the same *with us:* the record of these transactions is a testimony of what he is, and what he is ready to do in *our* behalf. And so, the prophet adds, by way of practical application, "Therefore turn *thou* to thy God: keep mercy and judgment, and wait on thy God continually."

Passing to New Testament times, the principle under consideration is both formally vindicated, and practically carried out. Not only does our Lord generally recognize as of God whatever was written in the Law and the Prophets, and recognize it as what he had come, not to destroy, but to fulfil—not only this, but he ever appeared as one appropriating, and, in a manner, living on the word contained in them. Thus, when plied by the tempter with the plausible request to turn the stones of the desert into bread, the ready reply was, "It is written, Man liveth not by bread only, but by every word which proceedeth out of the mouth of God"—*man* does it; man, namely, as the humble, docile, confiding child of

God—he lives thus; so it was written ages ago in the ever-living Word of God—written, therefore, also for him, who is pre-eminently such a man, as much as if it had been immediately addressed to himself. And the same course was followed in the other temptations: they were successively met and repelled by what was written aforetime, as equally valid and binding at that time as when originally penned.

To say nothing of the other apostles, who freely quote Old Testament Scripture, Paul both formally sets forth and frequently applies the same great principle:—sometimes in a more general manner, as when he affirms, that "the things written aforetime were written for our learning" (Rom. 15:3); or, more particularly, when speaking of the dealings of God with Israel in the wilderness, he states that "they happened unto them for ensamples [types], and are written for our admonition (1 Cor. 10:11); or, again, when identifying believers under the gospel with Abraham, he asserts that "they who are of faith are blessed with faithful Abraham" (Gal. 3:9)—the blessing pronounced upon him being regarded as virtually pronounced also upon those in later times who exercise his faith.

And still more striking is another exposition given to the principle, as connected with the Abrahamic blessing, in Hebrews, where, referring to the promise and the oath confirming it, it is said, God thereby showed "to the heirs of promise the immutability of His counsel," so that "by two immutable things, in which it was impossible for God to lie, we might have a strong consolation who have fled for refuge to the hope set before us"—not that *he* merely, to whom it was directly given, but that *we* too might have it. Therefore, the promise of blessing and its confirmatory oath, were, according to the author of the epistle, designed as well for believers in gospel times as for the father of the faithful; and why? Simply because they reveal the character and purpose of God in respect to the covenant of salvation, which, in all that essentially pertains to them, are independent of place and time, like their Divine Author changing not, but perpetually entitled to the faith and confidence of those who seek an interest in their provisions.

Such is the spirit or principle in which we are taught, on inspired authority—by Psalmists and Prophets of the Old Testament, by Christ and his apostles in the New—to regard and use that revelation of truth and duty, which comes to us bound up with the history of God's dispensations. If any thing can be deemed certain regarding it, it is that we must look through the external accompaniments of what is revealed to its heart and substance; in other words, that we must not allow what is merely circumstantial in the Divine communications to interfere with that which is essential, and which, from the organic unity pervading those communications, is properly of no age or time. The false principle, which in various forms has from early to present times been put forth, is to invert this relation—to employ the circumstantial as a lever to undermine or drive into abeyance the essential. Had such been our Lord's method of interpreting ancient Scripture, what would it have availed him to remember, in his hour of temptation, that man liveth not by bread only, but by every word of God, since that was written of Israel as redeemed from Egypt and fed with manna, while he was a stranger to both? Or, had it been Paul's, how should he ever have thought of transferring such special transactions and assurances of blessing as those connected with the faith of Abraham and the offering of Isaac, to believers generally of subsequent times? In acting as they did, they looked beyond the mere form and appearances of things, and entered into the faith of God's elect, which ever penetrates beneath the surface, and rather desires to know how much it is entitled to derive or learn from the written word of God, than to find how much it is at liberty to reject.

But if there be any portion of Old Testament Scripture which more than another should be dealt with after this manner, it is surely that master-piece of legislation—the ten words proclaimed from Sinai—in which the substance is so easily distinguished from the accessories of time and place, and the substance itself is so simple, so reasonable, so perfectly accordant in all its exacts with the dictates of conscience and the truest wellbeing of mankind, that there seems to be needed only the thoughtful and earnest spirit of faith, to say, Lord, here is the manifestation of thy most just and righteous will toward me—incline my heart to keep these thy laws.

2. But there is another and more extreme class of objectors, who make no distinction in this respect between New and Old Testament Scripture—who, as regards everything of a supernatural

kind that has a place in the sacred records, disallow any strict and proper obligation either to accredit what is testified, or to comply with its calls of duty. They were not personally present when the things so marvellous, so remote from one's every-day observation and experience, are reported to have taken place; and no evidence of a simply historical kind can give them a claim upon their conscience. A divinely inspired attestation might, indeed, carry such a claim, did we certainly possess it; but then inspiration belongs to the supernatural, and itself requires confirmation. So Mr Froude, for example: "Unless the Bible is infallible, there can be no moral obligation to accept the facts which it records; and though there may be intellectual error in denying them, there can be no moral sin. Facts may be better or worse authenticated; but all the proofs in the world of the genuineness and authenticity of the human handiwork, cannot establish a claim upon the conscience. It might be foolish to question Thucydides' account of Pericles, but no one would call it sinful. Men part with all sobriety of judgment when they come on ground of this kind."[2]

The objection is very adroitly put, and, if the alleged parallel instance from Grecian history were a fair one, the conclusion would be inevitable, that it were the height of absurdity to think of establishing on such a basis a claim of moral responsibility. One is only disposed to wonder that so palpable an absurdity did not suggest to such a writer as Mr Froude the possibility of some hitch in his own reasoning on the subject, and that it was scarcely probable the whole race of Christian apologists (comprising many of the most thoughtful and sagacious intellects of past as well as present times) should have committed themselves to positions which bespoke an utter absence of sobriety of judgment.

The argument is really one-sided and sophistical; it proceeds on the supposition of there being only one element requiring to be taken into account in the cases represented as parallel—the one, namely, that is, or might be, common to them both; while others, in which they differ, are thrown entirely into the background. The account of Pericles in Thucydides, and the evangelical narratives of

---

2 Essay on "Theological Difficulties."

Christ's person and work on earth, could easily be conceived to be alike genuine and authentic; but it would not thence follow that they stood upon a footing as regards their claim on men's moral responsibilities. For as men occupy no specific moral relation to the life and transactions of Pericles, they might be true, or they might be false, for any thing that concerns the conduct we have to maintain in this world, or the expectations we are warranted to cherish respecting the next; they might even remain to us a total blank, without materially affecting the course we pursue in respect either to God or to our fellow men. Therefore, let the facts themselves be ever so certain, and the account transmitted of them beyond the slightest shade of suspicion, they still do not in the least touch our conscience; we could at most be but somewhat less intelligent, if we refused to read or to accredit what is told of them, but we should not be one whit less happy or virtuous.

It is entirely otherwise, however, with the recorded life and works of Jesus Christ. These carry on the very face of them a respect to every man's dearest interests and moral obligations; if true, they bear in the closest manner on our present condition, and are fraught with results of infinite moment on our future destinies. And, unless the accounts we have of them present such obvious and inherent marks of improbability or imposture, as *ipso facto* to relieve us of all need for investigation, we are bound—*morally* bound by the relation in which the course of providence has placed us to them, as well as by the possible results to our own wellbeing— to consider the evidence on which they claim our belief, and make up our minds either to accredit or reject them.

There are undoubtedly persons who do assume the position just noticed, who hold the supernatural character of the events of gospel history as alone sufficient to warrant their peremptory rejection of its claims to their belief. With them the miraculous is but another name for the incredible. This, however, is not the aspect of the question we have here to deal with. Mr Froude's exception is taken against the facts of Christianity, as connected with our moral obligations, not because they are miraculous, but simply because they are facts—reported to be such—matters of historical statement, which, as such, he alleges, however authentically related, cannot bind the conscience, or constitute, if disowned, a ground of moral blame. Is it really so in other things? Do the properly parallel instances in the transactions of human life bear out the position?

Quite the reverse. A great part of men's obligations of duty, in the actual pursuits and intercourse of life, root themselves in facts, of which they can have nothing more than probable evidence. The whole range of filial duties, and those belonging to the special claims of kindred, are of this description; they spring out of facts, for which one can have nothing more than probable evidence, and evidence which sometimes, though fortunately not often, requires to be sifted in order to get assurance of the truth. In the department of political life, what statesman, or even comparatively humble citizen, can act in accordance with the spirit of the constitution—vindicate his own or his country's rights, provide against emergencies, devise and prosecute measures for the common good—without taking account of things near or remote, which he can only learn through the probabilities of historical testimony? And in the ordinary pursuits of business or commercial enterprise, every thing for men's success may be said to turn on their industry and skill in ascertaining what the probabilities are of things supposed to have emerged, or in the act of emerging—yea, in threading their way often through apparently competing probabilities; duty to themselves and their families obliges them to search thus into the facts they have to deal with, and to shape their course accordingly. Is not this, indeed, the very basis of Butler's conclusive argument in behalf of the *kind* of evidence on which all Christian obligation rests? "Probable evidence" (he says), "in its very nature, affords but an imperfect kind of information, and is to be considered as relative only to beings of limited capacities. For nothing which is the possible object of knowledge, whether past, present, or future, can be probable to an infinite intelligence; since it cannot but be discerned absolutely as it is in itself, certainly true, or certainly false. But to *us,* probability is the very guide of life."[3] And, as he elsewhere states in the application of this principle, "no possible reason can be given why we may not be in a state of moral

---

[3] "Analogy," Introduction.

probation, with regard to the exercise of our understanding upon the subject of religion, as we are with regard to our behaviour in common affairs." And the circumstance, "that religion is not intuitively true, but a matter of deduction and inference; that a conviction of its truth is not forced upon every one, but left to be, by some, collected with heedful attention to premises—this as much constitutes religious probation, as much affords sphere, scope, opportunity for right and wrong behaviour, as any thing whatever does."[4]

"The absurdity, if anywhere, is in the principle affirmed, namely, that God cannot have constituted it man's duty to *act* in cases of very imperfect knowledge; and yet we see that he has perpetually compelled him to do so; nay, often in a condition next door to stark ignorance. To vindicate the wisdom of such a constitution may be impossible; but the fact cannot be denied. The Christian admits the difficulty alike in relation to religion and the affairs of this world. He believes, with Butler, that probability is the guide of life; that man may have sufficient evidence in a thousand cases to warrant his action, and a reasonable confidence in its results, though that evidence is very far removed from certitude:—that, similarly, the mass of men are justified in saying, that they know a thousand facts of history to be true, though they have never had the opportunity or capacity of thoroughly investigating them; that the statesman, the lawyer, and the physician, are justified in acting, when they yet are compelled to acknowledge that they act only on most unsatisfactory calculations of probabilities, and amidst a thousand doubts and difficulties: all which, say we Christians, is true in relation to the Christian religion, the evidence for which is plainer, after all, than that on which man, in ten thousand cases, is necessitated to hazard his fortune or his life. . . . Those whom we call *profoundly* versed in the more difficult matters, which depend on moral evidence, are virtually in the same condition as their humbler neighbors.

"If, as you suppose, it cannot be our duty to act in reference to

---

[4] *Ibid.,* P. II. c. 6.

an 'historical religion,' because a satisfactory investigation is impossible to the mass of mankind, the argument may be retorted on your own theory [that, namely, of F. Newman, which, as with Mr Froude, would place its chief reliance on the inner consciousness]. You assert, indeed, that in relation to religion we have an internal spiritual faculty, which evades this difficulty; yet men persist in saying, in spite of you, that it is doubtful, first, whether they have any such; second, whether, if there be one, it be not so debauched and sophisticated by other faculties, that they can no longer trust it implicitly; third, what is the amount of its genuine utterances; fourth, what that of its aberrations; fifth, whether it is not so dependent on development, education, and association, as to leave room enough for an auxiliary external revelation—on all which questions the generality of mankind are just as incapable of deciding as about any historical question whatever."[5]

It is clear from such considerations, that certainty in religion cannot be attained by attempting to remove it from an historical to an internal, or strictly spiritual foundation; and also that the kind of certainty demanded to constitute the ground of moral obligation, is different from what is universally regarded as constituting such a ground in the common affairs and relations of life. Besides, the principle against which we argue, were it valid, would render a general and progressive scheme of revelation impracticable—since such a thing could be possible only by the historical element entering into the dispensation of religion, and the historical developments of one age becoming the starting-point of the next. Even in the more general field of the world's progress it would evacuate, for all essentially moral purposes, the principle, acknowledged also by the more thoughtful and observant class of theists, that "God is in history"—for this implies, that, as in the facts of history God reveals himself, so it is the duty of his rational creatures both to take cognizance of the facts, and to mark in them the character of the revelation. Much more must such be man's duty with the higher revelation which God gives of himself in Scripture, and which man needs for the relief of his profoundest wants, and the quickening of

---

[5] *Eclipse of Faith,* pp. 254-6.

his moral energies. For this, the history of God's kingdom among men has an important part to play, as well as the direct teaching of truth and duty. And for the greater and more essential acts of that history, the genuineness and authenticity of the sacred records must of necessity form the more immediate evidence and the indispensable guarantee. Not, however, as if this were the whole; for the facts which constitute the substance of the gospel, and form the ground of its distinctive hopes and obligations, are commended to our belief by many considerations, which strengthen the direct historical evidence—in particular, by a whole line of prophetic testimonies, of which they were the proper culmination; by the high moral aim of the writings which record them, and of the witnesses who perilled their lives in attestation of them; by their adaptation to the more profound convictions of the soul, and the spiritual reformation which the sincere belief of them has ever carried in its train. But the misfortune is, this varied and manifold congruity of evidence receives little patient regard from the literary, self-sufficient individualism of the age. And here also there is some ground for the complaint, which has been uttered by a late writer of superior thought and learning, in respect to the rationalistic criticism of Germany: "Men of mere book learning, who have never seen what the Spirit of God is working in the church, and who know little of life in general, take it upon themselves to pronounce final judgment upon the greatest revelations of spirit and life the world has ever seen; upon the greatest of men, and the greatest outward and inward conflicts; upon events which, more than all others, have moved the world; upon words and writings which, more than all others, have been productive of life. What does not occur in our days, or at least what is not seen by certain eyes, cannot (it is thought) have happened in an earlier age, the products of which yet lie before us the greatest in the world, and to which we have nothing even remotely similar."[6] Too manifestly, as the writer adds, there is in such things the evidence of an inward opposition to the truth, and hostility to the church of God.

---

[6] Auberlen, *The Divine Revelation*, p. 274. Trans.

BIBLIOGRAPHY:

Bright, John. *The Authority of the Old Testament.* Nashville: Abingdon Press, 1967, especially pp. 126-60, 184-212.

Bromiley, G. W. "History and Truth: A Study of the Axiom of Lessing," *Evangelical Quarterly.* XVIII (1946), pp. 191-98.

Lys, Daniel. *The Meaning of the Old Testament.* Nashville: Abingdon Press, 1967, pp. 119-72.

Part III
POETICAL BOOKS

INTRODUCTION

Wisdom, among the Israelites, developed herself in quite another direction from the philosphy of the Greeks. She did not give herself up to speculations upon the origin and nature of things. One word, resplendent with light, lying at the foundation of all the Jewish conceptions, set their minds at rest upon these matters: *In the beginning God created.* Hence the greater minds among the Jews directed their thoughts to the problems of practical life. The result of these labors is given us in five books, which form, as it were, the code of the Hebrew wisdom. The subjects treated in them relate, not to the study of Being, but to the purely practical question of *right living;* they even exhaust it. These books are—Job, in which is revealed the art of *suffering* well; the Psalms, which give us a model of true *prayer;* Proverbs, in which is taught the art of *acting* rightly in all circumstances; Ecclesiastes, which treats of the right manner of *enjoying* the good things granted to man here below; and finally, in the Song of Songs, the wisdom of the Israelites rises to the contemplation of the supreme art—that of true and pure *love.* What would the wisest of the Greeks have said, he who had himself, in opposition to all the pretended wise men of his age, made the art of right living the object of his researches—could he but have meditated upon the contents of this five-fold volume? Would he not have exclaimed, like one of his own countrymen, *Eureka!*

Among these five didactic books of the Old Testament, there are two connected with each other by profound affinities; the book of Job and the Song of Songs. Loving and suffering are emotions always closely allied. Is it not the very secret of suffering much to love much, and is it not by suffering more that love grows? It is not by accident that the series of the five books of the Hebrew wisdom opens with the book of Job and closes with the Song of Songs. Job is the personification of faith contending with the attacks of suffering; the Shulamite, of faith contending with the seductions of pleasure. One of these conflicts is the complement of the other. Love can only show itself to be invincible when it has undergone and overcome both.

—F. Godet

The following four essays will revolutionize the thinking of almost everyone. Job's Elihu will teach us to distinguish between punishment and chastisement. The Psalmist's imprecations will turn out to be prophetic teachings about God's attitude towards sin and the impenitent sinner. Even Ecclesiastes will be teeming with positive teaching when one sees that God built man for eternity and that man is personally and totally restless in everything he does and says until he finds the key to existence in the God who is everyman's source, support and end. Finally, the shepherd-hypothesis and the conclusion to the Song of Songs will teach us what true marital love should be.

There is very little in O.T. interpretation which compares to the precision in methodology and the fullness in theology that is to be found in these articles. They will remain as classics for all time.

VI

INTERPRETING THE BOOK OF JOB

by E. W. Hengstenberg

The very first verse of the Book of Job informs us as to the nature of its subject: "There was a man in the land of Uz, whose name was Job. The same was simple and upright, one that feared God and eschewed evil." The name Job (or more correctly Hiob) signifies *the much persecuted.* Understanding the name of the man, we are no longer astonished afterwards to find him surrounded and assailed on all sides by enemies, with Satan at their head, whose very designation, signifying *the adversary,* stands to that of Job in the relation of an *active* to a *passive. The much persecuted* is described as a thoroughly just man. Four several terms, designative of righteousness, are employed, in order to indicate its great breadth and completeness. According to the clue thus given, we should judge the theme of the book to be *the sufferings of the righteous*—how they are to be explained, and shown consistent with the divine righteousness; what should be the conduct of men so situated, and by what means the heart is then to be quieted and consoled.

The importance of this theme, and the great significance of the book, whose mission it is, as part of the marvellous organism of the canon of sacred Scriptures, to thoroughly discuss it, must be evident to all. If what Paul Gerhardt says is true "Until the grave, the rod of the cross will lie on us; but then it ends"—it is of the utmost practical consequence to have a clear understanding of this subject.

The solution of the problem in Holy Scripture depends on a twofold truth.

I. We must necessarily enter through much tribulation into the kingdom of God. For even in the righteous, that is, in him the main tendency of whose soul is Godward, and who keeps the divine law in his heart, there still dwells sin, and the necessary result of sin is suffering. This suffering is inflicted by the divine righteousness as punishment, by the divine love, as a means of improvement. The

91

common result of the two, this combination of *punishment*, which always proceeds from the principle of retribution, and of *love* whose design it is to further our salvation, is *chastisement*, to which the Holy Scriptures earnestly and lovingly admonish us to submit willingly, as being the unavoidable condition of our final redemption and glory. "My son," says Solomon, "despise not thou the chastening of the Lord, and be not impatient when he punisheth thee. For whom the Lord loveth he chasteneth, and he hath pleasure in him, as a father in his son." These words the Epistle to the Hebrews follows literally, adding, "if ye endure chastisement then are ye the children of God: for where is the son whom the father chasteneth not? but if ye be without chastisement, whereof all are partakers, then are ye bastards and not sons." Quite in the sense of the Scriptures Luther says in that Table-talk of his which contains so many deep and beautiful things, "therefore is it a foolish thing for reason and philosophy to say, 'it shall go well with the pious and righteous.' That is no true Christian conclusion. Because sin still remains in the flesh they must needs be chastised and plagued in order that it may be from day to day thoroughly swept out." In the same tone says one of Luther's most unfair opponents, De Maistre, in his *Soirèes de St. Petersbourg,* "I confess to them without shame that I can never reflect on this fearful subject without being tempted to cast myself on the earth, as a criminal begging for mercy; or else to call down all possible evils on my head as a slight recompence for the immeasurable guilt which I have contracted towards the Eternal Righteousness. And notwithstanding, they cannot believe how many times in my life it has been said to me that I am a very upright man."

II. The righteous are never visited with the cross, that is, with disguised grace, *alone.* The manifest grace of God is always in its company, and in its train. Although in the deepest outward trouble, they are still happier than the ungodly. "Thou givest me joy in my heart," said David, when compelled to flee before Absalom and when stripped of everything, "although, those have much wine and corn" (Ps. 4:8). And during the same hard times the Sons of Korah sang, as it were out of his own soul, "the Lord sendeth his goodness by day, and by night I sing to him and pray to the God of my life," *to be able* and to be permitted to do which, is a great mercy (Ps. 42:9.) But when sufferings have accomplished their purpose they are turned away by the Lord. The end always shows the difference between the righteous and the wicked. The proclamations which, according to 1 Peter 1:2, were made by the prophets, "of the sufferings of Christ and the glory which should follow," rested on the known experiences of the righteous. He who walks uprightly in the ways of the Lord, must have experienced that whenever he has stood on the brink of the abyss, the delivering hand has been stretched forth from above to preserve him from ruin, that his rescue has been effected just when he had gone so far that there was "only a step, nay, only a hair, between his life and death."

Now this solution, everywhere hinted at in Holy Scripture, when the problem is brought forward, is fully set forth in the Book of Job.

The book opens with a description of Job's life and character before the catastrophe, taking the two points which alone were of importance for his purpose, to wit, his prosperity and his righteousness based in piety. At the close of the opening part he describes Job's tenderness of conscience, which would not allow him to leave unatoned even apparently slight offenses, sinful thoughts, light discourse, useless words, such as men are used to utter in the merriment of social intercourse, and fits and ebullitions of worldly-mindedness. Job himself does not take part in the feasts of his children: he keeps himself in holy stillness and in priestly retirement. But when the feasts have gone their round, he comes forth, purifying and atoning, into the midst of his children, not seeking to force upon them his own views, but yet taking care that they shall not lose sight of the higher relations of life. Now he who stands thus in the midst of his family as a priest, ought, as it seems and as Job himself thought, to be sheltered from all the strokes of fate. But it happened otherwise; and that it did so, is to be explained from the fact that God's view of human nature is different from men's, that He discerns faults even in His saints. "Life often remains clinging to a straw, refusing to give itself up entirely to death." The praise given by the Holy Spirit to Job—"the same man was simple and upright, one that feared God, and eschewed evil,"—must of course have full truth. But when any one has attained to this degree, when he can say with truth, "I desire to have nought to do with the world; with that money, honor, pleasure, on which so much industry is spent," sin easily takes another shape; a man is threatened with the danger of being puffed up because of his righteousness, of being no longer willing to rank as a poor sinner, of becoming, in short, a proud saint. Then it becomes necessary for God to use His rod afresh, and to strike right sharply. For this disease is very hard to overcome. Lesser visitations serve often only to make it worse. Spiritual pride finds nourishment in becoming master of such attacks, in showing that they are unable to shake its faithfulness towards God.

The scene is then transferred to heaven. On the occasion of a solemn assembly of the angels before the throne of God, Satan also presents himself, raises doubts regarding Job's virtue, and demands that God shall prove him by suffering. God gives him power over Job, with the limitation that he is not to do him bodily harm.

Satan's desire and endeavor to destroy him shows that Job was a man of honest intent, that he belonged not to those who say, "Lord, Lord," but to those who sincerely strive to do the will of their heavenly Father. God's giving him up to Satan shows that there was still something in him to punish and to improve; that he still needed heavy blows, if he should escape the dangers by which his spiritual life was threatened.

From the necessity under which Satan is here represented as lying, to appear, like the angels, before God's throne, and to beg a formal permission, ere he brings suffering on Job, we may draw the consolatory truth that he is in his hatred entirely dependent on God, who pledges and proves His compassion and grace to His own children. Satan's intentions in laying upon them the cross are evil, it is true, but against his will he is forced to accomplish God's designs, which always at last remain victorious. The cross brings on a crisis in Job's history, whose final result is, to purge him from the dross of self-righteousness and pride. And this was that root of sin which still kept its seat in his inmost being. Every man has such a root of sin within him, and none dare say of Satan, what the only begotten Son of God said of him—"He hath nothing in me." Even the most

intimate disciples of the Lord, even the holy Apostles, were compelled to submit to Satan's request, that he might have them, to sift
them like wheat, and to be satisfied if only their faith did not fail
them.

Bengel says, "Satan is often concealed as an enemy where we
should never dream it." In the Scriptures, the punishments of the
wicked are directly traced back to the Lord and His angels, or to
Christ. Against the world, which is his friend, Satan seeks no ground
of complaint. In the chastisements, however, with which the righteous are threatened, Satan takes part. The Father in heaven turns,
as it were, his face away, and leaves to him the infliction of the pain
which his children need. Presupposing Satan to be absolutely dependent on God, there is something consolatory in the thought, that he
is placed in the matter of the cross between us and God. The
sufferings with which we are visited have, not unfrequently, what
may be almost described as a malicious character. It must also be
so, because it is intended that each one be assailed in his most
sensitive part, which frequently none knows save God, the afflicted
man himself, and that hateful Satan, who has a very keen eye for
the darker side of human nature. Still, it is a good thing that we
cannot trace our troubles directly back to God, that our heavenly
Father only permits, and that Satan devises and executes. The
question put by a savage, "Why then does not God strike Satan
dead?" could only have been retailed as apparently ingenious by
men who stood spiritually on a level with the savages. Satan is a
very important element in the divine economy. God needs him, and
He therefore keeps him until He shall have no more use for him.
Then will he be banished to his own place. The Scriptures call the
wicked heathen tyrant Nebuchadnezzar a servant of God. They
might give Satan the same name.

Job loses everything he has; first his property, then his children.
But he stands firm and immovable in the midst of these visitations.
"The Lord," says he, "gave, and the Lord hath taken away, blessed
be the name of the Lord." The Lord had not taken away from him
anything that was strictly his own; for he originally had nothing,
and had no right to lay claim to anything. God did but require back
that which He had lent of pure grace. Let it fall, then, as painfully

on Job as it might, how could he complain? Instead of murmuring because of what he had lost, he should give thanks for what he had received. But one thing is still lacking. Job had not advanced far enough to recognize in his sufferings the righteous punishment of his sins, and the chastisement necessary for his salvation. That was his Achilles-heel. And this it is which he must now be made to learn, and which, at the end of the book, we find that he has learned, after hard and severe conflicts and sad defeats. The final result is, that he is transformed from a dignified righteous man, into a poor sinner. Then, all at once, everything is made plain—he sees the meaning of his fate, and is therein to be counted far happier than the man who takes his flight into the other world with the sad words on his lips—"Then shall I clearly see and know, that which was hard and dark below."

Even after Satan's second attack, which was directed against his bodily health, Job did not become aware of his defect. The weakness of his wife, who up to that point seems to have held out and to have submitted patiently, even to the loss of all her children, must have served to set Job's strength in a clearer light. "Dost thou still retain thy piety," says she to him, "bless God and die." Death is inevitable and close at hand: God's grace is irrecoverably lost. Have God, then, at all events, blessed, and die and perish in a moment. Thou hadst long ago done more wisely to bid God farewell! The poor woman has been severely handled by commentators on account of these words. Spanheim calls her a second Xantippe, and maintains that she was left to Job as a thorn in his flesh after his recovery. J. D. Michaelis thinks she alone remained to Job in order that the measure of his sufferings might be full. It must, however, be taken into consideration, that her despair was rooted in the heartiest and tenderest love to her husband. In all their previous losses she had allowed herself to be kept in restraint by Job's own submissiveness. And had the pains of disease befallen herself, she would probably still have resisted her despair. Job, however, does not suffer himself to be dragged down by his wife; he finds means, on the contrary, of raising her up. "Thou speakest as the foolish women speak," says he to her; he does not say, "Thou art a foolish woman," but "thou art becoming unlike thyself, thou art entering into a circle to which thou hast hitherto remained a stranger." "Do we receive the good from God, and shall we not also accept the evil"; It is the same Giver who offers both; and he well deserves that we should take everything from him without question. As during the first stage of his sufferings, so also during the second, it is expressly remarked that Job "in all this sinned not with his lips." We expect now that something will soon occur to break Job's stedfastness, and to lead him to sin with his tongue. We do not, however, at once see what this can be, inasmuch as he has already lost everything without his submissiveness to God's will being shaken. The sequel tells.

Three friends of Job, Eliphaz, Bildad, and Zophar, hear of his misfortune and come to console him. They find him in a most mournful position, set themselves by his side in ashes, and remain seven days long, sitting speechless. After that Job opened his mouth and cursed his day.

How is it to be explained, that so great a change comes suddenly over Job; that he who just before was still all submission, and could even rush to the help of his wife, the weaker vessel, now all at once breaks out with the words—"Let the day perish when I was born!" and so forth? To curse one's existence, is to dispute with God, who gave it—is thanklessly to forget in the pain that blessing which, though often deeply concealed, never utterly fails—is, unbelievingly, to despair of the happy issue of our sufferings, and, consequently, of God's grace and righteousness.

The solution of the problem lies here. Where, in our English version, it is simply said—"And Job opened his mouth," we read in the original text—"And Job *answered* and said." His friends had not uttered a syllable; but they had clearly enough spoken to him by their looks. Job read in their countenances that their thoughts were busy with his righteousness; that they wished to deliver him a lecture of reproof; that they only waited the opportunity to enter on their work of advocacy of God. He read beforehand in their soul all that they afterwards uttered. That their stillness is not to be ascribed to the depth of their sympathy, is clear even from the words which give the reason of it—"for they saw that the pain was very great"—not "for their pain was very great." They could not straightway administer consolation to Job. According to their view, their prime duty was to bring him to a consciousness of his heavy guilt. They waited to catch him in a mood favorable for such a reproving lecture. Hence they held their tongues, until Job, irritated to the utmost by their long silence, himself began the conversation, and forced them to come forward with their view.

Job was now assailed on his weak side. To all other modes of suffering he had been equal, but that it should be adduced in proof of his guilt—that he should be robbed of his righteousness, that last possession to which he had so convulsively clung, and concerning which he himself exclaims—"My righteousness do I retain, and do not let go; not one of my days does my heart despise"—was too much for him. Because God, who had sent the sufferings, on whose evidence the charge was brought against him, was also the cause of this last and heaviest loss, he vents his indignation straightway against him. His friends he regards only as interpreters of the text composed by God.

The charge brought by Job against God gives rise to a dispute between him and his friends, which is carried on with ever increasing passionateness. This dispute is divided into three cycles. The first two fall into three subdivisions, comprising the discourses uttered by the three friends, and Job's separate answers. The last consists of two subdivisions only, the third friend, Zophar, having nothing more to say. Through his silence the author intimates to us the defeat of all three friends, who had made common cause.

The view taken by the friends is the following: that sin and suffering are measured out by God, as it were, ounce for ounce, so much sin, so much suffering. One man is just so much better than another, as he is happier. He who is as unfortunate as Job, must assuredly be, not merely a sinner, but a criminal. To doubt this is to do dishonor to God. And even if, in the case of a man suffering severely, like Job, we do not actually know of any great crime, we must still assume that he has committed one, in order to save God's honor. Nor may we allow ourselves to be deceived, even though appearances be of the fairest kind. These only show that the pretended saint is a thoroughly skilled hypocrite.

This view is characteristic of a *superficial piety*. Open ungodliness shuts out God entirely from earthly matters, and ascribes suffering to chance. The entire dispute is carried on in the book of Job from the point of view of the fear of God. But because this view is that of a *superficial* piety, it is, for that very reason, popular. In Elihu's discourse (32:19), it is expressly described as that of the "many": "Not the many are wise," says Elihu in reply. In the sphere of religion that saying, "*Vox populi, vox Dei,*" does not hold good. There, on the contrary, that which is popular is usually the superficial, the shallow. That this view is the popular one, the author intimates, in giving it no less than three representatives. The fundamental error of the three friends is a coarse, external conception of sin, which leads them to conclude, from Job's sufferings, that he has committed some palpable transgression. They are only acquainted with individual sins: of the essence of sin they have no knowledge. For this reason sufferings appear reasonable to them, only when they are meted out, piece by piece, to individual offenses. They have only an eye for such commands as, "Thou shalt not steal," "Thou shalt not commit adultery," which they do not consider in their roots, as did our Lord in the sermon on the mount, after the example of the prophets, and even of Moses himself: they only looked at the outward appearance. From that command, on the contrary, "Thou shalt love the Lord thy God with all thine heart, and with all thy soul, and with all thy strength," they turn away their eyes, or else give themselves up to the strangest delusions regarding it. Hence are they perfectly satisfied with their own fulfilment of the law, and find it perfectly orderly and just that things should go well with them. And when severe sufferings befall their neighbor, they look down upon him with lofty eyes, and search everywhere until they have discovered either the fact or the possibility of heavy guilt. The troubles of their neighbors seem in some way to do them good. They are the seal to their own excellence. Had Job's friends known human nature or themselves aright, they would have cried out when they beheld his sufferings, "If this is done in the green tree, what shall be done in the dry?" "God be merciful to us sinners!" A characteristic of the friends is their want of pitiful love. With unrelenting consequence they apply their theological prejudices to the case of their poor friend sitting in ashes, and smitten by the hand of God. They make no effort to enter into his position and feelings: they talk at him without intermission. He can only exercise compassion who has himself received compassion, and to this belongs a recognition of our own sins. All Pelagianism—or if the biblical name be preferred—all Pharisaism, where it is not a question of phrases, alms, and other such external matters, is at the bottom unmerciful, uncompassionate. Had the friends had any true pitiful love, they would have corrected their view by means of the very case before them. Perhaps the reason why the author gives such a vivid representation of this widespread view is, that he himself had formerly entertained it, and had skilfully applied it to poor sufferers whom he had encountered. The three friends, Job and Elihu, may be regarded as representing three different stages in the ways of the Lord, all which the author himself, without doubt, had passed through. First, he had stood proudly by the side of other sufferers; then he himself had wrestled with despair in suffering, because he was unwilling to renounce his self-righteousness; till at last he fought his way with Elihu to full and clear knowledge.

With all this there is no denying that there is an important element of truth in the discourses of the friends, and that usually they only err in the application of the general principle to the case in hand. This application the author lets them make silently, and hence their discourses, judged merely by their sound, express, for the most part, only truth. This high truth is *the knowledge of the close connection between sin and suffering,* of which a presentiment runs through the whole of the ancient world, and is ineffaceably impressed on the human heart. In solving the problem, the task is, to reconcile the element of truth, which lay on the side of the friends, with that which was on Job's side when he maintained his righteousness against those who charged him with coarse transgressions, and at the same time to trace back both errors to that common source out of which they plainly flow, namely, the want of a deeper knowledge of sin. The author recognized that there was truth in the discourses of the friends, as is plain, both from the free and full play which he allows them, and from the favorable light in which, on the whole, they are placed. So decided is this, that sayings have been adduced by the church in all ages from these discourses, as if they were fair representations of divine truth: for example, even the apostle Paul does so in 1 Corinthians 3:19, alluding to what Eliphaz advances in 5:13.

In the *discourses of Job against the friends,* a distinction must be drawn between that which flows from his own fundamental view, and that which belongs to the sphere concerning which he himself remarks—"to the wind are the words of him who is in despair." Further, "my sufferings are heavier than the sand on the sea-shore, therefore are my words irrational" (6:3.) In the warmth of his feelings, Job frequently goes so far as to represent God as the fierce enemy and persecutor of all the righteous on earth, as almighty arbitrariness and unrighteousness, and expresses accordingly, utter despair of a favorable turn in his affairs, and the conviction that God will never rest till He has brought him to complete ruin. It is a holy stroke of art on the part of the Holy Ghost, from whom the Scripture has its origin, that He allows free and distinct expression to all the thoughts of the pious, even to those which are due to the saddest weakness of the flesh, and then shows how they are to be overcome. Even a Byron was unable to outdo this book; it leaves him far behind. Then, again, when in a calmer mood, Job confesses that God's righteousness may usually be seen in the government of the world, and only represents his own sufferings as an incomprehensible exception. Here and there, too, he rises to a joyful hope—most gloriously when the confession burst from him, "I know that my Redeemer liveth" (chap. 19) as though the sun of faith had suddenly shone with full clearness through the clouds of pain and rebellion, only, however, alas! to be soon again darkened.

Job at last forces his friends to silence. Their case shipwrecks on their incapability of bringing proof of the crimes which they are compelled to lay to Job's charge, and on the fact that they are not only struggling against appearances, but, as they afterwards find out, against their own conscience also. It is owing to the character borne by Job's discourses previously mentioned, namely, to the interweaving of passion and conviction in them, that he is not allowed to quit the arena as soon as the friends give up the conflict. Before retiring, he lays before us, in the closing discourse (chaps.

27-31) a complete, calm and dispassionate statement of his views. Here we get the standard by which to try all his earlier discourses. Job declares, that he still keeps to the assertion of his own innocence, but that he notwithstanding recognizes how, usually, punishment follows on guilt; retracting whatever he had previously advanced in seeming conflict with this proposition. Did he not do this; did he on the contrary declare war in general against the eternally true proposition, that *sin is the ruin of men,* the lively carrying out and illustration of which gives the discourses of his friends so high a value—and in the heat of passion he had frequently done so before—then would Job be inferior to his friends, and there would seem to be no foundation for that final judgment of God's, whereby the very contrary was affirmed. Peculiar are the arguments by which Job supports the proposition in Chapter 28, a chapter which has often been misunderstood, and quoted in favor of that incomprehensibility of the course of divine providence the urging of which gave Rationalism a great show of piety. In the course of a brilliant picture, Job proves that wisdom is not one of the possessions attainable by men in their own strength, but one of the glorious privileges of God. From this he draws the conclusion, that it can only become ours in a moral and religious way, that is, through our entering into union with God and becoming participators of his spirit. If this be true, the ungodly are excluded from it; and are by consequence given over to unavoidable ruin. For whosoever lacks wisdom must rush blindly on destruction. The sea of this world hides so many rocks that a vessel whose rudder is not in the hand of wisdom must of necessity soon suffer shipwreck.

Notwithstanding Job's repeated efforts, the problem still remains to perplex him, the mystery of his sufferings still remains unexplained; a further examination is therefore absolutely necessary. He himself puts this clearly before us in the second part of his concluding discourse, in that he gives a detailed description of his uprightness and of his guiltless conduct, and sets in strong contrast therewith his severe afflictions. Examining the matter superficially, one can see no possibility of a satisfactory solution of the riddle, and may easily fall into the notion, that there is nothing for it but to refer all to the incomprehensibility of God's ways; a course which conducts to Atheism. If, however, we search more deeply, an outlet presents itself. Notwithstanding the apparent completeness of Job's enumeration of the sins he had avoided, notwithstanding the loftiness of his moral point of view, which led him to regard the confidence placed in gold as not less an execrable sin than idolatry, commonly so called—which made him consider it as a great sin to exult, whether in the greatness of our own possessions or in the misfortunes which befall our enemies; notwithstanding that Job unmistakeably considers sin as an inward thing, treating not merely the sinful act but also the first hidden germ thereof, namely, sinful desire (31:1), as worthy of condemnation and curse, still, he passes over one main class of sins in silence, evidently because his eyes had not yet been opened to see them. It is God's method to reveal to us by degrees the depths of our corruption; were he to do it all at once we should be liable to fall into despair. These sins were those of haughtiness, self-righteousness, pride in his own virtue. We expect that the impending decision of the dispute will turn on this point. And the fresh and complete exposition of the difficulties with which Job's concluding speech is occupied make us exceedingly eager to learn the nature of the decision. In distinction from the earlier ones it is marked by the calmness of its tone. Passion's storm is hushed, now that the friends who stirred it up, are forced to silence. A quiet sadness takes the place of the defiance, of the excited murmurs against God, of the questioning of his right, and of the challenges which were previously observable. We see throughout that Job is now in the mood to accept joyfully the solution which may be offered to him; for by himself he cannot find it, nor indeed can poor miserable man attain to anything unless it be given him from heaven. Everywhere there presses itself on our notice a presentiment that we are on the threshold of an explanation. We feel the soft breath of that grace which prepares the soul for the instruction to be communicated through Elihu. At the close of Chapter 31 it is said, "the words of Job have an end." The intimation is thus given us, that an entirely new section commences. Job was able to act a dignified part towards the friends, and having at last reduced them to complete dumbness, he now remained alone on the scene of conflict, and the words quoted are intended to mark the boundary line between him, on the one side, and Elihu, God's servant, and God himself, on the other side. The latter he finds to be indisputably his superiors. Job's time for speaking now ceases: the time to keep silence has begun. Henceforward he never opens his lips, save to express his readiness to keep silence and to lay his hand on his mouth. The three words (for there are no more in the original text) are rich in meaning. All words spoken against God, come, after a brief season, to an end, either of *grace,* as in Job's case, who begs that the folly of his discourses may be forgiven, or of *wrath,* when the mouth that uttereth great things is closed with violence.

Elihu now quits the circle of hearers within which he had quietly kept himself up to this point. Why he is described as a youth, may be learned from the words which the author puts in his mouth: "I thought, let days speak, and let the multitude of years prove wisdom. But the Spirit is in man [on that all depends!] and the breath of the Almighty giveth them understanding. Not the many are wise: neither do the aged understand judgment." Majorities are without weight in the church, and in spiritual things age does not at all carry the weight which belongs to it in the affairs of common life. *One* inexperienced youth *with* the Spirit of God is wiser than loud multitudes and grey heads, and even than the Coryphaei of wisdom without it. Besides, a youth is the most fitting representative of a truth which is here introduced with freshness and vigor into the midst of the Church of God.

Elihu's entrance is introduced as follows: "And the three men ceased to answer Job, for he was righteous in his own eyes. Then was enkindled the wrath of Elihu; against Job was his wrath kindled, because he declared his own soul to be more just than God. And against his three friends was his wrath kindled, because they found no answer, and therefore condemned Job." The situation is thus set distinctly before us. Job's fault is represented to be, that he was righteous in his own eyes. This necessarily and invariably leads those who are visited with severe afflictions, to the sad point of declaring themselves to be more righteous than God: which is to turn everything upside down. Self-righteousness deems itself to have fulfilled all its obligations to God. And because it can see in the sufferings, which are in reality inflicted because of sinfulness, and are capable of justification on that ground, only unrighteous arbitrariness, it sets forth God as less righteous than man, and so inverts the natural relation of the Creator to the creature. Access to the source of all consolation is thus cut off, and the way of the return of salvation barred. This is a very dangerous side of Pelagianism. In this respect most men live only on mercy. If God did not spare them, but visited them as he visited Job, they would fall into a state of formal rebellion against God, and would openly declare themselves his "personal enemies"; or else, which is the lowest stage of all, the stage when man renounces his true humanity, they would deny his existence. The friends could not heal Job's disease, because they themselves had a too superficial knowledge of human sinfulness. Not knowing how to meet Job's presumption in the right way, they reproach him with heavy individual crimes. To convince Job of the condemnableness of his self-righteousness, against which the friends had broken their power, is plainly the task which Elihu has now to accomplish.

Elihu agrees with the friends in recognizing that all suffering is a punishment: but diverges from them in that he shows suffering to have another aspect. There is a suffering which has its origin not merely in the divine righteousness, but at the same time also in the principle of love, and which therefore may, nay more, must be inflicted on the righteous, in order that he may see and be purified from the sin still cleaving to him, and be fitted for the higher blessings of redemption. In opposition to the bare idea of punishment, Elihu sets that of chastisement: an idea which modern times find, alas difficult of understanding. They speak only of trial, and of that mostly without any distinct conception of its nature.

As this portion is the very heart and life of the book, we shall quote the principal passages literally.

"For," says Elihu, "God speaketh once, yea twice, if man giveth not heed thereto. In the dream of the nightly vision, when deep sleep falleth upon men, in slumber on the bed; Then openeth he the ear of men, and sealeth their admonition. That he may withdraw man from his doings, and hide *pride* from the man. He preserveth his soul from the pit, and his life from falling under the sword."

Even he that standeth must take heed lest he fall. Especially in pride has the righteous still ever a dangerous enemy. God's compassionate love, therefore, sends from time to time emphatic *inward monitors,* as by significant dreams, which are here mentioned solely by way of example.

But the matter is not allowed to rest there. Inward monitions are but the prelude to *visitations,* and are meant to prepare the soil for these latter. He who walks uprightly in the ways of the Lord, will have found by experience that a heavy cross seldom falls on one who is unprepared for it, that the time chosen is usually one in which the heart has been peculiarly drawn upwards; but also, that it seldom fails to come when such a strong and gracious drawing has been felt. Elihu says further, "he is chastened also with pain on his bed, and the conflict in his bones is unceasing. And he loathes all manner of food, and his soul despiseth dainty dishes." And so forth, is a severe disease described, one being specified out of the whole number of painful visitations by way of example, just as the dream is made to represent inward monitions.

But that the ruin of the righteous is not intended, that in the infliction of suffering love goes hand in hand with righteousness, is made plain by the *issue,* which, when the sufferer does not by his own fault bar the way of salvation, separates the righteous from the wicked. Elihu proceeds, "If then a mediator-angel taketh his part, one of a thousand, that he may show unto man his duty. Then he is gracious to him, and saith, deliver him from going down to the pit, I have received a ransom [Repentance!]. He crieth to God and he showeth himself gracious to him, he beholdeth his face in joy, and God giveth back unto man his righteousness." The mediating angel represents *all influences from above,* by which the heart of the sufferer is awakened to genuine repentance. The ministering spirits which are sent forth to minister unto them who shall inherit blessedness, (Heb. 1:14,) stand invisible round about the sufferer's bed of anguish, and whisper in his ear. Were it not so, such earthly messengers of God, as Elihu, would speak to the winds. These latter however must also do their part, as we are vividly taught by the example of Elihu.

The second principal passage runs as follows: "and when they are bound in fetters and held in the cords of affliction. Then showeth he them by their work and their transgressions, that they have *become proud.* [This was another *nota bene* for Job.] He openeth also their ear to admonition, and commandeth that they return from iniquity. If they then hear and serve [submitting themselves to God's will and repenting], they spend their days in prosperity and their years in joy. But if they hear not, they perish by the sword, and die through their own folly. He saveth the wretched by his wretchedness, and openeth by oppression their ear." In these last words we have the quintessence of Elihu's entire argument. The friends also set before Job, in the case of his conversion, the prospect of a return of prosperity and salvation. But to them suffering appeared only as punishment, and they were very far from recognizing in it an outflow of the love of God, a disguised grace.

The carrying out of this view occupies the first of Elihu's four discourses. In the *second,* he shows that the position taken up towards God by Job, in maintaining that he has been unrighteously handled, is inconsistent with his own estimate of the divine nature. Job's weak and foolish attack on the divine righteousness makes shipwreck on the glory of the divine nature as manifested in the works of creation. The Omnipotence and wisdom of God, with which we everywhere meet, furnishes an indirect testimony to his righteousness. For the single attributes of the divine nature are all of them but as rays proceeding from the one center. Where one is, there also must of necessity the others be. How could the being which everywhere shows itself to be most perfect, lay itself open in such a way on this one point? Every witness therefore, in nature, to God's greatness as a Creator, rises against the accusers of God's righteousness. Whoever will bring a charge against God's justice, must first measure himself with the divine omnipotence. If this argumentation proves that God must necessarily be righteous, we shall be all the more ready to enter on the reasons contained in Elihu's second discourse, why God may be just, and yet the righteous suffer. At first sight it must occasion surprise, that the mind of the suffering righteous is directed to the wondrous formation of the clouds, of thunder and lightning, of snow, and afterwards, in the answer of God, to the war-horse, to the hawk, to the raven, to the behemoth or hippopotamus, to the leviathan or crocodile. And yet, more carefully examined, we see that such a course was fully adapted to its purpose. An almighty, all-knowing, and all-wise God, who is not at the same time righteous, is in truth an unthinkable thought. For this reason, those who doubt God's righteousness, are always on the high road to doubt His existence. Pelagianism leads not merely to the destruction of the true idea of God, but also to complete Atheism. It is, therefore, a great blessing to be, like Job, firmly rooted in God. Then, should we fall into error regarding one side of the divine nature, we shall be able to lift ourselves up by cleaving all the more firmly to another. By and by, even the dark side will become light.

Elihu's third discourse (chap. 35) lays hold on Job again from another side. Job had stood up as if he were in a position to lay claims, and plead merits. He had behaved towards God like an impatient creditor. What perversity! As little as man can harm God by his sin, so little can he benefit him by his virtue. Hence, when God rewards the righteousness of man, he does it out of pure grace: if he withholds rewards none can bring against him the charge of injustice. The All-sufficient One does not need man, and it is therefore foolish in us to demand and fume, and murmur. When sufferings come upon us, our only part is, to make sorrowful lament, humbly to beg, patiently to wait, and believingly to hope. Whoever is incapable of this, must blame himself if God does not hear, and the Almighty does not regard, his *vain cries,* that is, the empty pretensions expressed in his prayers.

Elihu's fourth and last discourse falls into two divisions. In the first (that is, up to 36:21) he carries out more completely what he had previously advanced to prove that the infliction of suffering was not inconsistent with the divine justice—that is, he shows how God afflicts the righteous in order to chastise, purify, and lead him to greater glory, if he allows tribulations to do their proper work. The second division is connected with the subject of the second discourse. God is great in nature: therefore must He also be just. Behold God is great in power: and therefore must He be of great justice and full of righteousness: He dealeth not wrongly. The

people must consequently fear Him; He regardeth not those who
are wise in their own eyes, nor such as in their self-righteousness
would tax him with wrong.

Elihu had apparently ended the dispute. For the friends had
previously retired from the arena, and Job, their conqueror, now by
his silence confessed himself conquered. Indeed, he had repeatedly
mentioned his silence as a sign of his overthrow (6:24, 25; 19:4 ff.).
Elihu also had regarded Job's silence as a token that he surrendered
himself prisoner: see 33:31-33, where he says, "If thou hast nothing
to say, then hear me and keep silence, I will teach thee wisdom."
But what still failed was the divine sanction. This alone could prove
to a certainty that Elihu had really stood up as the speaker for God.
Moreover it was not a mere question of doctrine. Job was to be
born again to a new life, and human efforts alone could not
accomplish that. God must directly reveal Himself to him. A true
and thorough cure of error in religious things, a real rise to a new
stage of the inner life, cannot be affected save by a vision of God.
Job himself confesses this in 42:5. "By the hearing of the ear I
learned from thee" (says he to God), "but now mine eye saw thee."
Job's earlier religious point of view, notwithstanding his great piety,
is thus characterized as a lower one, as one dependent on the
traditions of the Fathers and on the church; which, now that he,
having been prepared by his sufferings and by the penitential
discourse of Elihu, had been counted worthy of a divine manifestation, gives place to a relation to God which is mainly direct and
immediate. All religious doubts arise from our merely perceiving by
the hearing of the ear. When we have once seen with the eye, we
feel ashamed of our previous incomprehensible folly. It is the
greatest misfortune of the time that so few have seen with the eye.
For this reason, there are so few even among the well-meaning, who
walk with a firm and sure step. Hence also deep abysses of doubt lie
concealed behind a wall of orthodoxy. In an age of apostasy like
ours; in an age when Satan is again let loose from his prison, and
seduces the heathen in the four quarters of the earth, the mere
hearing with the ear, the mere leaning on the church, is much more
inadequate, than during the days of the dominion of the Christian
faith, when the temptations were far less. Now ought surely every

one who counts his own soul dear, to cry with Moses, "Lord, let me see thy glory," and not rest until his cry has been heard. Of course, the hearing with the ear is the first step. Had Job haughtily shut his ear to the authority of the church, his eye would not have seen. But thorough instruction must ever go before God's personal revelation of himself. Error, not truly overcome, bars the entrance like a bolt. It is God's method to communicate this instruction to men by means of men. To this end he has given the Holy Scriptures and founded in his church the office of teacher. In the present instance Elihu discharges the duty. From these observations it would appear that the thing of chief importance is God's *appearance,* not, what he may *say.* Still God cannot appear in silence. A discourse must accompany his appearance, as a kind of commentary thereon. And inasmuch as Elihu had been God's spokesman, God's discourse will naturally neither contradict that of Elihu nor contain anything essentially new. We may also anticipate beforehand that the substance of the divine discourse will be less comprehensive than that of Elihu's. In one portion of his discourses Elihu laid down a theory on the purpose of life. To enter upon such a subject would scarcely accord with the majesty of God. From it we should only expect the development of the main idea of the other principal part, the proof that Job's whole behavior was rooted in his failure to discern the glory of God manifested in all creation—a glory with which righteousness is ever inseparably connected. This subject is a more practical one. It affords constant opportunity for punishing and humbling. Who am I? and, Who art Thou? These two questions pervade the divine discourse, which indeed consists of questions, for questions are the proper mode of utterance, for majesty in wrath. Had Job in the first instance discovered within, the right answer to these two questions; had he seen that God, as the Almighty, must also be the Righteous One, that God therefore was of necessity in the right, and he himself ithe wrong, the second main portion of Elihu's discourse must sink ever deeper into his heart. For God *could* only be in the right, in case the view given by Elihu of the aim of sufferings was the correct one. The issue gave it a full and formal confirmation. Furthermore, the only means of thoroughly setting aside Job's inquiry was the element common to both the discourse of God and that of Elihu. The suppressed doubts would have ever again asserted their sway had it not been shown *how* God is in the right, as well as that he *must* be in the right because he is God, that he must be righteous because he is almighty.

God appears in the *storm* and speaks with Job. In the symbolical language of Scripture storms always bear a *threatening* character. By speaking out of the storm God shows that Job has sinned. God's discourse is an interpretation of the storm in which he appears. "Wilt thou condemn me in order that thou mayest be righteous?" is the voice of the storm, as to Job, so to all who like him murmur against God in sufferings.

The discourses of Elihu are impressed with the seal of a divine mission, by the fact that God's discourse is connected with them, not only by the sameness of idea, but even by the sameness of treatment. Elihu had proved God's glory, and his consequent righteousness, from the wonders on high, from the formation of the clouds, of the lightning, and of the thunder. The Divine discourse begins at the same point, and then descends to the earth, to the revelation of the glory of God in the animated creation, where the lion and the raven, the aristocracy and the proletariat of the world of beasts, rise up as witnesses against Job.

Job repents in dust and ashes. His repentance refers, first of all, to his discourses, and then to his entire conduct. Had he been previously himself pure in God's sight, his discourses would also have been pure. What now pains him in his own discourses is the assertion of his own perfect righteousness. The notion that he might lay claim to this had led him into error regarding God, and had thus prepared for him inexpressible suffering. Now his righteousness had become as dust and ashes. The brevity of Job's discourse is remarkable, in contrast with his previous prolixity. Depth of feeling, and especially thorough penitence, is simple in its utterances, and its words are as a tight and closely fitting garment.

The Lord now declares His anger against the three friends, and advises them to beg for the intercession and mediation of Job, who, through his awakening and repentance, had come into a much closer relation to God than formerly. They had deserved this humiliation. In their blindness they had held themselves to be better than Job, in the proportion in which they were happier. Whoso exalteth himself shall be abased; he who sits down at the head of the table of the kingdom of God shall hear the cry, "Give way to this man." To Job, too, was in this way the opportunity given, of showing, by his self-denying love, what inward gain his sufferings had brought him. Forgiving love towards those who had insulted him is made the condition of his restoration: here therefore we have the Old Testament basis of that saying of our Lord's "If ye forgive men their trespasses, your heavenly Father will also forgive you your trespasses."

Elihu's promise, that Job's repentance should be followed by the return of his prosperity, begins now to be fulfilled. But Elihu himself is no longer mentioned. God's spokesman retires, and God himself speaks by word and deed. Praise belongs not to him, for he had only uttered what God had given him. He has no merit; he has only to be thankful for the high grace which God had conferred upon him, in constituting him the medium of his revelations, and enabling him to lead back his wandering brother from the error of his ways. "When ye have done all, still say, we are unprofitable servants." God makes the fulfilment of his demand lighter for his servants, by treating them thoroughly as unprofitable.

James gives the sum of this book in the words, "Ye have heard of the patience of Job, and ye have seen the end of the Lord: for the Lord is merciful and compassionate." Job gave special proof of his patience or stedfastness, in that, when actually assailed by Satan on his weak side, he still, at the right moment, repented in dust and ashes, so that Satan was forced to retire ashamed, and lost the bet which he, as it were, laid with God at the commencement, when he said, "Of what avail is it, he will bless thee to thy face?" A joyful issue is that, when no one concerned receives harm save Satan himself.

VII

IMPRECATIONS IN THE PSALMS
by Chalmers Martin

It is usual to speak of "the imprecatory psalms," but it may well be questioned whether the phrase is not a misleading one, in so far, at least, as it seems to imply that there is a body of psalms in which imprecation forms a chief element. For this, of course, is far from being the case. There are in the whole Psalter not more than eighteen psalms that contain any element of imprecation, and, in most of these this element is a very minor one, embodied in a single line, it may be, or in a single verse. These eighteen psalms contain three hundred and sixty-eight verses, of which only sixty-five include anything that can be called an imprecation. Even in the case of the three psalms which show the largest measure of the imprecatory spirit, only twenty-three verses out of a total of ninety-five can be properly said to be imprecations. It is, therefore, more true to the facts of the case to speak of "imprecations in the psalms" than of "imprecatory psalms." But, of course, the real question is one, not of quantity, but of quality. It is not, How can we account for the presence of so many imprecations in the psalms? but, How can we justify it that there are any at all? And since this latter is the real question, it is fortunate rather than otherwise that the phenomenon with which we have to deal is one common in some degree to eighteen psalms instead of being confined to three or even to one. For we thus have a much wider basis for induction, and a much better chance, consequently, of arriving at the truth. Let us recall some of these expressions which have caused so much difficulty to readers of the Bible, not to say to many learned interpreters. Thus, for example, in Psalm 5:10, after describing the wickedness of his enemies, the psalmist prays:

> Hold them guilty, O God;
> Let them fall by their own counsels:
> Thrust them out in the multitude of their transgressions;
> For they have rebelled against thee.

In 10:15 he says:

Break thou the arm of the wicked;
And as for the evil man, seek out his wickedness
till thou find none.

In 28:4:

Give them according to their work, and according
   to the wickedness of their doings:
Give them after the operation of their hands;
Render to them their desert.

31:17, 18, sounds still more harsh:

Let the wicked be ashamed, let them be silent in Sheol.
Let the lying lips be dumb;
Which speak against the righteous insolently,
With pride and contempt.

In 40:14, 15, we read:

Let them be ashamed and confounded together
That seek after my soul to destroy it:
Let them be turned backward and brought to dishonor
That delight in my hurt.
Let them be desolate by reason of their shame
That say unto me, Aha, Aha.

Identically the same expressions are used in 70, which is one
with the latter part of 40 and language closely similar occurs also in
71:13. In 58:6ff. the psalmist cries:

Break their teeth, O God, in their mouth:
Break out the great teeth of the young lions, O Lord.
Let them melt away as water that runneth apace:
When he aimeth his arrows, let them be as though they were cut off.
Let them be as a snail which melteth and passeth away:
Like the untimely birth of a woman, that hath not seen the sun.

And he adds in verse 10:

The righteous shall rejoice when he seeth the vengeance:
He shall wash his feet in the blood of the wicked.

In 140:9, 10, other but equally dreadful figures are made use of:

As for the head of those that compass me about,
Let the mischief of their own lips cover them.
Let burning coals fall upon them:

> Let them be cast into the fire;
> Into deep pits, that they rise not up again.

But it is in Psalm 35, 69, and 109 that the difficulty presented by the seemingly malevolent expressions used appear in its most acute form. These three psalms constitute, as Delitzsch has observed, a fearful climax in this regard. In 35:4-6, for example, David prays:

> Let them be ashamed and brought to dishonor that seek after my soul:
> Let them be turned back and confounded that devise my hurt.
> Let them be as chaff before the wind,
> And the angel of the Lord driving them on.
> Let their way be dark and slippery,
> And the angel of the Lord pursuing them.

In 69:22ff. he says with regard to his enemies:

> Let their table before them become a snare;
> And when they are in peace, let it become a trap.
> Let their eyes be darkened, that they see not;
> And make their loins continually to shake.
> Pour out thine indignations upon them,
> And let the fierceness of thine anger overtake them.
> Let their habitation be desolate;
> Let none dwell in their tents.

> Add iniquity unto their iniquity:
> And let them not come into thy righteousness.
> Let them be blotted out of the book of life,
> And not be written with the righteous.

And once more, in 109:6-15, we come upon these terrible words:

> Set thou a wicked man over him:
> And let an adversary stand at his right hand.
> When he is judged, let him come forth guilty;
> And let his prayer be turned into sin.
> Let his days be few;
> And let another take his office.
> Let his children be fatherless,
> And his wife a widow.
> Let his children be vagabonds, and beg;
> And let them seek their bread out of their desolate places.

Let the extortioner catch all that he hath;
And let strangers make spoil of his labor.
Let there be none to extend mercy unto him;
Neither let there by any to have pity on his fatherless children.
Let his posterity be cut off;
In the generation following let their name be blotted out.
Let the iniquity of his fathers be remembered with the Lord continually,
That he may cut off the memory of them from the earth.

What shall we make of such expressions as these? It has, indeed, been contended by some that they are just what they seem at first sight to be, the language of a heart that cries for vengeance. David, it is said, was a man of like passions with ourselves, as more than one incident in his history amply proves. And if ever a man had provocation to speak unadvisedly with his lips it was he. Innocent of any crime, deserving on account of his talents and character, as well as of his splendid services both to Saul and to the nation, of the highest honors that the king could bestow, he found himself an outlaw upon whose head a price had been set; he could find safety only in the rocks of the wild goats; and while his own conscience testified his absolute loyalty to Saul, he knew that the king's jealous hate was daily being fed by the lying accusations of sycophants and intriguers such as Doeg the Edomite and Cush the Benjamite. What wonder, it is asked, if even a good man should, under such circumstances, be betrayed into occasional outbursts of fierce desire for vengeance upon enemies so mean, so false, so cruel! Such utterances were sinful, of course, but the sin was one for which much excuse may be made. The fact that David was guilty of it is to be put into the same category as the dissimulation of Abraham and Isaac with respect to their wives, or the anger of Moses when he smote the rock. Not everything is commendable which the Bible records; no more, it is suggested, is all the religious experience that finds expression in the psalms necessarily endorsed as pleasing in God's sight and meant for the imitation of those who read. Now while we may admit the greatness of the provocation which David had to anger against his persecutors, we can by no means accept this explanation of the expressions under consideration. For one thing, the psalms do not present us with an account of what David felt and uttered in the moment of extreme provocation. The psalms are literature, and literature of highly wrought, artistic form. However manifestly some of them may embody the thoughts and feelings begotten by such cruel experiences as David's outlaw life or his flight from Absalom, it is plain that they must have been composed at leisure; and while we may make excuse for harsh words uttered in the heat of anger, we cannot excuse the embodiment of the same words in permenent literary form. Imprecations on one's enemies should be repented of, not written down for others to read.

The explanation under review also fails in that it ignores the distinction between a lyric poem, not to say a hymn intended for use in the public worship of God, and a historical narrative. The latter may well claim to be a colorless, objective recital of facts (though in reality the Scriptural histories for the most part give clear intimation of the estimate proper to be put upon the facts which they record); but the former is in its very nature an expression of the poet's personal feeling, and involves an implicit claim that this feeling is in some sense true and right, such as others should sympathize with and, it may be, adopt as their own.

The attempt has also been made to account for these harsh expressions on the ground of the lower standard of morality which, it is alleged, obtained under the Old Testament dispensation. There were may things permitted, it is said, under the Old Covenant which are no longer allowable under the fuller light of the New. The polygamous arrangements of the Patriarchs, the exterminating wars waged by the Chosen People, are adduced as illustrations of the prevalence of such a lower standard. The injunction "Love your enemies, bless them that curse you, do good to them that hate you, and pray for them which despitefully use you and persecute you," had not been given. This was one of the "But I say unto you"s of Him who was also to pray for His murderers, "Father, forgive them, for they know not what they do."

But this explanation also falls to the ground in view of the fact that even the law of Moses forbids private vengeance, yes, commands kindness to enemies, witness Leviticus 19:18, "Thou shalt not avenge, nor bear any grudge against the children of thy people; but thou shalt love thy neighbor as thyself," and Exodus 23:4, 5, "If thou meet thine enemy's ox or his ass going astray, thou shalt

surely bring it back to him again. If thou see the ass of him that
hateth thee lying under his burden, and wouldest forbear to help
him, thou shalt surely help with him."

And it has been well pointed out that when Paul, in Romans
12:19ff., would forbid this very sin of a revengeful spirit, he does so
by means of two quotations from the Old Testament—one from the
Song of Moses (Deut. 32:35), "Vengeance is mine, and recompence," the other from the Book of Proverbs (25:21, 22):

> If thine enemy hunger, give him bread to eat;
> And if he be thirsty, give him water to drink:
> For thou shalt heap coals of fire upon his head,
> And the Lord shall reward thee.

Nor can we hardly doubt that David knew and understood these
injunctions of the law. The psalms everywhere bear evidence that
their authors' minds were saturated with the thought and language
of the Torah. Moreover, it is to be remarked that in two of the
three psalms in which the strain of imprecation is most pronounced
David protests the kind feelings he had for those who were perse-
cuting him. Hear him in 35:12ff.:

> They reward me evil for good,
> To the bereaving of my soul.
> But as for me, when they were sick, my clothing was sackcloth:
> I afflicted my soul with fasting;
> And my prayer returned into mine own bosom.
> I behaved myself as though it had been my friend or my brother:
> I bowed down mourning, as one that bewaileth his mother.

And so in 109:4, 5:

> For my love they are my adversaries:
> But I give myself unto prayer.
> And they have rewarded me evil for good,
> And hatred for my love.

Now, so far as David is concerned—and it is he principally among
the authors of the psalms that comes into consideration, since
thirteen of the eighteen psalms in which any imprecatory element is
found, and all three of those that are the *loci magni* in this regard,
are on good grounds ascribed to his pen—we can easily accept these
protestations as true. Rarely has a man of equal strength of charac-

ter and warmth of feeling shown himself so far from the spirit of revenge. The man who twice spared the life of his deadly enemy, and that, too, when others urged him to smite; who uttered the touching "Song of the Bow" when at last that enemy fell on Gilboa; who put to death the Amalekite who so far misjudged him as to think that the son of Jesse would rejoice in his rival's death; who treated honorably with Abner while he was still the mainstay of Ishbosheth's cause, and publicly avowed his horror at Joab's treacherous deed of blood; who visited a quick but just punishment upon the assassins who brought him Ishbosheth's bloody head; who would not suffer Abishai to carry out his purpose to cross the ravine and take off the head of scurrilous Shimei; who charged his captains as they went out of the gate of Mahanaim to deal gently with the guilty head of the rebellion, the young man Absalom—was this a man who would treasure up injuries in his memory, and breathe out his desire for vengeance in elaborate and many-sided maledictions? And if any one is disposed to find proof of such a savage temper in David's purpose to revenge himself on churlish Nabal, it is sufficient answer to point out that a few well-chosen words of remonstrance on the part of Abigail were enough, not merely to turn him from his purpose (since a comely and tactful woman with a handsome present at her back might well lead him to lay aside his intention of violence), but to prick his conscience and bring him to a solemn admission of his error. And if it still be urged that though David, after the overthrow of Absalom's revolt, spared Shimei and formally forgave him, he nevertheless afterward gave evidence of his lasting memory for injuries by charging Solomon to put the Benjamite to death, it may easily be shown that in giving this command David was acting not as a private person but as a king, who, as Keil says, "while he had forgiven the personal injury, had not forgiven, and as representative of the divine right in the theocracy could not forgive, the crime of high treason of which Shimei had become guilty by reviling the Lord's anointed." That David had faults, both as a man and as a king, is a fact which the Biblical writers take no pains to conceal; but surely, if they have given us a description of his character at all approaching the truth, a revengeful and implacable spirit was not one of those faults.

Nor ought we to overlook one further consideration which serves to show that these so-called "imprecations" are not mere outbursts of the spirit of vengeance. It is that the poems which contain them have the form of direct addresses to God; in other words, they are prayers, or if regard be had to their adaptation to use in public worship, they are hymns. These very psalms are full of earnest pleadings with God for help, with acknowledgments of dependence upon Him, with appeals to His mercy, His truth, His faithfulness, with thankful recognitions of past favors, with vows of grateful thanksgiving for deliverance, with humble confessions of sin, with professions of zeal for His honor. Let any one take Psalm 69, for example, and omit from it verses 22-28, and ask himself whether any other psalm strikes more squarely the note of real piety. Is it believable that words such as these, words of supplication, confession, adoration, are in truth only prelude and postlude to a horrid discord of angry curses sounding forth from a heart that can neither forgive nor forget?

But if these "hard sayings" are not longings for vengeance, what then are they? Before we attempt a positive answer to this question there is a preliminary consideration that deserves attention. It is that we are dealing here with poetry, not with prose, and with that form of poetry which more readily than any other takes on strong color, viz., the lyric. We are dealing, too, with Oriental poetry, the poetry of a people with whom hyperbole is the commonest and best-loved figure of speech. The value of this consideration to our present discussion has been happily illustrated by John DeWitt, lately professor in the theological seminary at New Brunswick, N.J., by means of a contrast between the attitude of David toward trouble and suffering as this is conveyed by the historical books, on the one hand, and by the psalms of suffering on the other. The former, he truly says, represent David as a man of the highest courage, the noblest fortitude; the latter set him before us as moaning, groaning, filling the air of night with complaints, making his couch to swim with tears, because of the attempts of his enemies. Now this contrast is to be explained, says Dr. DeWitt, not by assuming that there were two Davids, one of whom was a hero while the other was a coward, nor by assuming that one of these pictures is true and the other false, but simply by remembering that the historical books are prose while the psalms are poetry. With regard to the lamentations and the imprecations of the psalms alike, it is much to the point not to forget that we are dealing with the poetry of "the fervid, impassioned and demonstrative East, where to this day feeling of any kind is scarcely thought to be genuine unless it is expressed extravagantly."

Keeping this distinction between prose and poetry in mind, the first answer that may be given to the question we have raised is this: These so-called imprecations are *the expression of the longing of an Old Testament saint for the vindication of God's righteousness.* How much this subject of theodicy, or the justification of the dealings of God with man, engaged the attention of the Old Testament writers is well known. The whole Book of Job is devoted to it; it recurs often in the Proverbs and Ecclesiastes; it appears again and again in the Psalms. In Psalm 5, 7, 10 and 17 it comes prominently to view, while Psalm 37, 39, 49 and 73 are wholly given to the discussion of it. Now it is obvious that this puzzle, how to reconcile God's righteousness with the facts of human experience, had never been presented in a more striking form than in the history of David. That he, a man of true piety, of pure life, innocent of any crime, whom God's prophet had anointed as Jehovah's chosen king, and who was conscious of the moving of God's Spirit within him—that he should be for weary years a fugitive, an exile, an outlaw, while his enemies, men devoid of piety, of truth, of honor, were living in ease, safety, honor, at Saul's court—surely it would be hard to conceive how the contrast between what was and what ought to have been could be presented in more glaring colors. What wonder if, under such circumstances, David should feel his faith in God's goodness and righteousness put to a severe strain, and should long for such a reversal of these conditions as would set his doubts and the doubts of others forever at rest! And that this was really the case we have abundant evidence in those very psalms which contain the imprecatory clauses. Thus in 7:9ff. he cries:

> Oh let the wickedness of the wicked come to an end, but establish
>   thou the righteous:
> For the righteous God trieth the hearts and reins.

In 28:4 his prayer is that God will deal justly with the wicked:

> Give them according to their work, and according to the wicked-
>   ness of their doings:
> Give them after the operation of their hands;
> Render to them their desert.

Note what the result is that David hopes for from the overthrow of his enemies. Hear how in 58, after the request

> Break their teeth, O God, in their mouth. . . .

he adds:

> So that men shall say, Verily there is a reward for the righteous,
> Verily there is a God that judgeth in the earth.

To the same effect is 59:13:

> Consume them in wrath, consume them that they be no more;
> And let them know that God ruleth in Jacob,
> Unto the ends of the earth.

And still more striking is 69:6:

> Let not them that wait on thee be ashamed through me,
>   O Lord God of hosts:
> Let not those that seek thee be brought to dishonor through me, O
>   God of Israel.

Have we not in such passages the expression of the same feeling of perplexity at God's dealings and the same longing for the vindication of His righteousness that breaks forth in the opening lines of 94?

> O Lord, thou God to whom vengeance belongeth,
> Thou God to whom vengeance belongeth, shine forth.
> Lift up thyself, thou judge of the earth:
> Render to the proud their deserts.
> Lord, how long shall the wicked,
> How long shall the wicked triumph?
> They prate, they speak arrogantly:
> All the workers of iniquity boast themselves.
> They break in pieces thy people, O Lord,
> And afflict thine heritage.
> They slay the widow and the stranger,
> And murder the fatherless.
> And they say, The Lord shall not see,
> Neither shall the God of Jacob consider.

And from this point of view it is worthy of remark that, owing to the very vague knowledge of existence beyond the grave granted to David and the men of his time, they could not comfort themselves, with regard to these mysteries of Providence, with the thought in which we take refuge, that eternity will set right all the apparent inequalities of God's dealings with men in this world. As Delitzsch has said: "Theodicy, or the vindication of God's ways, does not yet rise from the indication of the retribution in the present time which the ungodly do not escape to a future solution of all the contradictions of this present world; and the transcendent glory which infinitely outweighs the sufferings of this present time still remains outside the field of vision." Does not this consideration make it easier to understand how the psalmists, in their anxiety for the vindication of God's doings, were moved to invoke fearful and striking temporal calamities on the heads of the wicked?

The second answer we may give to the question as to the real nature of these so-called imprecatory expressions is that they are, particularly in the mouth of David, *utterances of zeal for God and God's kingdom.* This will be the more plain when we remind ourselves that the kingdom of God existed at the time not under an ecclesiastical but under a political form—the form, namely, of a theocratic monarchy—and that to this divinely ordained kingship David sustained, and that consciously, a close official relation through the greater part of his life. He had been set apart in his youth by anointing at the hands of Samuel. During all the years of his outlaw life he carried in his breast the conviction, not merely that he was innocent of any fault against Saul, but also that he had been divinely designated to the kingly office which Saul was so foully misusing. When he came at last to the throne, he received confirmation of the sign given in his youth, not merely in the providential blessing that marked his reign, but more unequivocally in the great promise granted him through Nathan, in which God declared that he had established and would maintain the closest relations between himself, his name and cause, on the one hand, and David and his royal posterity on the other. How natural it was to David's mind and temper under such circumstances to invest himself with a sanctity far beyond that natural "divinity that doth hedge a king" we may discover by observing his attitude toward Saul. It was not merely military loyalty that restrained David in the cave from taking advantage of what seemed to his men a wonderfully providential opportunity to rid himself of his enemy. It was not admiration for Saul's splendid capacities, nor gratitude for favors received from the king in earlier and happier days, that held back his arm. It was not his covenant of friendship with Jonathan that made the sleeping Saul inviolably sacred. No; it was because Saul was the "Lord's anointed." "God forbid," this was David's awestruck reply to the urging of his men, "God forbid that I should stretch forth mine hand against the Lord's anointed." To have done so would, in David's esteem, have been to commit treason and sacrilege in one. Now it will easily be seen how a man who felt thus with regard to the theocratic office, even when it was being abused, when it was held by one from whom God had manifestly withdrawn his favor, would certainly, when this office had been conferred upon himself, regard himself and everything that concerned him in the light of this official relation to God and God's kingdom. Such an one was not, and could not be considered, even by himself, a mere private person. He was the representative of God, in a different way indeed from priest or prophet, but not less really than either. And as he was God's representative, his enemies ceased to be private enemies; nor were they guilty of treason simply. They must be accounted the enemies of God himself and of his cause on earth. As such David might anticipate for them, yes, he might even ask for them, a fate which he would never have desired for those who were mere personal opponents. And he could do this without sin, exactly as Paul could without sin write, "If any man love not the Lord Jesus Christ, let him be anathema maranatha."

But before turning to the psalms for proof that this was in fact David's attitude of mind toward his enemies, let me suggest a third answer to our question, one which is so closely allied to the one just presented that the evidence for both may best be sought at one time. It is this: *These fierce-sounding utterances are an Old Testament saint's expression of his abhorrence of sin.* Those against whom these hard sayings were directed were not, as we have seen, mere private enemies of David. They were not simple public enemies, as those would have been who should have plotted against the life of any other monarch of that day. They were not merely opposers of God and God's cause. They were also, in the psalmist's view, fearful embodiments of wickedness. And there is every reason to believe that his view of them was simple truth. For it must be remembered that the persons whom David had in mind in the psalms under review, which belong about equally to the time of his persecution by Saul and to that of Absalom's revolt, were not chiefly Saul, for whom he had high regard, and Absalom, his favorite son, but rather, as has been intimated already, the syco-phants and intriguers who gathered about these and urged them on to deeds of which neither would have been capable without such incitement. Doeg and Cush and Ahithopel are types of these vile men, in whom falsehood, treachery, cunning, greed, hate, cruelty, arrogance and pride had come to their perfect fruit. What wonder if to David's mind such seem the very incarnation of wickedness, against whom every righteous man, not to say a righteous king, ought to feel the deepest indignation and abhorrence. And if it be answered that David should have done what we recognize it as duty to do under like conditions, that is to say, that he should have pitied the sinner, even while he condemned the sin, the rejoinder is that this is just what David could not be expected to do, whether as a poet, a Shemite, a king, or an Old Testament saint. He could not do it as a poet, for poetry loves the concrete, so much so that had these sins lain before David's mind as abstractions he would have been compelled by poetic feeling to seek concrete forms under which to embody them. He could not do it as a Shemite, for the Shemitic mind has little taste for philosophical distinctions such as we make so readily. He could not do it as a king; for it is the duty of a king not only to hate evil but to punish evil-doers. A king, as Paul puts it, "is a minister of God, an avenger of wrath to him that doeth evil" (Rom. 12:4). Psalm 101, that ancient "mirror for magistrates," may show us what was David's feeling as to the relation which he as a king should sustain toward wicked men:

> Whoso privily slandereth his neighbor, him will I destroy:
> Him that hath an high look and a proud heart will I not suffer.

> Morning by morning will I destroy all the wicked of the land;
> To cut off all the workers of iniquity from the city of the Lord.

And lastly, this distinction between the sin and the sinner was impossible to David as an Old Testament saint. This impossibility arose out of the fact that the doctrine of Satan, which makes it easy for us to pity the sinner while we hate and condemn the sin, was then very imperfectly revealed. We pity the sinner because we view him as not exercising an unconstrained choice of evil, but as being the victim of a cruel compulsion. Behind him, urging him on, we see that dark spirit of evil who at the time of the Advent emerged so clearly into view. There is no imprecation in the psalms which Christians of to-day would not be willing to adopt with reference to this enemy of God and man. But to David and his contemporaries this mighty power of evil had only the most shadowy existence. They could not see behind the scowling features of Doeg or the cunning face of Ahithopel the hellish outlines that we see. They thought of these men as choosing evil simply because they loved it, and therefore as being worthy to be hated by all those who loved and chose the good.

Turn now to the psalms themselves and see the evidence that, in asking for the judgments of God upon his enemies, David regarded these enemies as at the same time and chiefly the enemies of God and the embodiments of sin. For example, take the very first expression of an imprecatory sort that the Psalter presents (5:10), and set it in its proper context. David's prayer is

> Hold them guilty, O God;
> Let them fall by their own counsels:
> Thrust them out *in the multitude of their transgressions:*
> *For they have rebelled against thee.*

And the implication of the italicized words is confirmed by a consideration of the psalm as a whole. It is true that once in the course of it David does speak of those whom he has in mind as "mine enemies," but it is not because they are his enemies that he desires their overthrow. It is because of their wickedness and opposition to God.

> For thou art not a God that hath pleasure in wickedness:

Evil shall not sojourn with thee.
The arrogant shall not stand in thy sight:
Thou hatest all workers of iniquity:
Thou shalt destroy them that speak lies:
The Lord abhorreth the bloodthirsty and deceitful man.

.   .   .   .   .

For there is no faithfulness in their mouth;
Their inward part is very wickedness:
Their throat is an open sepulchre;
They flatter with their tongue.

So 10:15 contains the fierce cry:

Break thou the arm *of the wicked;*
And *as for the evil man,* seek out his wickedness till thou find none.

But here again the italics are fairly representative of the true animus
of the expressions used. For while, on the one hand, the psalm
contains no intimation that the writer has any enemies, on the
other, the first two-thirds of it are occupied with setting forth the
irreverence, the arrogance, the rapacity, in short, the wickedness of
the ungodly. Or if we turn to the three psalms which all have agreed
upon as exhibiting the most striking illustrations of the phenomenon in question—I mean 35, 69 and 109—it is still the same. In the
first of these, for instance, we must note that David lays stress not
merely or chiefly on the injuries that his enemies have inflicted
upon him, but upon the causelessness of their hate; their oppressive
treatment of the poor, their untruth and ingratitude and malignity;
nor must we overlook it that in the end he connects the triumph of
his cause as a righteous person and a servant of God with the honor
of Jehovah himself. In Psalm 69 David feels himself to be in such a
sense the type and representative of all who fear God that his
overthrow must be a stumbling-block to them (v. 6); the reproaches
that have been heaped upon him have been inspired by his zeal for
God and God's house (vv. 7-9); deliverance granted to him will
become ground for thanksgiving and source of blessing for the
whole church (vv. 30-36). Or see, finally, how in Psalm 109, in
which these expressions reach their climax, emphasis is laid upon
the falseness, hate, ingratitude, unmercifulness, love of cursing, with

which the psalmist's foes were chargeable, and say whether we have
not basis for the assertion that the real thought of David in these
harsh-sounding utterances is that to which he gives voice in the
close of 139:19-22:

> Surely thou wilt slay the wicked, O God:
> Depart from me, therefore, ye bloodthirsty men.
> For they speak against thee wickedly,
> And thine enemies take thy name in vain.
> Do not I hate them O Lord, that hate thee?
> And am I not grieved with them that rise up against thee?
> I hate them with perfect hatred:
> I count them mine enemies.

And we may well ask in passing whether a man whose heart was full
of unholy enmity against personal foes would be likely to add:

> Search me, O God, and know my heart:
> Try me, and know my thoughts;
> And see if there be any way of wickedness in me,
> And lead me ithe way everlasting.

Once more, and finally, these so-called imprecations are *prophetic teachings as to the attitude of God toward sin and impenitent and persistent sinners.* The psalms are not merely lyric poems,
embodying the feelings of their authors; they are lyric poems
composed under the influence of the Spirit of Inspiration, and as
such are a part of God's revelation of himself. From them we may
learn, not only how David, for example, felt toward persistent and
high-handed sinners, but also and more particularly how God feels
toward such. David, as Peter informed his hearers on the day of
Pentecost, was a prophet. Nor was he a prophet simply in the
narrower sense of one who by Divine inspiration foretells future
events. He was a prophet in the wider sense of a spokesman for
God, an official teacher of God's will. David himself realized this, as
we may learn from the preface to what are called his "last words"
(2 Sam. 23:1-7):

> Prophetic utterance of David the son of Jesse,
> And prophetic utterance of the man who was raised on high,
> The anointed of the God of Jacob,
> And the sweet psalmist of Israel:

> The Spirit of Jehovah spake by me,
> And his word was on my tongue.

As an official communicator of God's will to men, David no doubt felt it to be an important part of his duty to warn men of the Divine wrath against sin and persistent sinners. Now it deserves notice that there is scarcely a single expression used by David in the so-called imprecations upon his enemies which may not be found in other psalms as simple statements of fact with regard to the fate of the wicked. In these places the form of the verb is not jussive; instead we find the simple imperfect or perfect: the statement is not of that which David desires God may do, but of that which God has done or will certainly do. Compare, for example, the prayer and the positive teaching in the following pairs of quotations:

> Let them be as chaff before the wind (35:5).

> The ungodly are not so,
> But are like the chaff which the wind driveth away (1:4).

> Break their teeth, O God, in their mouth:
> Break out the great teeth of the young lions (58:6).
> For thou hast smitten all mine enemies on the cheek bone;
> Thou hast broken the teeth of the wicked (3:7).

> Let destruction come upon him at unawares;
> And let his net that he hath hid catch himself (35:8).

> The nations are sunk down ithe pit that they made;
> In the net which they hid is their own foot taken (9:15).
> Let them be ashamed and confounded together that rejoice
>   at mine hurt;
>   Let them be clothed with shame and dishonor that magnify
>   themselves against me (35:26).

> All mine enemies shall be ashamed and sore vexed;
> They shall turn back, they shall be ashamed suddenly (6:10).

And not to seek further for exact verbal parallels between what is asked for in one set of psalms and what is predicted or asserted as fact in the other, let any one read 7:12-16:

> If a man turn not, God will whet his sword;
> He hath bent his bow, and made it ready.

He hath also prepared for him the instruments of death;
He maketh his arrows fiery shafts.
Behold, he (the wicked) travaileth with iniquity;
Yea, he hath conceived mischief, and brought forth falsehood.
He hath made a pit, and digged it,
And is fallen into the ditch which he made.
His mischief shall return upon his own head,
And his violence shall come down upon his own pate.

Or let him take note of the expressions that are used as to the fate of the wicked in 37:2, 9, 10, 15, 20, 35, 36, 38, or 55:23, or 63:9-11, or 64:7-9, and say whether David anywhere invokes upon his wicked foes any punishments more terrible than those which he sees to be in fact laid up for all the wicked. Now it is the duty of men to acquiesce in the righteous dealings of God, as well with the wicked as with the righteous. It was by divine command that all the people said amen to the fearful curses upon evil-doers that were pronounced from Mount Gerizim (Deut. 27:15ff.). Deborah was not less expressing a pious sentiment when, after the destruction of Sisera and his host, she sang:

So let all thine enemies perish, O Lord!

than when she immediately added:

But let them that love thee be as the sun when he goeth forth in his might (Judg. 5:31).

In view of these facts is it not easy to understand how David, with the terrible fate of the wicked before his eyes, should sometimes, not under the impulse of desire for revenge, but merely in the heat of poetic fervor, pass from the indicative to the optative, from the statement of a fact to the utterance of a wish? The form is different in the two cases, but the truth taught and intended to be taught is the same. This seems to be the view taken of the matter by our Lord and the apostles. For it may well make us cautious how we adopt the language of some who have felt themselves unable to justify the expressions under review—*e.g.,* Dean Stanley, who speaks of their "vindictive spirit" (*Lect. on the Jewish Church,* p. 170)—to remember what has been so strikingly put by Dr. Binnie, of Stirling (*The Psalms,* p. 285), that "except Ps. 1, 22, 110, 118, all great

Messianic hymns, no other psalms have been so largely quoted by our Lord and His apostles as these 'imprecatory psalms'. . . . The 69th, which bears more of the imprecatory character than any other except the 109th, is expressly quoted in five separate places, besides being alluded to in several more." And he adds: "The nature of the quotations is even more significant than their number. It would seem that our Lord appropriated this (69th) psalm to Himself, and that we are to take it as a disclosure of thoughts and feelings which found a place in his Heart during His ministry on earth. In the Guest Chamber He quoted the words of the fourth verse, 'They hated me without a cause,' and represented them as a prediction of the people's hatred of the Father and of Himself (John 15:25). When He drove the traffickers from the Temple, John informs us (2:17), His disciples remembered that it was written, 'The zeal of thine house hath eaten me up' (cf. Ps. 69:9), which implies that those words of the psalm expressed the very mind that was in Christ. When Peter, after mentioning the crime and perdition of Judas, suggested to the company of a hundred and twenty disciples that they ought to take measures for the appointment of a new apostle to fill the vacant place, he enforced the suggestion by a quotation, 'For it is written in the Book of Psalms, Let his habitation be desolate, and let no man dwell therein, and his bishopric let another take' (Acts 1:20)—manifestly on the supposition that this psalm and the 109th (for the quotation is from them both) were written with reference to Judas. In the Epistle to the Romans the duty of pleasing, every one of us, our neighbor to his good is enforced by the apostle with the argument (Rom. 15:3; cf. Ps. 69:9) that 'even Christ pleased not himself, as it is written, The reproaches of them that reproached thee fell on me'—an argument that has no weight if David alone is the speaker in the psalm, if Christ be not in some real sense the speaker in it also. Finally, we are taught in the same epistle to recognize a fulfillment of the psalmist's most terrible imprecations in the judicial blindness which befell the Jewish nation after the crucifixion of Christ (cf. Ps. 69:22, 23, with Rom. 2:9, 10)." All this proves that, if we are not to reject the authority of Christ and His apostles, we must take this imprecatory psalm as having been spoken by David as the ancestor and type of Christ. I do not say that the fact that these psalms are so unequivocally endorsed and appropriated by our blessed Lord explains the difficulty they involve. But I am sure that the simple statement of it will constrain the disciples of Christ to touch them with a reverent hand, and rather to distrust their own judgment concerning them than to brand such Scriptures as the products of an unsanctified and unchristian temper."

VIII

THE INTERPRETATION
OF ECCLESIASTES

by J. Stafford Wright

The Book of Ecclesiastes might be called the black sheep of the Bible. In olden days the Rabbinic schools of Hillel and Shammai disputed whether or not this Book "defiled the hands," that is whether it was a canonical Book that conveyed holiness when it was handled. To-day the examiner asks, "On what grounds would you defend the inclusion of Ecclesiastes in the Cannon?" In fact the history of the interpretation of the Book shows the profound suspicion with which it has always been regarded. It did, however, find its place in the Canon of Scripture, chiefly because of its Solomonic authorship and the orthodoxy of the final chapter. Yet today few of us would care to maintain that Solomon was the author, while many scholars reject the final chapter.

Ought the book then to remain in the Bible? Would it not be better to admit straight away that the contradictions and unorthodox statements, that have delighted skeptics and puzzled devout minds would have been far better employed in writing for the Rationalist Press Association than for the Library of the Holy Spirit. It is a question that must be faced. If there is no satisfactory interpretation of the book—satisfactory, that is, from the Christian standpoint—there is no logical reason for retaining it in the Bible.

I need not at this point enumerate the particular passages that have shocked the devout; we are familiar with the general tone of them. But it will be worth while to refer briefly to the methods of exegesis that Jews and Christians have employed to justify the retention of the book as part of the Word of God.

---

[1] A paper read at the Cambridge Conference of the Tyndale Fellowship for Biblical Research in January, 1945. This essay appears here with the kind permission of the Editor of *Evangelical Quarterly*, F. F. Bruce, and the author J. Stafford Wright.

Jewish expositors made use of three methods. (1) Some of them read the so-called Epicurean passages with a question mark after them, thus; "Is there nothing better for a man than that he should eat and drink, . . . ?" (2) Others adopted a legend that Solomon was driven from his throne in consequence of his disobedience to God, and held that this book was the product of his period of estrangement from God. The origin of this legend appears to be 1:12 which says, "I the preacher *was* King over Israel," implying that now he is no longer king. (3) The unorthodox statements were paraphrased and explained away, as they are in the Targum on this book. Thus such a verse as 9:7, "Go thy way, eat thy bread with joy, and drink thy wine with a merry heart, for God hath already accepted thy works," becomes in the Targum, "Solomon said by the spirit of prophecy before Jehovah, 'The Lord of the world shall say to all the righteous one by one, Go taste with joy thy bread which has been given to thee on account of the bread which thou hast given to the poor and the unfortunate who were hungry, and drink with good heart thy wine, which is hidden for thee in the Garden of Eden, for the wine which thou hast mingled for the poor and needy who were thirsty, for already thy good work has been pleasing before Jehovah.' " Paraphrase along these lines could make even Wellhausen a fundamentalist!

Early Christian commentaries used similar methods of allegorizing, paraphrasing, and explaining away. Jerome wrote a commentary on the book to induce a Roman lady to adopt the monastic life. According to him, the purpose of the book is to show the utter vanity of every sublunary enjoyment, and hence the necessity of betaking oneself to an ascetic life, devoted entirely to the service of God.

Martin Luther was probably the first to deny the Solomonic authorship. He regarded the book as "a sort of Talmud, compiled from many books, probably from the library of King Ptolemy Euergetes of Egypt." Grotius in 1644 followed Luther in the idea that the book was a collection, and once the idea of the unity of the book was broken, it became possible to follow a fresh line of interpretation. Thus Herder and Eichhorn (c. 1780) regarded the book as a dialogue between a refined sensualist and a sensual worldling, or between a teacher and a pupil. The successor to this theory to-day is the commonly adopted one of three hands in the book. First, there is Koheleth himself. Koheleth is the title assumed by the main author. Our English versions translate it as "The Preacher." Probably this is near enough to the correct meaning, but the commentaries commonly transliterate the Hebrew, so we shall do the same. Koheleth states doubts and problems that arise in his mind as he examines life. Then there is the Pious Man who interjects orthodoxy when he finds a saying of Koheleth that shocks him. Finally a Wise Man sprinkles in a few maxims and proverbs. It is, of course, possible to have many more writers than these three if you wish. Siegfried has a pessimist, a Sadducee, a wise man, a pious man, a proverbial anthologist, a Redactor, an Epilogist, a second Epilogist, and a Pharisee.

On the other hand some commentators hold strongly to the unity of the book. Canon Lukyn Williams in the Cambridge Bible accepts it almost entirely, as previously did such commentators as Delitzsch, C. H. H. Wright and Cornill. What interpretation on this view will justify the retention of the book in the Bible? Without concerning ourselves with details, the interpretation generally adopted is that here we have the struggles of a thinking man to square his faith with the facts of life. In spite of all the difficulties, he fights his way through to a reverent submission to God. The book then is valuable, since it shows that even with the lesser light of the Old Testament it was possible for a thinking man to trust God; how much more is it possible for us with the fuller light of the New Testament! Cornill thus regards the book as marking one of the greatest triumphs of Old Testament piety.

Another type of interpretation is worth mentioning. This stresses the phrase "under the sun," and holds that the author deliberately concerns himself only with the things of this world. Revelation and the world to come are laid aside for the purpose of the argument. Experience of the world leads only to pessimism. Where then is satisfaction to be found? The author does no more than hint that there is something more to be found in God. His purpose in writing is primarily negative—to cause dissatisfaction, so that men will turn in search of something that will satisfy.

Among those commentators who hold to the full inspiration of the Bible there is a certain hesitancy in dealing with Ecclesiastes. The introductory note in the Scofield Bible may be taken as fairly representative. "This is the Book of man 'under the sun,' reasoning about life; it is the best man can do, with the knowledge that there is a Holy God, and that He will bring everything into judgment. The key phrases are 'under the sun'; 'I perceived'; 'I said in my heart.' Inspiration sets down accurately what passes, but the conclusions and reasonings are, after all, man's."

Without being concerned with minor details, we have now reviewed the main lines of interpretation of this fascinating book. I do not know how far any one of them has satisfied you, but none of them completely satisfies me. This is not to say that there is no truth in them: obviously most of them contain some truth. But I do not feel that any of them has given a key that will unlock the book as a whole, though all assume that there must be a key somewhere. That is to say, Ecclesiastes cannot be treated as a string of texts, each of which may be interpreted in isolation. Even though we may conclude that the author jotted down different passages at different times, in the manner of a diary of his spiritual experiences, yet most of us will feel that there must be some underlying unity, some theme by which the whole is to be interpreted. At any rate I am proceeding on that assumption. So it is useless to take a text and ask "What does that mean?" unless we have in our minds some scheme for the whole book into which that test must fit. Most commentators have, of course, realized this. The point is, what is the scheme?

First of all there is one interpretation that I believe we must unhesitatingly reject. This is the conclusion that we have here the uninspired reasonings of the natural man or even of the skeptic. The theory of Scofield, and the theory of those who hold to several hands in the book, do not strike me as in the least likely. Koheleth is spoken of in the last chapter as a wise man. He evidently had a high reputation for wisdom. There is a proverbial saying that a fool can raise problems which a wise man cannot answer. If Koheleth was the skeptic whose doubts needed to be dealt with by the other two writers, I do not see that his wisdom is much greater than that of the modern tub-thumping objector to Christianity. Anyone who wants to fling doubts at religion has plenty of ammunition in the world around.

Moreover it does not seem to be worthy of God to occupy valuable space in the Bible with the arguments of the skeptic and of the natural man. We can buy those anywhere or have them for nothing. That is the difficulty with Scofield's theory. This objection, of course, does not hold good against those who, like Cornill, see in the book the triumph of piety over the arguments of skepticism. There is something very attractive in this view, but none the less I do not feel that it gives us the master key to the whole book.

Let us then turn to the book afresh, and try to examine it without prejudice. And let us see whether we can interpret it as a unity before cutting the Gordian Knot and dividing the book among three or more hands.

If you pick up a book and want to find the author's viewpoint, where do you turn? The preface is usually helpful—sometimes it saves you reading the book! The conclusion also in a well-written book generally sums up the point that the author has been trying to put over. When you look through the book, you may also be struck by something in the nature of a refrain, that by its continual recurrence tends to drive some point home. Suppose we apply these methods to Ecclesiastes.

The preface is a gaunt and stark announcement, "Vanity of vanities, saith the Preacher; vanity of vanities, all is vanity." That may be the grumblings of a pessimist. To me it is the trumpets sounding the opening theme of some colossal overture. "Vanity of vanities, saith the Preacher; vanity of vanities, all is vanity."

My opinion may be purely subjective; I do not ask you to accept it yet. But I do ask you not to dismiss the text as a sub-Christian verdict on life. It is sometimes said that Ecclesiastes is never quoted in the New Testament. But surely Paul has this verse in mind when he says in Romans 8:20, "The creation was subjected to vanity," and in the context he includes us Christians in the whole creation. In other words whatever may be the precise meaning of Koheleth's sentiment, there is a general agreement between him and Paul that everything is subject to vanity. Incidentally I wonder whether this text is a genuine utterance of Solomon's, handed down as his comment on life. Koheleth at a much later date is so struck by it that he proceeds to put himself in the position of Solomon, and examines life through Solomon's eyes, so as to see how far his verdict was justified. That, of course, is only an idea, and has no direct bearing upon the theme of the book.

From the preface we turn to the conclusion. Here again, not far from the end, we find the words of the preface recurring "Vanity of vanities, saith the Preacher; all is vanity" (12:8). But the final conclusion is definitely presented as the final conclusion: "This is the end of the matter; all hath been heard; fear God, and keep his commandments; for this is the whole duty of man. For God shall bring every work into judgment, with every hidden thing, whether it be good or whether it be evil" (12:13, 14). This conclusion is so orthodox that we hardly need any parallel quotations to support it, but we may notice the statement of Christ in Matthew 19:17, "If thou wouldest enter into life, keep the commandments," and that of Paul in I Corinthians 3:13, "The fire shall prove each man's work of what sort it is."

Now if this is the deliberate conclusion of Ecclesiastes, and if the book is a unity, it stands to reason that no statement elsewhere in the book can be interpreted as a final conclusion if it contradicts the statement at the end of the book. Or, to put it from another angle, if any statement in the course of the book is given as a final conclusion, it must be interpreted in the light of the ultimate conclusion at the end. This is not a matter of inspiration or non-inspiration; it is the treatment that we should give to any book written by a reasonable man.

The third way of finding an author's point of view is to see whether there is any statement that recurs as a kind of refrain. There are several of these in Ecclesiastes. The "Vanity" theme recurs a number of times: Koheleth keeps reminding us of his text. "Under the sun" is another theme. One might add also, as Scofield does, "I perceived," and "I said in my heart," and similar phrases that describe a personal experience. We can see how these refrains fit into the general argument.

But there is yet another refrain, and this is the one that causes most of the difficulty in the interpretation of the book. Six times over it comes, repeated in slightly different phraseology but reiterating the same sentiment. Its first occurrence in 2:24 is representative of all the six: "There is nothing better for a man than that he should eat and drink, and make his soul enjoy good in his labor." The other occurrences are in 3:12, 13; 3:22; 5:18, 19; 8:15; 9:7-9. In each case the statements appear to be made as final conclusions. So the solution to life is that of the Epicurean sensualist, "Let us eat, drink, and be merry, for tomorrow we die"!

Now something must have gone wrong with our deductions somewhere. For this is completely different from the ultimate conclusion of the book. We must face the contradiction and look at the alternatives which might resolve it. Koheleth may be a slipshod writer who does not worry about contradictions. But this is not a minor contradiction; the whole basis and argument of the book is at stake. Perhaps then the Epicurean sentiments represent a temporary mood, which is described, only to be rejected. If this is so, it is strange that the mood keeps recurring, each time in a dogmatic form that suggests a reasoned conclusion. At this point we may grow faint-hearted and adopt the counsel of despair, and dismember poor Koheleth, sending him to join the noble army of martyrs, among which will be found most of the books of the Old Testament. This dismembering is an easy way out of many Bible difficulties, so easy that no one seems to have wondered why the Hebrews were so much more careless with their literature than any other people have been.

But let us have one more look and see whether we can save the unity of the book. Why do we read Epicureanism into this refrain? Because we are familiar with the Epicurean slogan. But suppose that Koheleth was not familiar with the slogan. Would he then necessarily mean by his statement precisely the same as the Epicureans meant by theirs? Could he possibly mean something that would be consistent with his ultimate conclusion? This line of thought is worth following up.

There may be something in it. For at the beginning of Chapter 2 Koheleth describes Solomon's adventures in what we may call

Epicureanism—mirth, pleasure, laughter, wine, servants, silver, gold, music and love. What more could a good Epicurean want? But Koheleth's conclusion is that it is all vanity. He can hardly then be advocating a similar course of pleasure for all men, even on a lesser scale. What then does he mean? Let us return to the preface and to the conclusion.

"Vanity of vanities, all is vanity." "Fear God, and keep his commandments . . . God shall bring every work into judgment." The first is a verdict on all life. The second is counsel in view of the verdict. But is the verdict true? That is what Koheleth examines for us, turning life over and over in his hands so that we see it from every angle. And he forces us to admit that it is vanity, emptiness, futility; yet not in the sense that it is not worth living. Koheleth's use of the term "vanity" describes something vastly greater than that. All life is vanity in this sense, that it is unable to give us the key to itself. The book is the record of a search for the key to life. It is an endeavor to give a meaning to life, to see it as a whole. And there is no key under the sun. Life has lost the key to itself. "Vanity of vanities, all is vanity." If you want the key you must go to the locksmith who made the lock. "God holds the key of all unknown." *And He will not give it to you.* Since then you cannot get the key, you must trust the locksmith to open the doors.

Before we come back to the Epicurean refrain, I want us to be convinced that this really is the theme of the book and not just a fancy of my own. The statement in 3:10, 11 is instructive: "I have seen the travail which God hath given to the sons of men to be exercised therewith. He hath made everything beautiful in its time: also he hath set the world in their heart, yet so that man cannot find out the work that God hath done from the beginning even to the end." A number of commentators adopt the R.V. marginal rendering here, and translate the Hebrew *ha-'olam* as "eternity" instead of "the world," and, as this makes better sense, we may adopt it. The previous context deals with the occurrence of events at their right times. "To everything there is a season, and a time to every purpose under the heaven: a time to be born, and a time to die; a time to plant and a time to pluck up that which is planted."

And a long list follows. Then come the two verses that I quoted just now. God has given us a sore travail. Events happen to us from time to time, but God has given us a longing to know the eternity of things, the whole scheme; but, try as we will, we cannot see it, though we can declare by faith that each event plays its part in the beauty of the plan.

This is not an isolated thought. It occurs again in 7:14: "In the day of prosperity be joyful, and in the day of adversity consider: God hath even made the one side by side with the other, to the end, that man should not find out anything that shall be after him." Again it comes in 8:17: "Then I beheld all the work of God, that man cannot find out the work that is done under the sun, because however much a man labor to seek it out, yet he shall not find it: yea moreover, though a wise man think to know it, yet shall he not be able to find it."

This is not pessimism. It is the solemn truth—just as true to-day in Christian times as it was in the days of Koheleth. That eternal WHY hangs over our lives. It meets us at every turn. Our fondest hopes are shattered. Why? The Nazi hordes overrun Europe. Why? God allows the War. Why? A brilliant young Christian life is swept away, while a good-for-nothing wastrel is miraculously delivered. Why? Why? Why? Where is the sense in it all? And yet we must go on looking for the sense. It is incredible that life should make no sense. Every man who thinks at all believes that there is sense somewhere, if only he could find it. He may not look very far; he may settle down to an unworthy philosophy of life. Or he may plumb the depths of reason, of science, or of theology in an endeavor to find the plan. But he cannot find it. Joad has not found it. Huxley has not found it. Karl Barth has not found it. No one has. The moment we think we have it, something happens that does not fit into the scheme at all. But we go on looking. We must look. We cannot help it. "It is a sore travail which God hath given to the sons of men to be exercised therewith. . . . He hath set eternity in their heart, yet so that man cannot find out the work that God hath done from the beginning even to the end."

See how Koheleth develops his theme. We go through the world with him, looking for the solution to life, and at every turn he forces us to admit that here is only vanity, frustration, bewilderment. Life does not provide the key to itself.

Come with him in the first chapter, and study Nature, that great revelation of God. But Nature is a closed system, an endless round of sunshine, winds, rain, rivers, speaking of God, it is true, but not disclosing the plan of God. The key is not in Nature.

Then let us try Man. Perhaps the key will be found in the process of history or in the progress of science. But all we see is an endless chain of generation after generation, striving for this and for that, groping for something and finding no satisfaction, producing new inventions, which are but adaptations of what already exists in the closed system of Nature, and which never bring to light that new truth and solution to life that all men long for. The key is not in humanity.

But it may be in Wisdom. Surely the greatest minds have the solution, or what is Wisdom for? Does Wisdom satisfy? Koheleth faces the question in the second part of his first chapter. Even though you have the Wisdom of Solomon, the verdict is: "In much wisdom is much grief; and he that increaseth knowledge increaseth sorrow." Why should it be so? Verse 15 suggests the answer, "That which is crooked cannot be made straight: and that which is deficient cannot be made up." If we may paraphrase the last clause, the world is bankrupt and can do nothing about it. It is only the really wise man who realizes the bankruptcy of life. Philosophy may easily lead to despair. It has been said that it is better to be a discontented Socrates than a contented pig. Certainly your Socrates will always be discontented, because he knows that he must forever search for the key that he will never find.

But is there such a thing as a contented human pig? If there is, perhaps he has found the key dropped after all in the mire of his sty. So Koheleth looks there. In Chapter 2 he becomes the complete human animal. He runs the whole course of sensual pleasure, and his verdict is: "Vanity and a striving after wind." You can no more grasp the solution to life's eternal discontent there than you can grasp the wind in your fist.

Koheleth's mind sways to and fro. The clue is not in wisdom, but perhaps it may be in folly, in an attitude that closes its mind to all ideas? Is a fool the ideal man? No, cries Kohleth, I cannot admit that. "Wisdom excelleth folly, as far as light excelleth darkness." "Yet I perceived that one event happeneth to them all. . . . How doth the wise man die even as the fool! So I hated life." Now for the first time Koheleth faces us with that supreme vanity—death, death that beats at every man's door, death that comes when man least expects him, death that undoes man's finest plans. Death can make a man hate life, not because he wants to die, but because it renders life so futile, just as a child on the seashore may grow weary of the sand castles that he builds so patiently only to have them swallowed up by the inexorable sea. Koheleth gives an illustration in 2:18-23. A man gains wealth and power and makes an honored name for himself. If he could live forever, all would be well. But at his death all his possessions pass to another, and he may be a wastrel and a fool.

Pessimism of pessimisms: all is pessimism! God then has made us to dance like puppets, in a play that we must always be trying to understand but can never comprehend.

There seems to be no cure, but to cut the strings and end the play by suicide, or to dance to our own tune and call it God's. The last is the conclusion of Omar Khayyám, but neither of the two is the solution of Koheleth. And yet so nicely balanced are the ultimate conclusions of life and religion that there is in places only a hair's breadth between Koheleth and Omar Khayyám. Yet that hair's breadth puts Koheleth's book in heaven and leaves the Rubaiyat of Omar Khayyám tied to the earth.

Now at last we are ready to deal with the interpretation of the refrain to which we have already referred. But let us pause one moment more to ask ourselves what are the possible solutions to the problem of life that Koheleth raises, and what is the Christian solution? Suicide is a possible solution, we give life up in despair as a problem too great for us to understand. Few philosophers have accepted this solution, which is no solution at all. Popular Epicureanism is another solution which gives up the problem as insoluble. Some have believed this to be Koheleth's answer. But if it is, the closing verses of the book, and other passages in the course of the

book, must be ascribed to another hand and Koheleth himself
written off as a worldling. Fatalism may solve the problem. God is
the arbitrary Judge, or maybe he is no more than impersonal Fate,
working according to his whims and fancies. Omar Khayyám combines this Fatalism with Epicureanism. But what is this driving force
that compels our minds to turn again and again to the problem of
life? Is it no more than idle curiosity? Or is it part of our inheritance as those made in the image of God, so that we see that the
universe has a wholeness, and that it must make sense if only we
could find what the sense is?

The Christian answer is that the universe does make sense. There
is a plan and a purpose that has its center and its climax in Christ.
We as Christians have been predestinated to be an integral part of
that plan. We have been "created in Christ Jesus for good works,
which God afore prepared that we should walk in them" (Eph.
2:10). But not even to Christians has it been given to comprehend
the plan. Not even a Christian can explain how everything that
comes into his life takes its place in the plan. But, none the less, all
the time he is trying to catch a glimpse of a certain wholeness that
will link together all his individual experiences. But again and again
he is driven back to the position of Romans 8:28: "We know that
to them that love God all things work together for good, even to
them that are called according to his purpose"; or, if *ho theos* is
read in place of *ton theos*, "We know that God works all things for
good with them that love him." The Christian attitude then is one
of faith and confidence. The Christian says, "I know that all these
things must play their part in God's total plan. I long to know what
the plan is and to see it as a whole, and I shall always go on trying
to see it. But in the meantime I will live my life one day at a time,
believing that in the common round of life I am doing the will of
God. I will be content with what God gives me and take my life
from the hand of God."

If, as I believe, this is the Christian solution, it is also the
solution of Koheleth. If his refrain is interpreted in the light of the
rest of the book, it can only mean what the Christian means when
he says, "I will take the things that make up my life, my food, my
drink, my work from the hand of God. All things work together for

my good." Thus Koheleth says in 2:24: "There is nothing better for a man than that he should eat and drink, and make his soul enjoy good in his labor. This also I saw, that it is from the hand of God." Or again in 3:11-13: "He hath made everything beautiful in its time; also he hath set eternity in their heart, yet so that man cannot find out the work that God hath done from the beginning even to the end. I know that there is nothing better for them, than to rejoice, and to get good so long as they live. And also that every man should eat and drink, and enjoy good in all his labor, is the gift of God."

Now this theme is worked out, not only in the refrains, but continually throughout the book. There is the thought of the certainty of a divine plan, even though individual steps in the plan remain a mystery, and must be accepted by faith. But man must never lose the realization that there is a plan, and he must never begin to treat the common things of life, his food and drink and work, as though they were not the gift of God. Hence man must learn to serve God from his youth and he must remember that there is to be judgment. Judgment, of course, implies a divine plan. If our sins were not a falling away from the divine plan, it would be difficult to vindicate God's justice in bringing us to judgment. But if we are brought up to realize that we owe a responsibility to God, it will help us to make our daily lives from the hand of God. This is Koheleth's thought in 11:9, 10: "Rejoice, O young man, in thy youth and let thy heart cheer thee in the days of thy youth, and walk in the ways of thine heart, and in the sight of thine eyes; but know thou, that for all these things God will bring thee into judgment. Therefore remove sorrow from thy heart and put away evil from thy flesh; for youth and the prime of life are vanity." In other words, Koheleth advises young men to enjoy their lives, but not to forget that their pleasures should be regulated by a sense of accountability to God. They should put away all that would harm mind or body, and remember that youth is not the whole of life; it will give place to middle age, old age, and death. Could even a C.S.S.M. leader say more?

But this question of death needs a little more consideration. Once again Koheleth's statements must be interpreted against the background of the whole Book. Death is a salutary and sobering thing to Koheleth. See how he deals with it in 3:18-22. Man commonly tends to live as though he had unlimited time for doing the plan of God. It is an extraordinary fact that most of us live as though this life were to be prolonged indefinitely. Or, looking at it from another point of view, we dwell upon the immortality of the soul, and forget that the vehicle for the service of God now is the body, and, if we fail to serve God in the body now, we shall never be able to make up in the future for what we have failed to do now. But the body is a frail thing. It links man with the animal world. Animals and men both possess that which the mineral and plant world lack—body and spirit. It may sound rather shocking to say that animals possess spirit, but, if you are shocked, I believe that shows that you have misinterpreted Koheleth. Some Biblical psychology has failed to recognize different uses of the term "spirit" in Scripture. Hence Koheleth has been understood to teach in 3:21 that man perishes at death in the same way as the beasts perish; and in 12:7, when he says that the spirit shall return unto God who gave it, that man at death goes straight to heaven, and not to Sheol. But the face is that Koheleth is not discussing the survival of the personal spirit in either of these passages. All animal life, which includes human life, has two features in common—a physical body and a life principle which animates the body. The thought is expressed again in Psalm 104:29, 30: "Thou takest away their breath, they die, and return to their dust. Thou sendest forth thy spirit, they are created." This life principle, or spirit, is the gift of God, and, when the body turns back to dust, the life principle goes back to the Author of all life.

Thus, to return to the interpretation of 3:18-22, this body that we share with the animal world is a frail thing, yet it is the instrument with which we serve God. When an animal dies, where does it go? It goes to dust. What about its life principle? Can you assert that its destination is different from that of man? Are you, in other words, on a higher footing than an animal so far as the fact of physical death is concerned? Never mind about future opportunities of service. We are talking about service in the body. This life is the portion that God has given you. Here you must find your satisfaction and must realize yourself. For you will not come back again to this earth any more than an animal will.

I submit that that is a straightforward interpretation of the passage. And I should give a similar interpretation to 8:16—9:10. Here once again we find the longing to know the plan. "I beheld all the work of God, that man cannot find out the work that is done under the sun: because however much a man labor to seek it out, yet he shall not find it." Here too we have the acceptance of the plan by faith. "The righteous, and the wise, and their works, are in the hand of God." Here too is the bewilderment at individual events: "All things come alike to all." Those events that are beyond the individual's own control so often appear to happen in a haphazard way. The tower at Siloam falls on the good as well as on the bad. And then, looming ahead, is the one event for all mankind, the one event of death. And death closes all. "A living cur is better than a dead lion." "The living know that they shall die," and can make their plans accordingly. There is a sense in which it is never too late in this life to take up your part in God's plan. But the dead have run their course. They are waiting in Sheol for the judgment. They do not, like the living, know what is happening on the earth. They have no further opportunities of earning the Master's reward. Their bodies, the vehicles of the emotions of love and hatred and envy, have gone to dust, and no more can they share in life under the sun.

Now see how beautifully the refrain follows in verses 7-10. Take up the common things of life, and find your joy in the service of God there. Life is but vanity, but it is a vanity that may be turned to profit if only one grasps the opportunity while it is present. "Whatsoever thy hand findeth to do, do it with thy might; for there is no work, nor device, nor knowledge, nor wisdom in Sheol, whither thou goest." And if that last verse sounds sub-Christian, we may remind ourselves that Christ himself said, "I must work the works of him that sent me while it is day; the night cometh when no man can work" (John 9:4).

This emphasis upon doing our work with all our might is a necessary counterbalance to the thought of accepting our life as from the hand of God. We are not to live in a spirit of complete resignation to life, tamely submitting to the flow of events, saying

about everything, "This is the will of God." This is not Koheleth's
idea. The fact that he introduces the idea of moral responsibility,
with his warning of the Judgment, shows that we are to live our life
as free beings. Moreover the incidental pieces of proverbial wisdom
are intended to be a guide for the practical side of life. We have
reached the conclusion that the events of life by themselves do not
furnish the clue to their own meaning. "The race is not to the swift,
nor the battle to the strong, neither yet bread to the wise, nor yet
riches to men of understanding, nor yet favor to men of skill; but
time and chance happeneth to them all." So Koheleth says in 9:11
and, if we are honest, we must admit that this is the impression that
life makes on us. No one can guarantee success, and no one can
quite see how God will deal with him in the events of life. Therefore many things in life must be planned on this basis. As God's
people we may sincerely desire to arrange our lives for His glory,
but we find it very difficult to say for certain, "If I do such-and-
such a thing, I know I shall be conforming with God's plan, and he
will bless me in it." That is the point of Chapter 11. If you are a
merchant or a farmer, it is no use waiting for infallible guidance so
that you can invest all your possessions in one venture, or plant all
your seed with the prospect of 100 per cent success. You must
use your common sense, and make such provision as you can to
meet the unknown quantities in life. If you are a merchant, distrib-
ute your ventures over seven or eight schemes. If you are a farmer,
sow your seed at different times so as to make sure of one crop, if
not of more than one. This all sounds rather banal, but it seems to
me to be a true guide for life. Until such time as God gives us
infallible guidance, and as long as events in the world continue to
happen apparently indiscriminately, I do not see that we can do
anything else. Let us remember, however, that belief in the Providence of God does allow us to hold that there are exceptions to the
ordinary run of things. God can and does work miracles, which are
none the less miracles because they are brought about through
natural causes. His people are often miraculously delivered. But it is
fair to hold, as Koheleth held, that the vindication of God's way in
individual lives is the miracle, while the apparent chance—which to
us, as to Koheleth, is no more than *apparent*—is the normal rule.

But let us emphasize it once again, God has a plan, and at the end of it he will be vindicated. But until we have reached the ultimate end, we must not attempt to judge the plan from what we see by the way. Foolish men may try to do this and will be led to a false philosophy of life. Listen to Koheleth in 8:11-13: "Because sentence against an evil work is not executed speedily, therefore the heart of the sons of men is fully set in them to do evil. Though a sinner do evil an hundred times, and prolong his days, yet surely I know that it shall be well with them that fear God, which fear before him: but it shall not be well with the wicked, neither shall he prolong his days as a shadow [i.e., in quiet coolness after the fever of life] ; because he feareth not before God."

Here then is the case for Koheleth. As counsel for the defense let me adopt a sentence of Cicero in his *Pro Archia* and say, I hope I have caused you to say, not only that Ecclesiastes ought not to be struck out of the Canon, since it finds a place there, but that, if it had not been placed in the Canon, it ought to have been placed there. It is a unique book, and its omission from the Bible would be a definite loss. Quite obviously it is not the last word on the problems of life, for it belongs to the Old Testament and not to the New. But its solution is along the consistent Bible lines that appear in both the Old and the New Testaments. Is it only by chance that Paul in Romans 8, after speaking of the vanity of the whole creation, goes on to speak of the sufferings that create a problem even for the Christian, and the confidence of the Christian in his daily life that all things work together for good for him? "All things" means those fortuitous events that we share in common with all mankind, where the race is not to the swift nor the battle to the strong. The world is not weighted in our favor. But the same things, which break the man of the world, can make the Christian, if he takes them from the hand of God. Go on looking for the key that will unify the whole of life.

You must look for it: God has made you like that, sore travail though it be. But you will not find it in the world; you will not find it in life; in revelation you will find the outskirts of God's ways; in Christ your finger tips touch the key, but no one has closed his fingers on it yet. No philosophy of life can satisfy if it leaves out

Christ. Yet even the finest Christian philosophy must own itself baffled. But do not despair. There is a life to be lived day by day. And in the succession of apparently unrelated events God may be served and God may be glorified. And in this daily service of God, we may find pleasure, because we are fulfilling the purpose for which God made us.

That was Koheleth's philosophy of life. Was he wrong?

IX

THE INTERPRETATION
OF THE SONG OF SONGS

by F. Godet

Three principal systems of interpretation have hitherto been applied to the Song of Songs. The common feature of the two first is that they see in King Solomon and in the shepherd beloved of the Shulamite, one and the same person. But the two systems differ in this, that, according to one of them—the only one generally admitted in the synagogue and in the Church—the love which unites the Shulamite to his personage is of a purely spiritual nature; while, according to the other, all that is said of the relation between these two is to be taken literally, and is a picture exclusively of earthly love. From the former point of view, the Canticle is an allegorical description of the anguish and the emotions attending the union of Jehovah either with Israel, or with the Church, or with each individual soul. According to the second interpretation, it is the picture of an earthly and sensual love, which would render the book unworthy of a place in the Canon; or at least that of a love, natural indeed but honorable and ideally pure, before marriage, up to 3:5; in marriage, after 3:6. Delitzsch is undoubtedly the writer who has best succeeded in interpreting the Song of Songs from this latter point of view.[1] According to him, the idea of the Canticle is none other than that of the essential oneness of the marriage bond—true love as the moral basis of monogamy. It is the unfolding of the meaning of that saying in Genesis: *one* man and *one* woman; and an anticipation of the teaching of Jesus, who made of these words the first article of the Christian code of family life. It is the condemnation of polygamy, which was allowed in the East, and even among the Jews from the time of the patriarchs. The whole meaning of the Canticle would be summed up in that form of address, *my only*

---

[1] *Das hohe Lied,* 1851.

one, in which the well-beloved salutes the Shulamite. And it is by
going to the bottom of this idea, and not by following the false
track of allegory, that exegesis should discover in the Canticle the
depths of mystical love. For what the husband is to the wife as her
head, that Christ is to the Church (I Cor. 11:8).

We do not think that, either in the one shape or the other, the
interpretation which makes of Solomon and the shepherd one and
the same person can hold its ground against the objections which
are urged against it. In order not too much to forestall the future
stages of our argument, we shall quote only one passage, but one
which seems to us conclusive, because being placed at the end of
the drama, like the moral at the end of a fable, it ought better than
any other to sum up the meaning of the whole. The Shulamite,
leaning upon the arm of her beloved, exclaims:

> Many waters cannot quench love, neither can the floods drown it; *if a
> man would give all the substance of his house for love* it would utterly be
> condemned" (8:7).

Can no one fail to recognize in these words an allusion to the
magnificent offers made by Solomon to the Shulamite in the course
of the poem? Is not this evidently shown to be the meaning, by the
declaration which follows, in which she contrasts the trial she has
herself just undergone, with that which is one day to come upon
her younger sister?—

> I am a wall, and my breasts like towers; then was I in his eyes as one
> that found favor" (v. 10).

Who was this *he* of whom the Shulamite here speaks? The words
which follow point him out:

> *Solomon* had a vineyard at Baal-hamon.

There had then really been a quarrel between the Shulamite and
Solomon. The firmness of the young maiden had at last found favor
with the king, and she was allowed to return in peace to her home.
And now we see her as she comes forth from this formidable trial,
celebrating the invincible power of true love; of that which is a
flame, an inspiration *of Jehovah* (v. 6), and its victory over all those
external means of seduction which a rich and powerful man can

bring into play, to overcome attractions of a purer and nobler nature. Had we no other proof of the distinction between these two personages, this would be sufficient. The shepherd is the beloved; Solomon his rival; and the unconquerable faithfulness of the Shulamite represents the victory of pure love over every bond of union of which the spring is egoism.

We turn then now to the second principal class of interpretations—that which distinguishes and even contrasts Solomon and the beloved. The first author who opened the path to this exegesis was Jacobi (1771). It is the learned and ingenious Ewald who has since followed it out in the happiest and most consistent manner. Under his influence this method of exposition has acclimatized itself in France. M. Renan has completely adopted it in his work upon the Canticle (1860); M. Réville has also reproduced its essential features.[2] Unfortunately, Mr. Renan has introduced into the work of Ewald some alternations which have not improved it. He has, in some sort, materialized a series of pictures in which the German divine had had the good taste to see only simple dreams or visions of the Shulamite. According to the French writer, the shepherd appears often in the course of the story. Even in the very presence of Solomon, and in the midst of his seraglio, he makes the two lovers express their mutual love. From the tower of the harem the Shulamite addresses her beloved and sends kisses to him. Notwithstanding her captivity in the palace, she has full liberty to convey herself and her friend to the garden where they for the first time swore each other eternal love, there to sport freely with him. Then the next moment she finds herself in her royal prison, sighing at her separation from him. How are we to explain dramatic monstrosities such as these? M. Renan is himself, it is true, shocked at them, but he entrenches himself behind the idea of the imperfect character of the scenic arrangements in use at that remote period. But we ask whether the ancient stage ever did violence to common sense? There are some primary laws which not even the commonest theater could transgress without self-annihilation. To make of an oriental despot a calm spectator of caresses exchanged between his

---

2 *Revue de théol.,* vol. xiv.

favorite and his rival, to transform a seraglio into a room open to all comers, to make the actors of the interior of the harem pass thence to the garden, called the *vineyard*—such proceedings pass all licenses which ancient art could ever have allowed itself, even among the Hebrews. The truth is, that M. Renan has followed an entirely wrong track. Ewald maintains with reason that the beloved does not appear once upon the scene during the whole course of the trial— any more than Jehovah does in the book of Job—until the moment preceding the conclusion. It is this absence which constitutes the very strength and reality of the trial of the young maiden. And it is not until this trial is happily at an end, when the Shulamite has won the victory by herself, that the beloved at length makes his appear- ance, at the moment in which the heroine comes forward leaning upon his arm (8:1).

From M. Renan we must then return to Ewald; for it is in his view that we find that mode of interpretation of which we are speaking applied in the most attractive way.

The Shulamite, a youthful maiden of Shunem (or Shulem), of perfect beauty, finds herself a captive in the house of Solomon. He met with her during an excursion which he made with his court, and had her taken to his palace. But she resists all his flatteries and all his promises—even the offer of sharing his throne; and having exhausted upon her all the arts of seduction, and been unable to succeed in overcoming her noble resistance and her incorruptible faithfulness to the beloved one whom her heart has chosen, he at last sends her back free to her own people. Such is the simple result drawn out by Ewald with great skill from the luxuriant pictures of our poem. This is the slender canvas which carries all this rich and gorgeous embroidery.

Starting from this idea, Ewald dissects admirably the dialogue, and then the scenes and acts of the poem; and he shows clearly the dramatic character of the work. Only, as we have before pointed out, in many of those pictures of which M. Renan wrongly makes scenes of real life, Ewald sees only dreams and visions of the Shulamite, in conformity with a well-known usage in oriental poetry, attested by M. Renan himself, and which consists in identifying the vision of the beloved with his real self.[3] The Shulamite describes in appropriate terms these ecstasies, into which she falls many times, and it would seem periodically, in this remarkable expression:

> I sleep, but my heart waketh (5:2).

And this expression is explained by this other, which forms, as it were, the burden of the poem, and which indicates the moment when the Shulamite falls, or throws herself again into these states of ecstasy:

> I charge you, O ye daughters of Jerusalem, by the roes and by the hinds of the field, that ye stir not up nor awake my love, till he please (2:7).

In this way, all the dramatic improbabilities and all the moral incongruities which would result from M. Renan's realistic interpretation of certain scenes, disappear.

The position, then, according to Ewald, is this: On the one hand, a king in all the splendor of his glory, transported with admiration, overflowing with passion; on the other, the poor and simple shepherd to whom the Shulamite has plighted her faith; the former present, the latter absent; the maiden called to decide freely between these two rivals. Such is the conflict in all its moral grandeur. If it were not for the complete absence of the beloved, it would not be the ideal trial of faithfulness.

As to the external side of the picture we have no objection to make—taking it, at least, as a whole to Ewald's interpretation, and if we are unable to adopt it as it is, it is not that we deem it false in any essential particular, but only that it seems to us incomplete. It starts from the right point, but it does not lead to the end which has to be reached. It is like a still shapeless chrysalis, out of which is hereafter to come forth a brilliant butterfly.

---

[3] M. Renan, speaking of v. 2, says, "The vision of the beloved is in all that follows identified with the beloved himself, according to a figure, well-known to the Arabian poets, called *Thaif al Khaëal.* See *Journal Asiatique,* April, 1838, No. 378, and those which follow."

I appeal, in the first place, to the last speech which the poet puts
into the mouth of the Shulamite, at the moment in which she finds
her friend once more under the shades of the maternal home, and
when he invites her to sing:

> Thou that dwellest in the gardens, the companions hearken unto thy
> voice, cause me to hear it (8:13).

What does the Shulamite answer?

> Make haste my beloved, and be thou like to a roe, or to a young hart,
> upon the mountains of spices (8:14).

Can that be the last word of a romance of love? What a
conclusion, not to say what a fall, after so serious a conflict, and
one which has demanded of the Shulamite all the powers of her
moral being! Ewald, *pace* the French theologian, here again carries
off the palm of good taste. According to him, the Shulamite repeats
with delicacy—in a modified form no doubt—the love-song in which
she had lately invoked her beloved during the time of their separation: "turn my beloved, and be thou like a roe or a young hart,
upon the mountains of division" (2:17), she had said to him. This
song she now repeats, only substituting "flee" for "return." But
what is the object or meaning of this modification? we ask Ewald.
Is it merely a piece of sauciness? Such a conclusion would be
unworthy of the serious meaning which Ewald himself attributes to
the whole poem.

Ewald has done much in pointing out in the Canticle a progressive action, a conflict which takes place and which leads up to a
definite end. In our opinion we must go one step further; we must
recognize in this history a parable; in this visible drama which
unfolds itself before us, a riddle to which the reader is called upon
to find the answer.

The Song of Songs has to such a degree this enigmatical character peculiar to the time of Solomon, that it concludes with four
enigmas in regular form: [the apple-tree, the little sister, the two
vineyards, and the flight of the beloved] .

It appears to us that the action, in the Canticle, unfolds itself in
three acts, of which the first has for its scene Solomon's palace; the

second, the open place in front of the palace, then the palace itself; and the third, the garden of the Shulamite's own dwelling. The subject of the first two is the double victory gained by the young maiden in the two trials to which her fidelity is exposed; that of the third is her triumph after her victory.

The First Act

The first act comprehends the part of the poem which extends to 3:5.

It is composed of four scenes, of which the first takes place between the Shulamite and the young girls of the harem, and includes the seven first verses of the poem.

The Shulamite, a young peasant-girl—which is evident from these words, "My mother's children were angry with me; they made me keeper of the vineyards"—finds herself carried captive into Solomon's palace. The young girls of Jerusalem who are already there, form a kind of chorus, with whom the young maiden converses. This is a device for acquainting the reader with the situation. These young Israelites vie with each other in singing the delights of being the object of the attentions of such a prince as Solomon. In their enthusiasm they address him, although not yet present:

> Thy love is better than wine. Because of the savor of thy good ointments thy name is as ointment poured forth, therefore do the virgins love thee. Draw me, we will run after thee (1:2-4).

The Shulamite interrupts this discourse. We perceive the change of speaker by the fact of the king being spoken of in the third person:

> "The king hath brought me into his chambers."

The Shulamite awakes as out of a dream; she begins to perceive the critical position in which she is placed. The words of the young girls have but too clearly enlightened her mind on this point.

These latter, without noticing this exclamation, which is as it were an "aside" of the Shulamite, continue singing the loves of the master they serve, but addressing the Shulamite, as if it were their mission to persuade her to respond favorably to the advances of the monarch. Seeing herself the object of their attentions, and comparing her dark skin with the fresh faces of the young city maidens, the village girl is troubled, and exclaims:

> I am black, but comely, O ye daughters of Jerusalem, as the tents of Kedar, as the curtains of Solomon. Look not upon me, because I am black, because the sun hath looked upon me: my mother's children were angry with me; they made me the keeper of the vineyards; but mine own vineyard have I not kept (1:5, 6).

The expression "my mother's children," is somewhat strange. She thinks, at any rate, that they are bringing her rather rudely under the maternal roof. This circumstance may be compared with 7:1, where she is called a *prince's daughter*. Her brothers have employed her in the rough work of dressing the vines. This to her is a kind of social degradation. And this first misfortune has been followed by a second. She possesses—no doubt as a heritage from her father—a vineyard, of which mention will be made again, later on, in one of the enigmas at the conclusion of the poem (8:11, 12). Of this inheritance she has not taken the care she ought. But what are these misfortunes, compared with that which she now sees falling upon her? She is separated from her beloved. Her heart seeks him in these magnificent apartments, but he is elsewhere; at this hour of noon he "makes his flock to rest" in some shady spot upon the mountains. In thought she beholds him under the cypresses and cedars which border the pastures, and in the simplicity of her love and the vividness of the impression made upon her mind, she addresses him as if he could hear her, and says:

> Tell me, O thou whom my soul loveth, where thou feedest, where thou makest thy flock to rest at noon: for why should I be as one that turneth aside by the flocks of thy companions (1:7).

She fears that if she goes to seek him upon the mountain, and is driven to enquire from others the place where he is resting, she may be taken for an immodest woman.

The young girls are amused at this outburst of tenderness, this sweet dream, by the help of which the Shulamite escapes from the dreadful reality; and as if to keep up in her this play of the imagination, they invite her, if she is simple enough to prefer the condition of life of a shepherdess to that of mistress of the brilliant monarch, to lead her little flock of goats up the slopes of the mountain:

> If thou know not, O thou fairest among women, go thy way forth by the footsteps of the flock, and feed thy kids beside the shepherds' tents (1:8).

A new scene here opens upon us. Solomon enters the apartment. He addresses the young maiden, and pays his tribute of admiration to her beauty; but his emphatic manner of speech is that of one of the great ones of the earth, who thinks it easy to dazzle a simple girl with a few gross compliments:

> I have compared thee, O my love, to a company of horses in Pharaoh's chariots. Thy cheeks are comely with rows of jewels, thy neck with chains of gold (1:9, 10).

To his flatteries he thinks it well to add some promises, but he risks no great expense for them:

> We will make thee borders of gold with studs of silver (1:11).

Listening to such words, which are repulsive to her, the Shulamite becomes reserved, and, speaking to herself, declares that at the very moment when the king is so addressing her from the divan on which he is sitting, she is caring but for one thing, the love of her beloved:

> While the king sitteth at his table, my spikenard sendeth forth the smell thereof. A bundle of myrrh is my well-beloved unto me; he shall lie all night betwixt my breasts. My beloved is unto me as a cluster of camphire in the vineyards of En-gedi (1:12-14).

Solomon answers:

> Behold, thou art fair, my love; behold, thou art fair; thou hast doves' eyes (1:15).

The Shulamite, her spirit becoming more and more fired, addresses to him she loves, the echo of the praises which Solomon lavishes upon her:

> Behold, thou art fair, my beloved, yea, pleasant (1:16).

She imagines herself transported already to his side:

> Our bed is green. The beams of our house are cedar, and our rafters of fir. I am the rose of Sharon, and the lily of the valleys (1:16, 17; 2:1).

This means clearly enough that she prefers the carpet of verdure and the shades of the forest to the gilded rooms in which she finds herself a prisoner. She is a flower of the field, and feels herself out of place in this magnificent palace. Solomon does not discourage her:

> As the lily among thorns, so is my love among the daughters (2:2).

The Shulamite, excited, answers him with an increasing vivacity:

> As the apple-tree among the trees of the wood, so is my beloved among the sons. I sat down under his shadow with great delight, and his fruit was sweet to my taste (2:3).

The vision of her beloved reaches here to its full intensity. Detaching herself entirely from the surrounding circumstances, she forgets her captivity; she fancies herself with him again in the places in which the young men and maidens used to make merry. Her heart gives way in this imagined bliss. The strong effort she has just made to resist the seductions to which she has been exposed, the vervor of her love, which has been intensified by this struggle with the passion of which she is the object, have exhausted her strength. She fancies herself falling into the arms of her beloved, in whose presence she imagines herself, and, closing her eyes, she entreats the maidens who are about her, in the name of everything that is lovely and tender in rural life, to respect the bliss into which her love has thrown her, and not to recall her to the sad reality, before she awakes of herself out of this sweet, unspeakable ecstasy:

> He brought me to the banqueting house, and his banner over me was love. Stay me with flagons, comfort me with apples: for I am sick of love. His left hand is under my head, and his right hand doth embrace me. I charge you, O ye daughters of Jerusalem, by the roes, and by the hinds of the field, that ye stir not up, nor awake my love, till he please (2:4-7).

Here, then, we see the Shulamite wrapped in her blissful dream. This is the point at which, properly speaking, the first act should close. But the author reveals to us the Shulamite's visions during this state of trance. The curtain falls for a while upon the external world, but at the same moment it rises upon what is passing in her soul. The two scenes which are to follow, are two ecstasies of the young maiden, closely connected with each other, and which form the conclusion of this first act.

The first—the third scene of the poem—comprehends 2:18—17. It is a morning scene. The Shulamite is in her mother's house. She fancies she hears the voice of her beloved calling to her, and catches sight of him through the lattice:

> The voice of my beloved! behold, he cometh leaping upon the mountains, skipping upon the hills. My beloved is like a roe or a young hart: behold, he standeth behind our wall, he looketh forth at the windows, shewing himself through the lattice (2:8, 9).

He is inviting her to a walk with him into the country, which is beginning to clothe itself in its vernal beauties:

> My beloved spake, and said unto me, Rise up, my love, my fair one, and come away. For, lo, the winter is past, the rain is over and gone; the flowers appear on the earth; the time of the singing of birds is come, and the voice of the turtle is heard in our land; the fig tree putteth forth her green figs, and the vines with the tender grape give a good smell (2:10-13).

But the Shulamite does not accept this invitation; she does not show herself. The beloved likens her to a dove hiding in the clefts of the rocks. If she cannot follow him, at least he begs to see her face, to hear her voice; he asks her for a song:

> Arise, my love, my fair one, and come away. O my dove, that art in the clefts of the rock, in the secret places of the stairs, let me see thy countenance, let me hear thy voice; for sweet is thy voice, and thy countenance is comely (2:13, 14).

She replies by a song in which she reminds him of the commands of her brothers, which oblige her, as well as her younger sister perhaps, or other young girls, to guard the tender shoots of the vine against the depredations of the little foxes. Thus do we hear echoing on through the ecstasies of the Shulamite all the emotions, pleasing or painful, of her past state of watching:

> Take us the foxes, the little foxes, that spoil the vines: for our vines have tender grapes (2:15).

Hence she is obliged to defer until the evening the walk to which she is invited. But her heart is none the less united to her friend; and when evening comes, and she will have finished attending to her rough work, she expects to see him coming towards her with eager steps, that they may enjoy the last hour of the day together.

> My beloved is mine, and I am his: he feedeth among the lilies. Until the day break, and the shadows flee away, turn, my beloved, and be thou like a roe or a young hart upon the mountains of Bether (2:16, 17).

Did ever any poetry surpass the dazzling brilliancy of this picture?

The second trance of the Shulamite which forms the fourth and last scene of the first act, is described in 3:1-5.

The evening has come; the beloved has not made his appearance. Night reigns around the Shulamite, and in her heart. We must remember that the scene which follows is entirely imaginary. That which would be shocking were the Shulamite speaking and acting in this way while in full possession of her faculties, will appear but natural, if we remember that it is an ecstasy or trance which the author is describing. It is important to notice here the use of the plural, *the nights* (3:1), which many of our translators have wrongly changed into the singular. This use of the plural is an insuperable difficulty in the way of any interpretation coarsely realistic. Finally, in order to understand the picture which follows, we must remember the custom of the oriental shepherds, who whenever they fear any nocturnal danger, bring their flocks back into the shelter of the towns and pass the night with them in the public places. Hence we understand how it comes to pass that the Shulamite went in search of her shepherd in the solitary streets in the middle of the night:

> By night on my bed I sought him whom my soul loveth: I sought

him, but I found him not. I will rise now, and go about the city in the
streets, and in the broad ways I will seek him whom my soul loveth
(3:1, 2).

Poor Shulamite! The hard rules of law do not easily accom-
modate themselves to the impulsive movements of a lover's heart.
She falls into the hands of the watch, but this time she escapes with
only a fright; and soon finding the object of her search, she brings
him into the house, into her mother's room; a little feature in the
narrative of exquisite delicacy, admirably leading the reader to
contrast this scene with the picture which opened the drama, that
of the young Israelitish maidens left alone in the harem of the
palace:

> I sought him, but I found him not. The watchmen that go about the
> city found me: to whom I said, Saw ye him whom my soul loveth? It was
> but a little that I passed from them, but I found him whom my soul
> loveth: I held him, and would not let him go, until I had brought him
> into my mother's house, and into the chamber of her that conceived me
> (3:2-4).

Then the Shulamite feels herself lost once more in the ineffable
bliss caused by the conscious presence of her beloved. And from the
midst of this happiness, on which rest the eye and the blessing of
her mother, she repeats the prayer which she has before addressed
to the young maidens around here when she had felt herself falling
into the trance, and once more adjures them to respect the sacred
repose of love, and not to tear her violently from this blissful
dream:

> I charge you, O ye daughters of Jerusalem, by the roes, and by the
> hinds of the field, that ye stir not up, nor awake my love, till he please
> (3:5).

Nothing can be more consistent, it seems to me, than the
conception of this first act, so understood.

The Second Act

The second song of the poem, or the second act of the drama,
extends from 3:6 to 8:4. It is the repetition of the trial to which
the Shulamite's fidelity is exposed, but in an intenser form. The

scenes correspond almost exactly with those of the first act. The first represents her brought in, as it were, in triumph, upon the portable throne which Solomon has had made. She arrives at the gates of the palace, admired by the people of Jerusalem who surround the procession. She is received by the king, who introduces her into the palace. The dialogue between her and the king then begins. Solomon pours out his admiration and his passion. He hopes that even that very day the Shulamite will give herself to him. She shall be his *only one* in the midst of all the other queens, and all the beauties who fill his harem. She replies to all these grand offers as she had done, in the first act, to promises less magnificent. But in this violent contest between the passion of the king and her own true and sincere love, which the contact with this alien fire only kindles into greater intensity, she falls again into one of those fits of absence which are in her the introduction into the state of ecstasy; and it is with this condition of the Shulamite that this act continues and concludes. We see, then, that the second act is a repetition of the first, in larger proportions. Let us go into the details.

The first scene, that of the coming in of the Shulamite on Solomon's throne, is described in 3:6-11.

The inhabitants of Jerusalem express their surprise and admiration at the sight of the procession as it approaches:

> Who is this that cometh out of the wilderness like pillars of smoke, perfumed with myrrh and frankincense, with all powders of the merchant? Behold his bed, which is Solomon's; threescore valiant men are about it, of the valiant of Israel. They all hold swords, being expert in war: every man hath his sword upon his thigh because of fear in the night. King Solomon made himself a chariot of the wood of Lebanon. He made the pillars thereof of silver, the bottom thereof of gold, the covering of it of purple, the midst thereof being paved with love, for the daughters of Jerusalem. Go forth, O ye daughters of Zion, and behold king Solomon with the crown wherewith his mother crowned him in the day of his espousals, and in the day of the gladness of his heart.

The first words might be perfectly rendered by the neuter: "What is that?" instead of "Who is this?" and be made to refer, not to the Shulamite herself seated on the palanquin, but to the portable throne, all enshrouded in the clouds of incense which they are burning around it. The only indication of the presence of the Shulamite is the address of Solomon, at the moment when the procession arrives. Nevertheless, we have translated it in the feminine on account of the parallelism between this passage and the analogous question of 8:5: "Who is this that cometh up from the wilderness?" where there can be no doubt as to the meaning of the Hebrew pronoun.

What had happened between this act and the preceding one? Had Solomon, on meeting with such determined opposition from the young maiden, sent her back to her mother? Is it there that he now, for the second time, sends this magnificent procession to fetch her, hoping that the royal splendor in which she is brought back will dazzle her, and prepare the way for the victory which he still makes sure of winning? This supposition seems to us more natural than that which makes the Shulamite remain in the palace after the preceding ecstasy; how, in the latter case, are we to account for the procession which brings her?

With 4:1 the second scene opens—the dialogue between Solomon and the Shulamite.

> Behold, thou art fair, my love.

This is a repetition of 1:14. Then, up to verse 6, the king enthusiastically describes her beauty. The Shulamite interrupts him as she had done before (1:12, 16). She hopes that when the evening is come she will be at liberty to climb the mountain of myrrh and the hill of frankincense, where her beloved feeds his flock. Solomon replies with expressions more and more impassioned. Does he allude, in the words which follow, to the Shulamite sitting on his throne in the palace, from which she casts at him glances full of pride? or is he here imitating the language of the shepherd, who, in 2:14, had compared her to a dove which hides itself in the clefts of the rocks?

> Come with me from Lebanon, my spouse, with me from Lebanon: look from the top of Amana, from the top of Shenir and Hermon, from the lions' dens, from the mountains of the leopards.[4] Thou hast ravished

---

4 Solomon's throne was surrounded with massive golden lions. 1 Kings x. 19, 20.

> my heart, my sister, my spouse: thou hast ravished my heart with one of
> thine eyes, with one chain of thy neck (4:8, 9).

His passion kindles more and more. It overflows from his lips
like a torrent of fire. The heart of the Shulamite gives itself up to
the same emotion, but it is for another than the monarch before
her. And when Solomon, in the paroxysm of his love, cries:

> A fountain of gardens, a well of living waters, and streams from
> Lebanon (4:15).

She answers at once, under the sway of her own passion:

> Awake, O north wind; and come, thou south; blow upon my garden,
> that the spices thereof may flow out. Let my beloved come into his
> garden, and eat his pleasant fruits (4:16).

Solomon, in his excitement, takes courage and dares to apply to
himself this outburst of love:

> I am come into my garden, my sister, my spouse: I have gathered my
> myrrh with my spice (5:1a).

And as if already confident of victory, he invites the young people
around him to share his joy:

> Eat, O friends; drink, yea, drink abundantly (5:1c).

But, oh wonder! She to whom this transport is addressed, lies
before him as an almost lifeless body. While he was yet speaking, his
captive had escaped from his power. She has fallen again into a
trance like that which had ended the first struggle. She herself tells
him so in these words:

> I sleep, but my heart waketh (5:2a).

Here opens a scene of a kind analogous to the visions described
in the two corresponding scenes of the first act, but even more
extraordinary.

First, from verses 2 to 7, we have a vision which combines in
itself many features of the two which precede it. It is announced in
the same manner:

> The voice of my beloved (5:2b).

He comes to seek her as he had done in the first vision, but this time it is in the night:

> The voice of my beloved that knocketh, saying, Open to me, my sister, my love, my dove, my undefiled; for my head is filled with dew, and my locks with the drops of the night (5:1).

The Shulamite replies with an exquisite modesty:

> I have put off my coat; how shall I put it on? I have washed my feet; how shall I defile them? (5:3).

She then relates how she had seen the hand of her beloved coming through the "hole of the door" and drawing near the latch.

Then she rose to open to him, and touching the handle of the latch she became conscious that it was dripping with myrrh—myrrh from the hand of her beloved. Then she opened the door, but he was gone—vanished. She continues:

> My soul failed when he spake: I sought him, but I could not find him; I called him, but he gave me no answer. The watchmen that went about the city found me, they smote me, they wounded me; the keepers of the walls took away my veil from me (5:6, 7).

Here again we may notice a step in advance upon the corresponding ecstasy in the preceding act, where the watchmen had let her pass without molesting her.

And in this condition she addresses the Jerusalem maidens, not this time to adjure them to leave her to her happiness—for she is not now blessed with the presence of her beloved—but to entreat them, should they meet him, to tell him how she longs for him:

> I charge you, O daughters of Jerusalem, if ye find my beloved, that ye tell him, that I am sick of love (5:8).

Just as, in the first scene, the young maidens had made a sport of entering into the Shulamite's imaginative dreams, spurring on, in some sort, the travail of her soul, the chorus here interposes, and answers her in the same spirit:—

> What is thy beloved more than another beloved, O thou fairest among women? what is thy beloved more than another beloved, that thou dost so charge us? (5:9).

Thereupon the lips of the Shulamite open, and overflow. She pours forth enthusiastic praise of the beauty of him she loves, and finishes by saying:

> This is my beloved, and this is my friend, O daughters of Jerusalem (5:16).

The young maidens carry on this singular conversation, as one might answer a child talking in its sleep; they amuse themselves in taking parts in this drama which is being played in the mind of the Shulamite. They ask her:—

> Whither is thy beloved gone, O thou fairest among women? whither is thy beloved turned aside? that we may seek him with thee (6:1).

If we were in the prose of actual life, the Shulamite would have to answer that she knows nothing about it, for her beloved had vanished suddenly without giving her time to see whither he was gone. But we are in the world of visions, where imagination quickly fills up all *lacunae:*

> My beloved is gone down into his garden, to the beds of spices, to feed in the gardens, and to gather lilies. I am my beloved's, and my beloved is mine: he feedeth among the lilies (6:2, 3).

If the preceding apparition were not a mere vision, there would be no meaning in this answer. Shepherds do not pasture their flocks in the middle of the night.

Here (6:4) opens the third scene, which extends to 8:4, and in which, if we compare it with the corresponding scene of the first act (the fourth), we may notice again a gradation not less marked relatively to this last. Solomon re-appears. He is about to make a last effort. He renews rather emphatically his flatteries, comparing the Shulamite to the two fairest cities in his kingdom, Tirzah and Jerusalem. Then, in allusion to the proud demeanor of his prisoner contrasted with the tenderness of her invocations to her absent friend, he exclaims:

> Thou art . . . terrible as an army with banners. Turn away thine eyes from me, for they have overcome me. . . . There are threescore queens . . . and virgins without number. My dove, my undefiled is but one; she is the only one of her mother, she is the choice one of her that bare her.

The daughters saw her, and blessed her; yea, the queens and the concubines, and they praised her. Who is she that looketh forth as the morning, fair as the moon, clear as the sun, and terrible as an army with banners? (6:4-10).

We have already seen how, during the Shulamite's ecstasies, there returned upon her memory the impressions of her state of watching, and the outward circumstances which had produced them. She seems at this moment to be recalling some memory, and trying to picture to herself the events which have brought her to her present condition. She had gone down to her garden, which was in a retired valley, to enjoy the sight of the growth of the spring vegetation. And there, without knowing how it happened, she found herself in the midst of the chariots of a royal procession:

> I went down into the garden of nuts to see the fruits of the valley, and to see whether the vine flourished, and the pomegranates budded. Or ever I was aware, my soul made me like the chariots of Ammi-nadib (6:11, 12).

Did this imprudence on the part of the Shulamite take place before her former captivity, or was it the cause of the triumphal but compulsory return which forms the subject of the opening of the second act? It is difficult to decide between these two alternatives, but the general sense of the words is evident; she reproaches herself for having allowed her curiosity to draw her too near the escort of the young king, who, with all his court, was on a party of pleasure in the neighborhood of the place where she lived; and she acknowledges that it was thus she brought upon herself what has now happened. The memory of this moment becomes so vivid in her mind that she tries to fly now, as she ought to have done in reality when the event occurred. Still in her state of trance, she rises and endeavors to escape. Only so, it seems to us, can we explain that invitation, so pressing and four times repeated, by the surrounding assembly:

> Return, return, O Shulamite; return, return, that we may look upon thee (6:13).

The Shulamite replies with a charming modesty:

> What will ye see in the Shulamite? (6:13).

The assembly answers:

> As it were a dance of Mahanaim (6:13).

From our point of view, the interpretation no longer presents any difficulty. In her trance, which is a kind of somnambulism, the Shulamite, who was on the point of taking flight, begins slightly to move, in presence of the company. The effect she produces upon all who see her in this mysterious state, is that of a being hovering between heaven and earth, a supernatural apparition; and it is to this that allusion is made in that strange expression, "like a dance of Mahanaim," that is to say, of a host of angels. The chorus then begins singing the praises of her grace and beauty (7:1–5). This enthusiastic description has often been put into the mouth of the king, but the contrary is shown by the expression in verse 5:

> The hair of thine head is like purple; the king is entangled in its curls.[5]

What proves undeniably that it is the sight of the measured march, or, if you will, the dance of the Shulamite which charms the spectators, is that the description begins with the walk and the shoes of the Shulamite, and ascends gradually to her hair:

> How beautiful are thy feet with shoes, O prince's daughter (7:1).

Does this title, *prince's daughter,* refer only to the nobleness and dignity of the whole bearing of the young maiden, or does it not also contain an allusion to her high birth?

Excited to rapture by this sight, the young king gives vent without restraint to his passion:

> How fair and how pleasant art thou, O love, for delights! . . . Thy stature is like to a palm tree. . . . I said, I will go up to the palm tree, I will take hold of the boughs thereof . . . and the roof of thy mouth is like the best wine. . . . (7:6-9).

Suddenly the Shulamite interrupts him, as she had done before in the first act, and adopting his own expression, finishes by applying it to her lover:

> ". . . for my beloved" (7:9).

---

[5] Eng. version, "held in the galleries." Tr.

And now, in her turn, abandoning herself to the intensity of her feeling, she opens her mouth to say things which in her waking state she would never have uttered. Her beloved is present; she is his. She invites him to an excursion into the country; then she will bring him again into her mother's house, and there she will serve him with the fruits new and old which she has been keeping for him. Oh! why is he not her brother? Then she could at any rate live with him, and show him her love, without anybody having a right to blame her—sit at his feet in her mother's house, and let him teach her all she does not know. Then she in her turn will offer him spiced wine and the juice of her pomegranates. And at this delicious thought she feels herself again falling into a swoon, but she thinks it is in the arms of him whom she fancies close to her; and as she loses consciousness, in the ecstasy to which she resigns herself, she repeats the burden of her song—the words which each time give notice of rest after the struggle:—

"I charge you, O ye daughters of Jerusalem, that ye stir not up, nor awake my love, until he pleases" (8:4).

Thus has the faithfulness of the Shulamite triumphed in two terrible conflicts with the three great powers of which the apostle speaks; the lust of the flesh, the lust of the eye, and the pride of life. She has preferred the love of a man, poor but sincere, to the passion of one selfish, however magnificent. The love of him who gives nothing—but himself, has seemed to her better than the love of him who gives everything—except himself.

The Third Act

The third act is the triumph which follows victory. It comprehends the last chapter, from verse 5, and is composed of four short scenes, in which all the personages connected with the Shulamite make their appearance, as in a kind of review, each one uttering, or else listening to, words which sum up the truth of her condition.

The first of these short scenes naturally refers to the relations between the Shulamite and her beloved. The chorus see in the distance two personages approaching—a youth with a maiden who is leaning upon him in trustfulness and tenderness:

> Who is this that cometh up from the wilderness, leaning upon her
> beloved? (8:5).

This corresponds with the Shulamite's appearance in the preceding act (3:6), when she was arriving at the palace in Solomon's
palanquin, and surrounded by his guard. Now she has regained her
liberty, and has hastened to seek her friend. She has found him
asleep under an apple tree, near the paternal house. As she comes
upon the scene with him, she addresses to him these words:

> I raised thee up under the apple tree: there thy mother brought thee
> forth: there she brought thee forth that bare thee (8:5).

And now that she has found him, her sole wish is to remain
indissolubly united to him:

> Set me as a seal upon thine heart, as a seal upon thine arm:[6] for love
> is strong as death; jealousy is cruel as the grave: the coals thereof are
> coals of fire, which hath a most vehement flame. Many waters cannot
> quench love, neither can the floods drown it: if a man would give all the
> substance of his house for love, it would utterly be contemned (8:6, 7).

How could M. Renan bring himself to put these burning words
into the mouth of a sage, of a pedant, who was to utter them on the
stage like the moral of a fable? It is the Shulamite herself who is
here celebrating the strength of the feeling which has made her
victorious, of that true love which is as a flame proceeding from
Jehovah Himself, into which no selfish element can enter, and
whose unconquerable vehemence is only equalled by the power of
death, and the insatiableness of the grave.

If this poem were only a love-song, it would finish with this its
highest burst of feeling. We are not surprised, therefore, to find
many interpreters who take this view of it, rejecting all that follows
as added at a later date. But this is an arbitrary hypothesis, which
finds no support from the manuscripts. We proceed, therefore, to
the second scene: the Shulamite and her younger sister.

At her mother's house, the Shulamite finds herself confronted
with her brothers who had educated her so sternly; and there she
converses with them about a younger sister, whose age for the

---

6 The ancients used to hang their seals to the neck, or to the wrist, by a chain.

present protects her from a trial like that to which she has herself been just exposed. But for her, too, the hour of trial will soon come (8:8–10). The meaning of it is this: if the young maiden keeps firm she shall be crowned, but if she gives way, shame and sevitude await her. In order to develop moral energy in her young sister, the Shulamite holds out her own example; did she not, like an impregnable citadel, at last force the besieger to make peace with her?

Who is this besieger? If the whole poem did not make it plain, the sequel would show it clearly enough. The Shulamite settles her account with Solomon himself. She addresses him as if he were present (8:11, 12).

The king has (*hajah,* which properly means *there has come to him*) a large vineyard in a place called *Baal Hamon.* As to this place, of which the name means *master of a multitide,* it would be as useless to look for it in the map, as it would be to look for the mountain, from the top of which the Devil showed Jesus all the kingdoms of the world. This domain is let out to tenants, and it brings the king large revenues. For each of these tenants has engaged to pay him a thousand shekels. Well, the Shulamite also has a vineyard of her own. She has not, it is true, been able to keep possession of it (1:6). She has lost it by her own fault, and given it to Solomon. Nevertheless, she will not take back the gift she has made. Let him also take his thousands from her vineyard, but let two hundred shekels be reserved for the "keepers" of this property. It is a sort of will. The Shulamite makes a bequest in Solomon's favor, but at the same time charges the property with a permanent rent for those whom she recognizes as tenants of her vineyard in perpetuity.

Finally, the shepherd, who has just made his appearance for the first time, opens his mouth, and utters the only words attributed to him in the whole drama. He asks the Shulamite, as a favor to his friends who have come down with him from the spiced mountains, on which he has his dwelling, for a song. He addresses her as the *inhabitant of the gardens.* We must take care not to substitute here, as M. Renan does, the singular for the plural, and translate, "Fair one, who inhabitest *this garden.*" He is not speaking of any garden in particular, but of gardens in general. It is the Shulamite's kind of life, as opposed to his own, which the shepherd wishes thus to define. The gardens symbolize social life and its restraints; the pasture-lands complete liberty:

> Thou that dwellest in the gardens, the companions hearken to thy voice: cause me to hear it (8:13).

Then it is that the Shulamite, complying with the wish of her beloved, sings to him those mysterious words, which seem to indicate a secret fear, inspired, perhaps, by the thought of the presence of the mighty Solomon:

> Flee, my beloved, and be thou like to a roe or to a young hart upon the mountains of spices (8:14).

She gives up the thought of accompanying him herself. There is still a bond which holds her to these gardens; that lower domain of the monarch's kingdom. But there is nothing to keep him back. Let him spread his wings, and return to his natural sphere! Let him re-ascend to where he can breathe once more the pure air of perfect liberty.

And it is in face of this last verse that M. Renan has the courage, to say no more, to bring his analysis of the poem to an end with these words: "The Song concludes *therefore*(!) quite naturally with the peaceful re-union of the two lovers."

BIBLIOGRAPHY ON POETS:

Clarke, Arthur G. *The Song of Songs.* Kansas City, Kansas: Walterick Publishers, n.d. (An exceedingly useful commentary based on the shepherd hypothesis.)

Kidner, Derek. *The Proverbs: An Introduction and Commentary.* London: Tyndale Press, 1969. (Especially the introduction, pp. 13-56).

Kline, Meredith. "Song of Songs," *Christianity Today*, April 27, 1959, p. 39.

Lewis, C. S. *Reflections on the Psalms.* New York: Harcourt, Brace and Company, 1958. (Especially pp. 20-34 "on cursing" and pp. 90-96 "about praising.")

Osgood, Howard. "Dashing the Little Ones against the Rock." *Princeton Theological Review* I (1903), pp. 23-37.

Snaith, Norman H. *The Book of Job: Its Origin and Purpose.* Naperville, Illinois: Allenson, Inc., 1968. (Good for history of exegesis of Job.)

Woudstra, Sierd. "Song of Solomon" in *The Wycliffe Bible Commentary* (eds. Charles F. Pfeiffer and Everett F. Harrison), Chicago: Moody Press, 1963, pp. 595-604.

Yamauchi, Edwin, "Cultic Clues in Canticles?" *Bulletin of the Evangelical Theological Society,* IV, (1961).

Part IV
PROPHETICAL BOOKS

X

THE PROPHECY
OF THE VIRGIN MOTHER

by Willis J. Beecher

Editor's Introduction

A veritable Babylon of interpretations has been offered on the identity of the Servant and the meaning of the Almah. *Overly zealous evangelicals have assigned double meanings to these two figures in the text, thereby leaving the Old Testament field to whatever seems best in the eyes of current scholarship so long as the New Testament Messianic reinterpretation is still allowed. This solution fails to account for the Biblical authority of both testaments.*

The end of the see-saw battle among Christian and non-Christian exegetes can be charted by adopting the Scripture writer's point of view. No author in modern times has outlined this solution more clearly than Willis J. Beecher. If any progress is to be made in this difficult area of hermeneutics, expositors will need to return to Beecher's analysis and programmatic suggestions.

Hebrew. "Behold [thou] the virgin art pregnant, and bearing a son, and shalt call his name Immanuel."

Septuagint. "Behold the virgin shall be pregnant, and shall bear a son, and shalt call his name Immanuel."

Matthew 1:23. "Behold the virgin shall be pregnant, and shall bear a son, and they shall call his name Immanuel."

There are some variations of reading in the copies of the Septuagint, but none that affect any point to be considered here.

The Hebrew lexicons tell us that the word *almah,* here translated virgin, may denote any mature young woman, whether a virgin or not. So far as its derivation is concerned, this is undoubtedly the case; but in biblical usage, the word denotes a virgin in every case where its meaning can be determined. The instances are, besides the text, that in the account of Rebekah (Gen. 24:43), that of the sister of Moses (Exod. 2:8), the word used in the plural (Ps. 68:26 [25] ; Cant. 1:3; 6:8), its use in the titles of psalms (Ps. 46; I Chron. 15:20); and its use in Proverbs 30:19. The last passage is the one chiefly relied on to prove that the word may denote a woman not a virgin; but, "the way of a man with a maid" there spoken of is something wonderful, incapable of being traced or understood, like the way of an eagle in the air, a serpent on a rock, a ship in the sea, and it is only in their application to that wonderful human experience, a first love between a man and a virgin, that this description can find a full and complete significance. The use of the word in the Bible may not be full enough in itself to prove that *almah* necessarily means virgin, but it is sufficient to show that Septuagint translators probably chose deliberately and correctly, when they chose to translate the word, in this passage, by the Greek word that distinctively denotes a virgin, and that Matthew made no mistake in so understanding their translation.

This word has the definite article, in both the Hebrew and the Greek, and it is an error to omit the article in translating. In Matthew, the King James version commits this error, and both versions, in Isaiah, remit the definite sign to the margin.

The question whether the sentence in Isaiah is in the second person or in the third depends properly on the verb "call." The two English versions represent a very respectable consensus of opinion when they render the passage in the third person, though the King James version rather inconsistently puts into the margin the alternative reading "thou [O virgin] shalt call." It seems to me, however, that the following reasons are entirely decisive in favor of rendering the verb "shalt call," and making the whole sentence correspond with it. First, the verb is *qarath*, the regular form of the feminine second person singular for verbs of this class; the third feminine would be *qar'ah;* if this verb is third person, it is a quite unusual form for the Hebrew. Secondly, this particular form of this verb occurs only here and in Jeremiah 3:4, Genesis 16:11, and Isaiah 60:18, and in all these other instances it is in the second person feminine; while the third person feminine occurs, in the regular form for it in Genesis 29:35; 30:6, I Chronicles 4:9. Thirdly, the Septuagint translator renders the verb in the second person. As the Greek stands, it makes Ahaz, and not the virgin, the subject of the verb; it does not follow that the translator regarded the verb as second person masculine, for it is quite as likely that he neglected to notice that the lack of a feminine designation for the Greek verb would render the meaning of the Greek different from that of the Hebrew. And fourthly, it is a fact that has been neglected that the phraseology of this verse is quoted from older phraseology; and this fact not merely accounts for the use here of the second person feminine, but shows this use to be a necessary part of the structure of the sentence. This will be clear, if we compare our passage with the statements made concerning the birth of Ishmael (Gen. 16:11), the birth of Isaac (Gen. 17:19), and that of Samson (Judg. 13:5, 7). In the following translation, the words that are identical in English represent words that are identical in Hebrew:

Isaiah 7:14. "Behold [thou] the virgin art pregnant, and bearing a son, and shalt call his name Immanuel."

Genesis 16:11. "Behold thou art pregnant, and bearing a son, and shalt call his name Ishmael."

Judges 13:5, 7. "Behold thou art pregnant, and bearing a son."

Genesis 17:19. "But Sarah thy wife is bearing to thee a son, and thou shalt call his name Isaac."

In this exhibit of the verses, I have put "thou" of the first line in brackets, as being supplied in translation; but it really would be more correct to regard it as implied in the verb, and omit the brackets. In this line, the words "the virgin," used in the second person, correspond to the pronoun used in the other lines.

From this we see the true explanation of the second person feminine as here used by the prophet. He was not, as some have supposed, addressing some woman then present, but was using, by quotation, phraseology that was somewhat familiar, and he used it in the grammatical form in which it had become familiar.

What did the prophet mean by this statement? What did those who originally heard it understand him to mean?

The words occur in the midst of the prophetic discourse which might fairly be entitled The Discourse of the Three Children (Isa. 7—12), which consists of several brief recapitulations of earlier prophecies uttered at different times, followed by a fresh prophecy based on these. The words which connect the recapitulated prophecies with the fresh prophecy are:

"And I will wait for Jehovah, the one hiding his face from the house of Jacob, and will hope in him. Behold I and the children whom Jehovah has given me are for signs and for prodigies in Israel, from Jehovah of hosts, the one dwelling in Mount Zion" (8:17, 18).

The three children mentioned in the discourse are, First, Shear-Jashub, *Remnant-will-return* (7:3; compare 10:20, 21, 22; 11:11, 16). Second, Immanuel, *God-with-us* (7:14; compare 8:8, 10), and third, Maher-shalal-hash-baz, *Haste-spoil-swift-prey* (8:1, 3, 4; compare 10:2, 6). Each of the three is the subject of one of the recapitulated introductory prophecies, and each is again introduced later into the argument of the discourse. So far, Immanuel is on the same footing with Shear-Jashub and Maher-shalal-hash-baz.

The introductory prophecy in which Immanuel is mentioned is the passage 7:10-25. Apparently Rezin and Pekah were still threatening Jerusalem, and King Ahaz, instead of relying on Jehovah's promise of rescue, was sending to Tiglath-pileser, King of Assyria, for aid (7:1-9; 2 Kings 16:5-18, 3 Chron. 28:5-21). To lead Ahaz to a better course Isaiah offered him the privilege of asking a sign from Jehovah, and on his refusal to ask gave him the prophecy concerning Immanuel as a sign. Before the child should be old enough to choose good and reject evil, the deliverance from Rezin and Pekah would be accomplished; but although Jehovah would thus keep his promise, this sign-rejecting Ahaz should find that the Assyrian whom he thus insisted on calling to his aid would prove to be a worse scourge than the other invaders had been. Here again the child Immanuel is, within certain limits, on precisely the same footing with the other two children of the discourse. Considered merely as a sign to Ahaz, this case is entirely parallel with that of Maher-shalal-hash-baz; perhaps, indeed, the two are identical. The sign to Ahaz, so far as the matter directly in hand was concerned, was simply the fact that a child that moment conceived would not become old enough to tell good from bad before Jehovah's promise would be fulfilled.

But at this point Immanuel parts company with the other two children. The significant names of the other two appear in the second part of this discourse, in the passages already referred to, but no dignity or importance is ascribed to the children themselves. With Immanuel the case is different. His name does not appear in the second part of the discourse, but appears in the fourth of the short introductory prophecies (8:5-10). There the mention of Immanuel is personal in its character and presents him as a wonderful and awe-inspiring person. Ahaz has persisted in his refusal. He has sent for Tiglath-pileser. The latter has come up and conquered Damascus, and Ahaz has gone thither to pay him homage. He has there committed himself to the principle that he will worship the gods that have smitten him; that is, the Syrian gods who give rejoicing to Rezin and the son of Remaliah (2 Chron. 28:23; 2 Kings 16:10-16; compare Isa. 9:12 [13]; 10:20). In these circumstances, I suppose, Jehovah's message came to the prophet:

"Because this people have refused the softly flowing waters of Shiloah" (that is, the waters that were sent them), "and [have chosen] that which rejoices Rezin and the son of Remaliah, therefore behold the Lord is bringing up upon them the strong and many waters of the river, even the King of Assyria and all his glory; and it shall come up above all its channels, and shall go over all its banks, and shall glide on into Judah, shall overflow and pass on, shall reach unto a man's neck, and its outstretched wings shall fill the width of thy land, O IMMANUEL" (8:6-8).

But on recapitulating this message, though it bears on the face of it a threat that the Assyrian shall be successful, the prophet breaks out in the next verse into exclamations of exulting defiance:

> Be ye evil, O ye peoples, and be ye broken in pieces!
> And give ear all ye far places of earth,
> Gird yourselves, and be ye broken in pieces,

> Gird yourselves, and be ye broken in pieces!
> Devise ye counsel, and let it be broken,
> Speak ye a word, and it will not stand;
> For—IMMANUEL!   (8:9).

This conception of Immanuel as a being of such a character that Judah can appropriately be called Immanuel's land, this conception of him as himself constituting a reason why, even when Jehovah's people are in the flood up to the neck, their representative can exult in the assured overthrow of those who do them evil, differentiates him as widely as possible from Shear-jashub and Maher-shalal-hash-baz.

The fact already considered, that the phraseology of the promise of Immanuel is that used in the older Scriptures, in the accounts of certain theophanic appearings of Jehovah, also marks a clear difference between this child and the other two children of Isaiah's discourse. The fact presupposes that the older phraseology was familiar to some of the prophet's original hearers, and that they would thus be led to associate the offered sign with Jehovah's earlier and well-known promises to his people.

In its general meaning this idea of the birth of a child as a realization of the truth, "God is with us," re-appears in this discourse in the two sections (9:1-6; 11). The first of these sections includes the passage:

> For a child is born to us,
> A son is given to us,
> And the dominion is upon his shoulder,
> And his name is called Wonderful, Counsellor, a hero God,
> Eternal Father, Captain of Peace.
>
> To the multiplying of the dominion and to peace there is no end,
> Upon the throne of David, and upon his kingdom,
> To prepare it and to found it in judgment and in righteousness,
> From now, and even forever;
> The jealousy of Jehovah of hosts will do this.

The second of the two sections begins thus:

> And there shall come forth a shoot from the stem of Jesse,
> And a branch from his roots shall bear fruit,
> And the spirit of Jehovah shall rest upon him. . . .

In each of these passages we have the mention of a child born in fulfillment of the promise that had been made to David, to the effect that his seed should be eternal—should have eternal dominion—and in that dominion should wield a peaceful scepter. In this second half of his discourse on the three children Isaiah thus reiterates the promise that had been made to David, and insists upon it. He makes it the foundation of his rebukes to the people for their corruptions, and of his encouraging exhortations to the "disciples," now that the predicted calamities from the Assyrian have come upon the nation. But there can be no doubt that the same ideas were familiar to him and others a few years earlier when he spoke to Ahaz the prophecy concerning Immanuel. Reaching this point we reach, I think, the true reply to the question that Isaiah was understood to mean by that prophecy.

Those who heard him understood that when Ahaz refused to ask the offered sign the prophet repeated to him, in a new form, Jehovah's promise concerning the seed of David, and made that to be a sign that Jehovah would both keep his present pledge and punish Ahaz for his faithlessness. It may be doubted whether any of them had in mind the idea of just such a person as Jesus, to be born of a virgin, in some future century; but they had in mind some birth in the unending line of David which would render the truth, "God with us," especially significant (compare Luke 1:31-33). If to them the word almah strictly meant virgin it gave something of mystery to the prediction, suggesting, however, that things which are naturally impossible are yet within the power of Jehovah for carrying out his appointed purpose. In fine, this prophecy falls into rank with most of the Messianic prophecies quoted in the New Testament, in that it is a repetition of the one great promise made to Abraham, to Israel, to David—that promise which was always being fulfilled in the older history, but always looking forward to larger fulfillment in the future.

XI

THE SERVANT

by Willis J. Beecher

The prophetic literature says that the calling of Abraham from Ur of the Chaldees was the beginning of Israelitish history. At that time, these writings say, Yahaweh made a promise to Abraham, the benefits of which extend to all mankind. This promise was the heart of the creed of what the prophets regard as the true religion of Yahaweh in Abraham's time. This literature further affirms that the promise was renewed to Israel when Israel became a nation, still with the necessary implication that it constituted the heart of the creed of those who most truly worshipped Israel's God. There was another distinguished renewal of it, these writings say, to David the king, making his line central in Israel in the fulfilment of the promise. In David's time and the centuries that followed, they say, there arose in Israel a large number of singers and other prophets, and these generally made this promise, already well known, the basis of their religious and political teachings; and in doing this they unfolded and illuminated the promise itself.

Now if this is true, we should expect to find in the writings of these singers and other prophets a considerable number of technical terms, set apart to the uses of this teaching. The evolution of such terms would in the circumstances be inevitable, under the known laws of human speech. Similar phenomena mark our own habits of thinking and utterance. A dictionary which should include all our technical religious terms and phrases, with an exhaustive classification of the uses of each term, would be a large volume. It is incredible that the teaching of the prophets concerning the promise should have been maintained generation after generation without giving rise to such terms. As a matter of fact, the literature is marked by them. In the course of time certain words came to have a partly technical sense when used in the treatments of the promise-doctrine. Especially do we find personal terms denoting the "seed" through whom the promise and its benefits are transmitted, for

187

example, Servant, Son, Chosen one, Branch, Holy one, Messiah; and other terms denoting his relations to human history, for example, the kingdom, the last days, the day of Yahaweh. In most instances the roots of this use are pre-Davidic. There is a strong development of it in the Psalms that are assigned to the times of David. The use remains to the close of the Old Testament.

Taking up these terms in the order of their conspicuousness, we should perhaps expect that "Messiah" would come first; but that is not the case. On the whole, the term "Servant" is the most prominent and is the best fitted to stand as a representative of the rest in any brief statement of the matter. In the King James version this term is occult in the New Testament, but it appears in the revised version.[1] Aside from its use elsewhere in the Old Testament, it characterizes the last twenty-seven chapters of Isaiah, and in our consideration of it we will mainly confine ourselves to these chapters. They are more cited in the New Testament as messianic than any other Scriptures except those that contain the promises to Abraham and to David.[2] I should say that there is no room for dispute over the use of the term "Servant" in these chapters were it not for the fact that it is actually very much in dispute. Owing to this we shall have to make a study of the term, though necessarily an incomplete one.

I. We shall simplify the study if we begin with two auxiliary points.

1. First, the author of these chapters of Isaiah, being a Hebrew-

---

[1] For example, Peter says: "Ye are the sons of the prophets, and of the covenant which God made with your fathers, saying unto Abraham, And in thy seed shall all the families of the earth be blessed. Unto you first God, having raised up his Servant, sent him to bless you" (Acts 3:25-26. See also 3:13, 4:27, 30, etc.).

[2] As the word "servant" is one of the words most frequently used in the Hebrew literature, we cannot always easily differentiate its technical use, that is, its use as a messianic term. It is used untechnically of the patriarchs and of Moses, Caleb, Samson, David, and others (see concordance). In the later prophetic books the word "servant" is used in the singular of such men as Moses and Daniel and Nebuchadnezzar, and in the plural of the prophets. But these facts do not disturb the fact of the technical use. Something like the technical use occurs in personal references to David and to the patriarchs (e.g., Acts 3:26 RV, perhaps Gen. 26:24, and concordance of both Testaments). It is used of Israel and of the house of David in other prophetic writings than the last twenty-seven chapters of Isaiah (e.g., Jer. 30:10; 33:21, 22, 26; 46:27, 28; Ezek. 28:25; 34:23, 24; 37:24, 25; Hag. 2:23; Zech. 3:8).

speaking person, follows the Hebrew idiom when he applies a personal name to a nation. That is, he thinks of the nation as a personality rather than as personified. In English we think of a business corporation as an artificial person, created by law. There is a Hebrew conception of a nation that is as personal as our idea of a corporation.

We personify a country in the feminine. We say America expects her sons to be loyal. The Hebrew does the same. Our prophet might speak of Judah as expecting the return of her sons. In mentioning national characteristics, we speak of a typical individual. We say, The Spaniard is proud, or, The German is plodding. The Hebrew uses the same form of expression, but rather with the conception of a national personality than of an individual typifying a nation. In Hebrew one would say, in the masculine singular, the Canaanite, or, the Moabite, meaning thereby the collective body of the Canaanites or Moabites, speaking of them as if they constituted a single person.

But the Hebrew carries this a step farther. In Hebrew one speaks of a nation precisely as of a person, using the name itself, and not merely its gentile adjective. When one says Asshur or Mitsrayim, you have to look at the context to see whether he means the founder or the country or the nation or the persons who compose the nation. If the agreeing words are feminine singular, he means the country. If they are masculine plural, he means the persons who compose the nation. If they are masculine singular, he may mean either the founder or the nation. He talks of the nation as a person precisely as he talks of the founder as a person.

This point in Hebrew diction is important in the study of these twenty-seven chapters. Through inattention to it, wrong inferences have been drawn from the strongly personal way in which these chapters speak of "the servant of Yahaweh."

2. Second, these chapters are saturated with the ideas and the diction of Genesis and of the other parts of the Old Testament where the promise-doctrine is taught.

They are familiar with the creation story, using the word "create" twenty times, about as many as all the rest of the Old Testament together, leaving out the narratives in Genesis. They make much of Abraham (41:8; 51:2; 63:16). They magnify the covenant (42:6; 49:8; 54:10; 55:3; 56:4, 6; 59:21; 61:8).

They refer repeatedly to the incidents of the exodus: the crossing of the sea, the passage through the wilderness, the water from the rock, Yahaweh's Spirit with Moses, and the like. They lay stress upon Yahaweh's choosing of Israel.

While Abraham and Israel are thus to the front in these chapters, David is not neglected. Mention is made of "the sure mercies of David" (55:3). The promises to David:

> "There shall not be cut off to thee a man from upon the throne of Israel" (I Kings 2:4; 8:25; 9:5),

finds its echo in the passages that speak of the everlasting name that shall not be cut off (48:19; 55:13; 56:5).

Just as the pentateuch and 2 Samuel emphasize the thought of the "seed" of Abraham, of Jacob, of David, so the second part of Isaiah emphasizes the same term.

The second part of Isaiah, like the other writings that emphasize the promise, lays especial stress on the point that the promise is to be eternally operative. To say nothing of other phraseology in which eternity is mentioned (e.g. 45:17; 54:8-9; 65:18, 22), the word *olam* occurs thirty-four times in these chapters.

These chapters, like the other Scriptures that treat of the promise, make much of the fact that the promise is for the nations. The word "nation" occurs thirty-six times in these twenty-seven chapters.

> Thy seed also had been as the sand (48:19).
> He shall see seed (53:10).
> And thy seed shall possess nations (54:3).
> The seed of the adulterer. A seed of falsehood (57:3, 4).
> Out of the mouth of thy seed, or . . . of thy seed's seed (59:21).
> And their seed shall be known among the nations . . . for they are a seed that Yahaweh hath blessed (61:9).
> And I will bring out from Jacob a seed (65:9).
> For they are a seed of those blessed of Yahaweh (65:23).
> For as the new heavens . . . stand before me . . . so shall your seed and your name stand (66:22).

In Exodus 19 we are told that Israel was to be "a kingdom of priests," thus sustaining a peculiar relation to Yahaweh, the owner of all the earth. This priestly character of Israel as compared with the other nations appears in the last chapters of Isaiah.[3]

And in many other matters of detail these chapters are full of the promise made by Yahaweh to the nations through Abraham and Israel and David. The one supreme, ever recurring idea is that Israel, however unworthy he may be, or however desperate his condition, is nevertheless Yahaweh's Chosen one, chosen for a purpose, a purpose that will surely be accomplished.

II. From the point of view thus gained we approach the main question, the question of the use of the term "Servant" in these chapters.

With all the differences of opinion that exist, I suppose that the following statements of fact would be accepted by all who have studied the subject. The word "servant" occurs twenty times in the first fourteen of these twenty-seven chapters, always in the singular number, and eleven times in the last thirteen of the chapters, always in the plural. In but one of these thirty-one places is it used as an ordinary common noun.[4] In twelve of the twenty instances in which it is used in the singular it is defined in the context as denoting Israel. In all the cases in which it is used in the plural it

---

[3]And strangers shall stand in waiting,
   and shall shepherd your flock,
 Sons of a foreigner being
   your husbandmen and your vineyardmen;
 While ye yourselves shall be called
   the priests of Yahaweh.
 The ministers of our God!
   shall be said to you (61:5-6).

 A robe of righteousness hath he made me wear,
   as when the bridegroom acteth the priest, garlanded (61:10).

 And they will bring in all your brethren
   out of all the nations (61:20).
 And I will also take of them for the priests,
   for the Levites, saith Yahaweh (61:21).

[4] "Servant of rulers" (49:7). But even this is hardly an exception, for the meaning is determined by the implied contrast of "servant of rulers" with "Servant of Yahaweh." The instances in 44:26 and 50:10 are not exceptions, even if any one thinks that the Servant in these verses is the prophet.

denotes Israelites, though in some of the cases those who are
Israelites by adoption (e.g., 56:6).

1. From this general survey we turn to details. We look first at
instances in which the Servant is expressly said to be Israel.

The twelve instances occur in the following eight passages:)

> And thou Israel my Servant,
>   Jacob whom I have chosen,
>   seed of Abraham my friend!
> Whom I firmly laid hold of from the ends of the earth,
>   and called from the distant parts of it,
> And to whom I said, Thou art my Servant,
>   I have chosen thee, and have not cast thee off;
> Fear not, for I am with thee!
>   be not dismayed, for I am thy God! (41:8-10).

> And now hear thou, Jacob my Servant,
>   even Israel whom I have chosen:
> Thus saith Yahaweh thy maker,
>   even thy fashioner from the womb, who helpeth thee,
> Fear thou not, my Servant Jacob,
>   even Jeshurun whom I have chosen.
> For I will pour water upon a thirsty [field],
>   and streams upon dry land;
> I will pour my Spirit upon thy seed,
>   and my blessing upon thy offspring (44:1-3).

> Remember these things, O Jacob,
>   and Israel, for thou art my Servant.
> I fashioned thee, Servant to me thou art,
>   thou, Israel, wilt not be forgotten of me (44:21).

> For the sake of my Servant Jacob,
>   and Israel my Chosen one,
> I have called thee by thy name,
>   I surname thee though thou hast not known me (45:4).

This is spoken to Cyrus, who is in the context called Yahaweh's
"anointed," but is distinguished from the Servant.

> Yahaweh hath redeemed his Servant Jacob (48:20).
> And he said to me, Thou art my Servant,
> O Israel, in whom I glorify myself (49:3).

In the instances thus far cited the defining context is separated

from the word "Servant" by only a few clauses at most; in the two
following instances the defining context is a little more remote, but
it is unmistakable.

> Hear, ye that are deaf,
>   and look, ye blind, that ye may see!
> Who is blind as my Servant,
>   and deaf as my Messenger whom I am wont to send?
> Who is blind as the Perfected one,
>   and blind as the Servant of Yahaweh? (42:18-19).

> Let them give their witnesses, that they may be justified,
>   that men may hear and may say, Truth.
> Yourselves are my witnesses, saith Yahaweh,
>   and my Servant whom I have chosen,
> To the end that ye may know, and may believe me,
>   and may discern that I am he (43:9-10).

All this the poet brings in for the consolation of Israel, as a part
of the riches included in his great theme, "The word of our God
standeth forever."

We fail, however, of rightly understanding this, if we neglect to
notice that the poet is here looking at Israel from the point of view
of the promise. This is an important matter, and one that has been
too much neglected. Neither in the instances just cited nor elsewhere in these twenty-seven chapters is the term "Servant" ever
applied to Israel considered merely as an ethical aggregation of
persons. It implies, indeed, that Israel is an ethical aggregation, but
also that he is something more. When the prophet uses the term, he
is invariably thinking of Israel as Yahaweh's own people. We have
already seen that these chapters are saturated with the idea—the
same idea that appears in the pentateuch and in 2 Samuel—that
Yahaweh has made an eternally operative covenant with Abraham,
Israel, David, in virtue of which he will bless all nations through
them. It is in this character of promise-people, covenant-people,
that the chapters speak of Israel as the Servant, not in the character
of a mere political aggregation.

This distinction is not in all respects new. Paul long ago wrote:

> For they are not all Israel which are of Israel; neither, because they
> are Abraham's seed, are they all children; but, in Isaac shall thy seed be

> called. ... It is not the children of the flesh that are children of God,
> but the children of the promises are reckoned for a seed (Rom. 9:6-8).

As interpretations of Paul's word, we are familiar with such phrases as "the Israel within Israel," "the ideal Israel," "the spiritual Israel." Whatever phrase you use for it, the distinction is genuine. I think that the best of these phrases is "the Israel of the promise," or, "Israel regarded as the promise-people." This corresponds most closely to the facts, and to the phraseology of the Old Testament, and to Paul's term "the children of the promise."

Israel the Servant is therefore Israel regarded as the promise-people, Israel regarded as Yahaweh's Chosen one. From one point of view he is identical with the political aggregation known as Israel, while from other points of view he is something entirely different. It should not surprise us if we find Israel the Servant and Israel the political aggregation sometimes spoken of as two, or even as having relations one with the other.

2. We turn to a second class of passages, those in which the word "servant" is used or implied without an explicit contextual identification with Israel.

At the outset we may lay aside all anxiety as to the bearings of these passages on the claims of the New Testament. If the passages represent the Servant to be a person different from Israel, then the New Testament claims that what is said concerning that person is fulfilled in Jesus. If on the other hand we find that the Servant, in these passages, is still Israel, we shall also find that the New Testament claim is that Jesus Christ is Israel the Servant in his highest manifestation. In either case the passages are messianic, and in either case the New Testament claims that they are fulfilled in Jesus the Messiah.

(a) Study first a group of two passages. The first consists of the lines that introduce the mention of Cyrus (44:25-26).

> He breaketh impostors' signs,
>   and maketh diviners mad.
> He maketh wise men return backward.
>   and maketh their knowledge folly.
> He raiseth up the word of his Servant,
>   and fully performeth the counsel of his messengers.

> That saith to Jerusalem, She shall be made to abide;
>   and to the cities of Judah, They shall be builded;
>   and, Her ruinous places I will rear up.

At a superficial glance it is natural to say that "the word of his
servant," here placed parallel with "the counsel of his messengers,"
must, of course, be the word uttered by the prophet, the prophet
being here the servant. This will afford a passable interpretation of
the whole passage. But it is not a necessary interpretation. It is
possible to regard the genitive as objective, so that "the word of his
Servant" will be Yahaweh's word concerning his Servant. This
makes good parallelism with "the counsel of his messengers," for
Yahaweh's word concerning his Servant is an important part of his
counsel as transmitted through his prophetic messengers. So far,
therefore, as parallelism and syntax are concerned, we may translate:

> He established his word concerning his Servant,
>   and fully performeth the counsel announced by his messengers.

This is clearly the meaning that best fits the logical and poetic
requirements of the whole context. The writer uses the word
"Servant" here in the same sense in which we have found him using
it elsewhere.[5]

The same peculiarities appear in the remaining instance.

> Who is there among you fearing Yahaweh,
>   hearkening to the voice of his Servant,
> That hath gone in darknesses,
>   there being no brightness for him?
> Let him trust in the name of Yahaweh,
>   that he may stay himself in his God (50:10).

We have here again the objective genitive. "The voice of his Servant" is the voice concerning his Servant, the word "voice" being
used as in Isaiah 40:3, 6. Cheyne is correct in regarding the
preceding verses as spoken by the Servant, and is therefore wrong in

---

[5] Some have held that the Servant is here the prophet, but the prophet as the
representative of the true Israel, who is properly the Servant. This gives in part the same
result as the interpretation I have proposed, but it seems to me less feasible.

thinking that there is here an arbitrary break, and that the tenth
verse is perhaps spoken by the prophet in his own person.

(b) Taking the passages in the order of the obviousness of their
meaning, we notice next those in which the word "servant" is used
in the plural.

We have already touched the fact that this word occurs only in
the singular in these chapters up to the fifty-third, and only in the
plural from the fifty-fourth onward. Of course, scholars who regard
the later chapters as written at a different period from the earlier,
and from a different viewpoint, will count these plural instances as
irrelevant; but at all events they will not prejudice the argument.
The instances are as follows. Observe that in each case the servants
are Israelites either by birth or by adoption.

> Return thou for the sake of thy servants,
>   the tribes of thine inheritance (58:17).

> And the sons of the foreigner that join themselves
>   upon Yahaweh, to minister to him,
> And to love the name of Yahaweh,
>   to be to him for servants (56:6).

> So will I do for the sake of my servants,
>   in order not to destroy the whole;
> And I will bring out from Jacob a seed,
>   and from Judah one possessing my mountains,
> That my chosen ones may possess it,
>   while my servants have their dwelling there.

> *   *   *   *   *   *

> And you, ye forsakers of Yahaweh,
>   those forgetting my holy mountain,

> *   *   *   *   *   *

> Behold my servants shall eat,
>   and ye shall be hungry;
> Behold my servants shall drink,
>   and ye shall be thirsty;
> Behold my servants shall be glad,
>   and ye shall be ashamed;
> Behold my servants shall sing aloud
>   from gladness of heart,

> And ye for your part shall cry out
>   from sorrow of heart,
> And from breaking of spirit ye shall wail.
> And ye shall deposit your name
>   for an oath to my chosen ones;
> And the lord Yahaweh will slay thee,
>   and will call his servants by another name (65:8-15).

The two remaining instances are like the others, though less
·marked.

> This is the heritage of the servants of Yahaweh,
>   their righteousness being from with me,
>   saith Yahaweh (54:17).

> And Yahaweh's hand with his servants shall be known,
>   and he will spurn his enemies (66:14).

In this second group of instances, therefore, the servants are
Israelites, regarded as the persons in whom the promise stands firm.
This is not quite the same as to say that they are the faithful in
Israel, though perhaps the difference after all is not very great.

(c) We will take next the instances in which the Servant is
presented as speaking in the first person. In these instances it is
quite generally true that the Servant is differentiated from the
actually existing Israel, and is represented as having a mission to
Israel. The most distinct instance is that in Chapter 49:1-7.

> Hearken ye coastlands unto me,
>   and be attentive ye peoples from afar.
> He that called me from the belly is Yahaweh;
>   from the bowels of my mother he made mention of my name.
> And he placed my mouth as a sharp sword,
>   in the shadow of his hand he hid me,
> And he placed me as a polished arrow,
>   in his quiver he concealed me.
> And he said to me, Thou art my Servant,
>   thou, Israel, in whom I glorify myself.
>
> And I, I said, Vainly have I toiled,
>   for nought and vanity have I used up my strength.
> Verily, my judgment is with Yahaweh,
>   and that which I have wrought is with my God.

> And now [be ye attentive] : Yahaweh hath said—
>   he that formed me from the womb for a Servant to him,
> For bringing back Jacob unto him,
>   and that Israel may be gathered to him,
> So that I might be honored in the eyes of Yahaweh,
>   my God being my strength—
> He hath said, It is too light a thing,
>   thy being Servant to me
> To raise up the tribes of Jacob,
>   and to restore the preserved of Israel;
> And I will give thee for a light of nations,
>   that my salvation may be unto the end of the earth.
>
> Thus saith Yahaweh,
>   Israel's redeemer, his holy one,
> To one despised of soul, to one abhorred
>   of a nation, to a slave of tyrants:
> Kings shall see and arise,
>   captains, and they shall worship,
> For the sake of Yahaweh who is faithful,
>   the Holy One of Israel who hath chosen thee.

In the beginning of this passage Israel is the Servant. Farther on the Servant has a mission to Israel. The Servant is to be honored for bringing back Jacob and gathering Israel to Yahaweh. What he is Servant for is in part the raising up of the tribes, and the restoring of such Israelites as have been preserved.

Who is this Servant that has a mission to Israel? Is he the same who has just been called Israel? Verbally he is presented as different from Israel, and as a person doing personal acts rather than as a personification. Does this prove that he cannot possibly be Israel? Who is he? Is he a new character introduced here without warning? or is he the Israel of the promise, differentiated in thought from the merely ethnical Israel, and conceived of as having relations with him?

The second of these alternatives is the true one. Israel is here represented as having relations with himself. There is nothing strained in this way of stating things.

This one clear instance in which the Servant is introduced as speaking in the first person, and as having a mission to Israel, though also he himself is Israel, may serve to interpret four other instances, and may in turn be interpreted by them. In these four other instances the word "Servant" is not used; but a character, not Yahaweh, is introduced speaking in the first person.[6] In each of them the speaker is in commission from Yahaweh. One of them is very brief; in each of the others the speaker identifies himself with Israel, but may be differentiated from Israel. In each it is plausible to say that the speaker is the personified Israel of the promise, as in Chapter 49.

(d) One group more remains. It consists of three instances, in two passages which are very prominently quoted in the New Testament.

The first is found in Isaiah 42:1-4.

> Behold my Servant whom I uphold,
>   my Chosen one in whom my soul delighteth.
> I have given my Spirit upon him,
>   he will bring out judgment to the nations.
>
> He maketh no outcry, nor lifteth up
>   nor publisheth his voice in the street.
> A bruised reed he breaketh not,
>   and a flickering wick he quencheth not.
>
> Of a truth he will bring out judgment,
>   he will not flicker nor be broken,
> Until he put judgment in the earth;
>   meanwhile coastlands wait for his law.

This is quoted somewhat in full and applied to Jesus, in the gospel by Matthew (12:18-21). Notice that the emphatic statement in these three stanzas is that the Servant shall be the supreme judge of the nations. This is spoken of in the first stanza; its inconsistency with the manifested meekness of the Servant is suggested in the second stanza; and the third stanza four times affirms that it is nevertheless a fact. The point illustrated in Matthew is the meekness of the person spoken of, in contrast with his victoriousness and his being the hope of the nations.

---

[6] One of these instances is Chapter 61 read by Jesus in the synagogue of Nazareth, with the comment: "Today hath this scripture been fulfilled in your ears" (Luke 4:16-21; cf. Isa. 50:4-9; 48:16; 63:7-64).

The other passage is the complete section concerning the humiliated Servant (Isa. 52:13-53). It occupied a remarkably large place in the thinking of the first preachers of Christianity.[7] Its full messianic significance cannot be appreciated except through a thorough study of the entire passage. But we must be content with citing briefly the two places in which it uses the word "Servant."

> Behold my Servant dealeth wisely,
> Is high and exalted and lofty exceedingly (Isa. 52:13).

> It being Yahaweh's will to bruise him, making him sick;
>   even if thou regard his soul as a trespass-offering,
> He shall behold a seed, shall prolong days,
>   the will of Yahaweh prospering in his hand.
> Of the toil of his soul he shall behold, shall be sated;
>   in knowing him shall my Servant, righteous,
> Give righteousness to the many,
>   and their iniquities himself shall bear as a load (53:10-11).

In this passage Yahaweh represents the Servant's being stricken as the result of the transgression of "my people" (53:8). That is, this section, like Chapter 49, makes a distinction between Yahaweh's people and the Servant, that is, between Israel the Servant and Israel the aggregation of persons. But it goes farther in this direction than Chapter 49. It distinguishes the Servant from his generation, his unspeakable generation, and represents him as cut off from the earth, as having a grave, as experiencing "deaths" (vv. 8-9). So far as these representations go, he is not an unending succession of persons, but is one Person. Later we shall meet again this figure of the Person of the promise, wonderful both in his sorrows and his exaltation.

This passage brings out into strong relief an experience of the Servant that is also much emphasized elsewhere, namely, his humiliations and sufferings; but it brings out an aspect of this experience that is presented in other places only by allusion or implication. The sufferings of the Servant are vicarious and mediatorial in their

---

[7] It is formally cited at least nine times, in at least the six books Luke, John, Acts, Romans, Galatians, 1 Peter; and is informally cited much oftener. See the reference Bibles. Probably the most familiar instance is that it was the passage which the Ethiopian eunuch was reading when Philip joined him (Acts 8:32-33).

character. In many of the passages heretofore cited we find Israel suffering for his own misdoings, and this is the case in some of the passages in which he is called the Servant. But in Chapter 53 we find a different view. Over and over the passage reiterates that the Servant is blameless. It is not as the result of his own sins that he suffers, but of those of his people and of the many nations. The result shall be their being made righteous from their sins, and this shall eventuate in such victory and glory and joy for the Servant as shall more than compensate him for all his sorrows.

III. We must not dismiss the term "Servant" without recurring to the point that this is the one messianic term that is best fitted to stand as representative. What is true of the term "Servant" in its messianic use is typically true of the other terms that have the same signification. For this reason let us ask here, in regard to the Servant, two or three questions which we shall have to repeat, later, in regard to the whole body of messianic prediction. It is no reason against this procedure that we thus catch a glimpse of certain still distant goals toward which our study is moving.

Who is the Servant spoken of in these Isaiah chapters? A certain interpretation replies that the Servant clearly is the people of Israel, and therefore is not Jesus of Nazareth. It is Israel, this interpretation affirms, whom Yahaweh chose, separated from the peoples, led through a career of mingled suffering and victory, set for a light to the nations, and made to be, in very important senses, the world's redeemer. It is Israel whose mission of good to mankind has so largely resulted from his sufferings, from his being scattered among the peoples, and subjected to undeserved contempt and ill treatment. This is not an ignoble interpretation, and it agrees with most of the facts as we have been studying them. But it does not, unless supplemented by something else, account for some of the personal experiences attributed to the Servant, nor for the degree of the exaltation ascribed to him.

This interpretation is contradicted by another which affirms that the Servant is Jesus Christ, and therefore is not Israel. This view fully accounts for the personal terms, the exaltation of the Servant, his being sometimes separate from Israel and in relations with Israel, and the wonderfully minute identity between the characteristics and experiences of Jesus and those of the Servant; but it necessitates a dreadful amount of difficult explanation when it is called upon to account for the passages which explicitly declare that the Servant is Israel.

The truth is, that both interpretations are correct in what they affirm, and incorrect in what they deny. If the Servant is Israel, that does not prove that the Servant is not Christ. If he is Israel, then he is Israel thought of as the promise-people, Israel in all the fulness of his mission to the world, and not in some relatively narrow and circumscribed portion of it. The prophet was dealing with what he regarded as the eternally operative promise of Yahaweh. He is speaking constantly of the future of Israel and Servant, though, of course, not to the exclusion of the past or the present. He holds that the promise has been fulfilling in the past, is at present in process of fulfilment, and will continue to be fulfilled in the future, without limit of time. He holds this as an article of religious doctrine, independent of any power which he may possess of miraculously foretelling the future. The statements he makes concerning Israel the Servant do not terminate their effect with the Israel of his own time. By their very terms they look forward. They apply especially to any future portion of Israel's history which shall be especially the manifestation of God's purpose toward mankind through Israel. They so apply if the prophet had a definite knowledge as to the events in which the manifestation would be made; and equally they so apply if his knowledge of the coming events was vague—merely a conviction that Yahaweh would somehow accomplish the word he had spoken.

It follows that there is no contradiction between the statement that the Servant is Israel and the statement that the servant is Jesus Christ, provided Jesus Christ is the most significant fact in the history of Israel as the people of the promise; and this Christianity claims that he is.

This may be variantly stated. The prophetic use of the term "Servant" has such a character of universalness that really it might be applied to any person of any race or time, provided he is characteristically the agent of the divine purpose for mankind. It might be applied to the personified aggregate of all such persons, or to any lesser aggregate. In the Old Testament, as a matter of fact, it denotes Israel regarded as such an aggregate. It might be properly applied to any Israelite who is in this respect typical, and it is so applied to Moses and Caleb and David and others, though perhaps not in all cases in its full meaning. In particular, the Servant might be any priest or prophet or other public man, brought into such relations with Yahaweh that he is the representative of the Israel of his generation. If the New Testament writers are correct in regarding Jesus as preeminently the representative Israelite, as the antitype of all types, then they are correct in applying directly to him what the prophets say concerning Israel the Servant.

It will help to give us a steady grasp of these facts if we take a glance forward to our own times, and the fulfilment now in progress of the things that are said concerning the Servant. Israel the Servant is now in very important senses the light of the nations, as the prophet said he would be. His being so consists in three things, and it is a mistake to omit any one of the three from our consideration. First, the promise-people is in a unique degree a blessing to mankind if we consider only what Israel the race has accomplished and is accomplishing in business and commerce and governmental administration and learning and literature and art. If Israel's contributions of this kind to the civilization of the twentieth century could be suddenly obliterated, the world of mankind would come to a standstill. Second, the work of the promise-people for mankind is being wrought in what the religion of Israel and its daughter religions, Christianity and Islam, are accomplishing. And third, these two great things become insignificant when compared with the person and work of Jesus, provided Jesus is the Son of God that we Christians believe him to be. The career of Israel the Servant includes all the beneficent things that God has wrought through him, including God's supreme manifestation through him in the person of Christ the Lord. Defining thus, we Christians should accept, instead of rejecting, the statement that in all the instances Isaiah's Servant of Yahaweh is Israel.

BIOGRAPHY ON PROPHETS

Beecher, Willis J. *The Prophets and The Promise.* Grand Baker Book House, 1969 (r.p.). (This entire work is worthy of careful study and reflection.)

Culver, Robert D. "The Identity of the Servant of the Lord in Isaiah, 40-53" in *The Suffering and The Glory of The Lord's Righteous Servant*. Moline, Illinois: Christian Service Foundation, 1958, 127-71.

Kaiser, Walter C., Jr. "The Eschatological Hermeneutics of Evangelicalism," *Journal of Evangelical Theological Society*, XIII (1970), pp. 91-99. (Note especially the section on I Peter 1:10-12: the prophets did know what they were predicting!)

Wilson, Robert Dick. "The Meaning of Alma (A.V., Virgin) in Isa. VII:14," *Princeton Theological Review*. XXIV (1926), pp. 316ff.

Young, Edward J. *Studies in Isaiah*. Grand Rapids, Eerdmans, 1954.

Part V

ETHICS AND OLD TESTAMENT THEOLOGY

XII

THE ETHICS OF THE OLD TESTAMENT

by William Brenton Greene, Jr.

Editor's Introduction

While the Bible is in part a book about morality and ethics, many suspect that due to the primitiveness of the times and simplicity of thought, its earliest expressions in the Old Testament offend and contradict its higher statements and actions in the New Testament. William Brenton Greene, Jr. gives a sample of the questions asked and the answers available from his lectures on ethics.

The Objections to Old Testament Ethics

1. The leading objections to the ethics of the Old Testament may be reduced to the following seven:

a. God is represented sometimes in the Old Testament as partial, fickle, hateful, revengeful, and otherwise morally unworthy.

For example, in Genesis 6:5-7 we read that when God saw the wickedness of man it repented him that he had made him. This, however, is not becoming in God. Indeed, it is impossible. As the Scripture itself says elsewhere, "God is not a man, that he should lie; neither the son of man, that he should repent: hath he said, and shall he not do it? or hath he not spoken, and shall he not make it good?" Again, God's dealing with Pharaoh, as recorded in Exodus 7-14, are inconsistent with any just conception of deity. He is represented as hardening Pharaoh's heart toward Israel, and then as overwhelming him in the Red Sea for his treatment of Israel; whereas the Bible itself says in another place "God cannot be tempted with evil, neither tempteth he any man" (James 1:13); and it is impossible for us to think of him as punishing anyone for sin which he himself has caused. So, too, in 1 Kings 22 God is described as deceiving Ahab, and in Ezekiel 14:9 as deceiving false prophets. These are but specimens of many objections of the same kind that might be adduced and that will, doubtless, occur to you. It cannot be denied that they are serious difficulties. If for no other reason, this would be so because unbelievers make great capital out of them. The deist Bolingbroke says: "It is blasphemy to assert that the Old Testament writers were inspired, when they attribute such things to divinity as would disgrace humanity"; and Col. Ingersoll was continually sneering: "If the best that can be conceived of God is what the Old Testament represents him as being, then there can be no God."

(1) The representation of God which is largely predominant in the Old Testament is that he is infinitely exalted, and absolutely perfect in moral excellence. He is "the Lord, the Lord God, merciful and gracious, long suffering, and abundant in goodness and truth, keeping mercy for thousands, forgiving iniquity and transgression and sin, and that will by no means clear the guilty" (Exod. 34:6-7).

Even the objector concedes that this is the representation of God characteristic of the Old Testament. His argument is that its God cannot by its own showing be the true God, for he contradicts himself.

Is the objector's course, however, a just one? Because a comparatively few of the Old Testament's representations of God seem to be at variance with the exalted character which it usually ascribes to him, they conclude either that the character as a whole is so inconsistent as to be impossible, or that the predominant representation is false and the exceptional one true. Ought they not rather to infer that, if either must be false, it is the exceptional one; and that if the exceptional one fairly admits of two interpretations, then that one which harmonizes with the characteristic representations must be the true one. We have no right to assume that the author is inconsistent. If his statements can be harmonized, we are bound to do so. No one insists more strenuously than does the objector that his own utterances should be treated thus.

(2) To harmonize is possible and usually easy, if we take into account the context (according to our first principle) as well as the contents of each passage, the idioms of language, and the characteristics of the oriental mind. For example, the objectionable expression, "It repented him" in Genesis 6:6 must be interpreted by the

explanatory phrase in the context "it grieved him." "This shows," says the excellent commentary of Keil and Delitzsch, "that the repentance of God does not presuppose any variableness in His nature or purpose. In this sense God never repents of anything 'because,' as Calvin has written, 'nothing happens unexpectedly to Him or unforseen by Him.' The repentance of God is an anthropomorphic expression for the pain of the divine love at the sin of man, and signifies that, as Calvin has also added, 'God is hurt no less by the atrocious sins of men than if they pierced His heart with mortal anguish.' "

Indeed, when, as in John 3:10, "repent" used in connection with God does indicate change, it does not mean a change in God's attributes and character, but only in his manner of treating men. It is not a change of will, but a will to change that is intended. This will to change, moreover, is in this case, the expression and the condition of a changeless will in the sense of disposition. Thus, if God had willed to treat the Ninevites after their repentance as He had threatened to treat them before their repentance, this would have proved him mutable. It would have revealed him as displeased, at one time with impenitence and at another time with penitence.[1] In this way it appears that in this case, as in many others, the objectors do not know what they are objecting to. Their objection is that when God repents he must be changeable, whereas he would be changeable, if in these instances he did not repent.

Again, take the objectionable phrase in Exodus 10:27, "But the Lord hardened Pharaoh's heart." This is evidently to be interpreted by the explanatory phrase occurring often in the context, "And Pharaoh hardened his heart." Nor may it be said that there is as much reason why this phrase should be interpreted by the other and objectionable one. The latter is inconsistent with the Old Testament's characteristic representation of God. It should, therefore, as has been already implied, be interpreted by the clearly parallel and explanatory phrase that would remove the inconsistency. Moreover, the idiom of the language shows, that, independently of the question of consistency, the interpretation just suggested is the one required. According to the Hebrew idiom a positive statement is often used as equivalent to the mere negation

---

[1] Vide, also, Jer. 18:7-10.

of its opposite. Thus in the Hebraistic Greek of the New Testament hate in Romans 9:13 ("Jacob have I loved, but Esau have I hated") does not mean what we mean by hate, but only the absence of that special love which God feels for those whom, out of his general love for all sinners, he has chosen to be his adopted sons. So in Matthew 10:37 to hate father and mother is the same as to love them less in comparison than Christ. In like manner, the meaning of harden is not to soften. When God hardens a man's heart, he simply leaves him alone and lets him do what we are told that Pharaoh did; viz., harden his own heart. "Pharaoh," says Luther in his *Table Talk,* "was hardened because God with his Spirit and grace hindered not his ungodly proceedings, but suffered him to go on and have his way." As Edwards says, "When God is spoken of as hardening some of the children of men, it is not to be understood that God by any positive efficiency hardens any man's heart. there is no positive act in God, as though he put forth any power to harden the heart. To suppose any such thing would be to make God the immediate author of sin. God is said to harden men in two ways: by withdrawing the powerful influences of his Spirit, without which their hearts will remain hardened and grow harder and harder; in this sense he hardens them as he leaves them to hardness. And again, by ordering those things in his providence, which, through the abuse of their corruption, become the occasion of their hardening. Thus God sends his word and ordinances to men which, by their abuse, prove an occasion of their hardening."[2]

Nor may it be objected that this is forcing into phrases the meaning that we wish them to have. If you were living in Turkey, you would not say, "I missed my steamer"; but you would say, "I caused my steamer to run away." Neither would you allow that you were giving an arbitrary meaning of your own to the phrase when you explained it as meaning only that you had missed the steamer. The idiom of the language would lead you to speak as you did, and it is not otherwise when God is said to have hardened Pharaoh's heart.

Once more, take the case in which God is reported to have deceived Ahab (1 Kings 22), or that in which he is represented as deceiving false prophets (Ezek. 14:9). Here the solution of the

---

[2] *Works,* Vol. IV, p. 548.

difficulty is not in a peculiarity of the Hebrew idiom, but in a popular conception. This is that whereby we are commonly conceived as doing what in strictness we only permit. Thus if a physician has neglected a patient who has died, he is said to have killed him; yet it is not the physician's neglect but the sick man's disease that is the efficient cause of his death.

God is represented as having deceived Ahab, for example, only because the popular mind does not discriminate between what one does and what he only permits and also because it overlooks the great difference between the sovereign God's relation to the permission of evil and ours. It is true that in 1 Kings 22 God seems to do more than simply permit the deception. He is represented as saying in heaven, "Who shall persuade Ahab, that he may go up and fall at Ramoth Gilead? And one said on this manner and another said on that manner. And there came forth a spirit and stood before the Lord, and said, I will persuade him. And the Lord said, Wherewith? And he said, I will go forth, and I will be a lying spirit in the mouth of all his prophets. And he said, Thou shalt persuade him, and prevail also: go forth, and do so." What else, however, does this mean than that, as God's eternal plan contemplates both the existence and the development of evil; so it provides for its own accomplishment by the foreordained permission of evil on the occasions when and in the ways in which evil can by its own working serve the divine purpose? This is not saying that God does evil that good may come. It is saying that he takes evil *already* here, evil actually in manifestation, evil that, if left uncontrolled by him, would of itself hinder the good; and then so overrules the tendency of this evil that of itself, though contrary to its own intention, it advances truth and righteousness. What does this indicate but a being as ethical as he is wise and powerful?[3]

Nor may the objector reply that, while all this may be so, it is at least immoral for God in what claims to be his inspired Word to use these pictorial representations, popular phrases, and anthropomorphic expressions. If so, then it is immoral for the father to speak to his little boy as if he were himself a child, or for the scientist to lecture in the language of the people.

b. The second objection to the ethics of the Old Testament is

---

[3] *Westminster Confession of Faith*, chap. V, Sec. 4.

that it often gives the divine endorsement to character not approved by our moral sense. Not only is God, as we have seen, represented as immoral himself, but even as distinctly approving what is immoral in others. Abraham is exalted as the most striking example of faith, yet he told lies. David is made the great type of Christ, yet he committed adultery and commanded murder. In general, the Patriarchs were not men whom we would care to invite to our homes; the Judges, so far from ornamenting modern society, would be almost sure to land in the lock-up. The Kings were not above the average of oriental monarchs; the Priests were only too evidently tainted with professionalism; the Prophets often exhibit spiritual imperfection; in a word, the men whom God chose to represent him in the sphere of politics and religion were not such as we would suffer to serve us even in menial positions. This is one of the stock infidel objections. Now without pausing to show, what could easily be shown, that these charges are almost as false as they are malicious, it will be sufficient to remark by way of refutation as follows:

(1) Divine approbation in many of these cases where God's approbation is expressed, is explicitly based on and restricted to certain specified and admittedly commendable aspects of these characters. Thus it is as Abraham lives the life of faith that he is "the friend of God." This is made perfectly clear.

(2) In no case is divine approbation extended to those qualities which provoke our moral censure. Abraham is never praised for deceitfulness, nor is Jael praised *by God* for cruelty.

(3) In many cases divine disapprobation is pronounced upon those points of character which we denounce, and the sins are visited with severe judgments. Thus the early deceit of Jacob was avenged through all his later years by the withering influence of the fear of man. The one great crime of David caused the evening of his glorious day to be darkened by the clouds of lust and blood. This connection between sin and suffering in the case even of the most illustrious and most specially chosen servants of God is brought out so clearly and is traced with such evident purpose that it seems impossible to escape the conviction that God would thus put himself on record as condemning what is bad in *all,* and specially in all on whom he has set the mark of his peculiar approval.

In a word, the sufficient answer to the objection under consideration is the principle already approved and illustrated; viz., commendation of a character need not imply commendation of every element of that character.

Nowhere, perhaps, is it more necessary to keep this principle in mind that in the interpretation of the passages in which, as it is often alleged, deceit and lying are commended. Such, for example, are Exodus 1:17-21 and Joshua 2:4, and 6:25, the case of the Hebrew midwives and that of Rahab the harlot. Thus God dealt well with the midwives, not because they lied to the Egyptians; but, because, though they lied to protect themselves, they feared him rather than the king of Egypt and saved the men-children of the Israelites alive. Indeed, this is expressly affirmed to be the ground of his treatment of them. So, too, Rahab the harlot was spared in the sack of Jericho, not because she lied to her fellow citizens concerning the Hebrew spies, but because, as Hebrews 11 informs us, of her faith in the God of Israel. These and like cases, moreover, point the important and often forgotten truths, that no one is so bad that there is not some good in him, and this good ought always to be appreciated even when mixed with the bad.

c. A third objection to the ethics of the Old Testament is that it endorses, not only characters that we cannot justify, but even expressions of individual feeling towards one's fellows that are offensive to our moral judgments. These endorsements appear specially in the "Imprecatory Psalms," some fifty in number. All these, though not nearly to the extent charged, contain sentiments that shock us: and certain of them, as Psalm 35, 59, 109 and 137, we can scarcely bring ourselves to read in private; and we could not, I suppose, and certainly should not read them in public worship without explanation. Nevertheless, most of the difficulty will be removed in their case by the following considerations:

(1) The style of these psalms means much more to us than it did to the authors. "The eastern minstrel employs intense and figurative words for saying what the western logician would put in tame and exact language. The fervid oriental would turn from our modifying phrases with sickness of heart. We shudder at the lofty flights which captivate him. But he and we mean to express the same idea." The occidental philosopher affirms that God exercises benevolence

toward good men. Isaiah, however, means only this when he cries out, "As the bridgegroom rejoiceth over the bride, so shall thy God rejoice over thee" (Isa. 62:5). In like manner the denunciatory phrases of the Old Testament are far more unqualified than we should select. The Hebrew poet sings: "The righteous shall rejoice when he seeth the vengeance: He shall wash his feet in the blood of the wicked." Yet these glowing words would not mean more than the precise terms that we would employ, such as, "Good men will rejoice when they see virtue triumphant, even if its prosperity be attended with the just and needed sufferings of the vicious." Another illustration in point is the last verse of Psalm 137, "Happy shall he be that taketh and dasheth thy little ones against the rock." This expression on the part of the captives in Babylon means something altogether different from the utterly unchristian sense commonly given to it and that it seems to us to have. Inasmuch as Babylon was on a plain where there were no rocks, the literal meaning cannot be the true one. As Dr. Howard Osgood correctly renders the passage the sense is "Blessed shall every one be whom God shall use to destroy to the uttermost Babylon and her children that chose and followed in her sins."[4]

(2) In the imprecatory psalms, and especially in the objectionable phrases in them, the psalmists identify their enemies with God's enemies. "Do not I hate them, O Lord, that hate thee? and am not I grieved with those that rise up against thee? I hate them with perfect hatred: I count them mine enemies" (Ps. 139:21, 22). Their own cause, therefore, the psalmists feel to be God's. Hence, in opposition to themselves they see opposition to him. In this, and not in anything merely personal do we lay bare the root of their indignation.

Now will it not be much more so in the case of sin against God? How may we remain neutral when, as in this instance, the contest is between our loving Father and gracious Saviour, on the one hand, and his rebellious children, on the other?

(3) The imprecations in the Psalms rest in general on divine denunciations and predictions with respect to evil. They simply call

---

4 *Princeton Theological Review* I (1903), p. 37.

on God to do in the case of his enemies what he has declared that he will do and what, therefore, ought to be done. It is not a desire, for personal vengeance, but a longing for the vindication of the divine justice in the divine way that is expressed. This distinction is most important. The mob that clamors for the murderer that by torturing him they may wreak their vengeance on him we cannot condemn too strongly. The mass meeting, however, that passes resolutions calling on the authorities for the strictest enforcement of the laws we cannot praise too highly. Or shall we temper our praise, if, in the course of the resolutions, crime is denounced in the most vigorous language and the infliction of the extreme penalties of the criminal code is most earnestly and even vehemently demanded. We can scarcely insist too strenuously on what we know ought to be done. In like manner, may the imprecatory psalms be fully justified. They simply call on God to do what He has said ought to be done.

(4) Nor is the idea which they thus give of God inconsistent with his character as set forth elsewhere in the Bible. This is true even of God as revealed in Christ. Isaiah predicts him as one "who shall smite the earth with the rod of his mouth and with the breath of his lips shall slay the wicked" (11:4). And when Christ came he was anything but the synonym of weak gentleness. Indeed, it is precisely from him that the most withering denunciations of wickedness ever uttered proceed, and it is just He who represents Himself as pronouncing at the great day on those who would seem to have been only negatively rather than positively his enemies, the most terrific sentence ever passed: "Depart from me, ye cursed, into everlasting fire prepared for the devil and his angels" (Matt. 25:41). Nor did this escape the attention of those who knew him best. The imprecatory utterances of the New Testament, though not so numerous, are quite as fearful as those of the Old. "I would that they were even cut off which trouble you," wrote Paul (Gal. 5:12). "Alexander the coppersmith did me much evil: the Lord reward him according to his works" (2 Tim. 4:14), he also said. Even the Apostle of love portrays the martyrs as crying with a loud voice, and saying: "How long, O Lord, holy and true, dost thou not judge and avenge our blood on them that dwell on the earth!"

(Rev. 6:10). Indeed, the general spirit of the New Testament overawes us by its references to God as a "consuming fire," "into whose hands it is dreadful to fall"; "for if he that despised Moses' law died without mercy under two or three witnesses, of how much sorer punishment, suppose ye, shall he be thought worthy who hath trodden under foot the Son of God?" (Heb. 10:28, 29). So far, therefore, from these imprecatory psalms putting the Old Testament out of harmony with the New, it would be out of harmony, did it not contain the imprecatory psalms or something like them.

Now the New Testament is, as we have seen, characteristically, though not exclusively, the gospel of the grace of God. Divine grace, however, is supported by divine justice, and divine justice prepares for divine grace. Without the latter, grace, God would lack the most glorious trait of his moral character. Without the former, justice, the fundamental attribute of his essential nature would be wanting. In order, therefore, to the truth, both the justice and the grace of God, his wrath against sin and his mercy to sinners, must be emphasized.

d. A fourth objection to the ethics of the Old Testament is that, in addition to endorsing, as we have just seen, expressions of individual feeling that offend our moral judgments, it represents God as explicitly requiring in some instances acts condemned by our moral sense. For example, Abraham is commanded to sacrifice Isaac; Moses, to deceive Pharaoh with reference to letting the people go; the people to deceive their Egyptian neighbors by pretending to borrow jewelry from them when they had no intention of returning it. This objection culminates in the charge that God expressly required courses of action towards nations and races, which courses of action are utterly abhorrent to our better feelings. Thus with reference to the Canaanites the divine command to Israel was: "Thou shalt not seek their peace nor their prosperity all thy days forever" (Deut. 23:6). Indeed they were charged to drive them out summarily; to destroy them utterly, "showing no mercy, to save alive nothing that breathed." They were to exterminate absolutely all who stood in the way of their undisputed possession of a land to which they had no claim either in law or equity, at least from the human standpoint.

And this mission Joshua strictly fulfilled. Acting on the command of Moses, which was received from God, he smote all the cities "with the edge of the sword, and utterly destroyed all the souls that were therein; he left none remaining." Moreover, the subsequent neglect to execute this ordinance was named as criminal disobedience to Jehovah, and for it Israel had to pay a terrible penalty.

Nor is the difficulty a sentimental one only. At first sight, it is more perplexing to the intellect than it is distressing to the heart. These wars seem to involve cruelty, and to proceed from and to express a cruel disposition on the part of Israel. They appear also to be unjust. The innocent perish with the guilty, and the command is that it should be so. Respecting Amalek, God told Samuel to "slay both man and woman, infant and suckling, ox and sheep, camel and ass" (1 Sam. 15:3).

We should observe:

(1) In all cases in which God is charged with having commanded lying, etc., a correct exegesis will, it is believed, refute the charge. For example:

The Israelites were not told to *borrow* of the Egyptians on the eve of the exodus, neither did they pretend to borrow. What they did, and what God told them to do, was to *ask*. So the Hebrew verb *shā'al* means; so the LXX *eiteo* signifies, with the added idea of demanding; so is the Vulgate *postulo;* and finally such is now the rendering of our Revised Vision. "And it shall come to pass," it reads, "that when ye go, ye shall not go empty: but every woman shall *ask* of her neighbor, and of her that sojourneth in her house, jewels of silver and jewels of gold, and raiment: and ye shall put them upon your sons, and upon your daughters; and ye shall spoil the Egyptians."

Nor may it be urged that the request of the Children of Israel would be regarded by the Egyptians as a demand for a loan and that, therefore, deception was really to be practiced, though a lie was not formally to be uttered.

> Still less could the Israelites have had merely the thought of borrowing in their mind, seeing that God had said to Moses, "I will give the Israelites favor in the eyes of the Egyptians; and it will come to pass, that

when ye go out, ye shall not go out empty." If, therefore, it is "natural to suppose that these jewels were festal vessels with which the Egyptians furnished the poor Israelites for the intended feast," and even if "the Israelites had their thoughts directed with all seriousness to the feast which they were about to celebrate to Jehovah in the desert"; their request to the Egyptians cannot have referred to any borrowing, nor have presupposed any intention to restore what they received on their return. From the very first the Israelites asked without intending to restore, and the Egyptians granted their request without any hope of receiving back because God had made their hearts favorably disposed to the Israelites.[5]

Nor, I should add, may the morality of their thus despoiling their oppressors be questioned. It was done by the command of God; and he whose "are the silver and the gold and the cattle on a thousand hills" has the right to dispose of them, consistently with his own absolutely holy nature, to whomsoever he will.

Nor would it be difficult to discern a righteous reason for the exercise of this right in this particular case. It was but just that the nation which had brought the people of God into bondage should be required to help them on the occasion of their exodus, that thus the wrath of man should be made to advance the kingdom of the Most High.

Equally susceptible of vindication is the petition of Moses to Pharaoh that the people be allowed to go into the wilderness to sacrifice. This did not involve deception. God did not mean that the people should get permission to go away to sacrifice and then should avail themselves of the opportunity to escape. On the contrary, he told them to seek permission to sacrifice because, as he himself said, he was sure "that the king of Egypt would not let them go, no, not by a mighty hand." Indeed, so far from God's course being the tricky one that many have tried to make it out to be, it was prompted by both justice and mercy. Mercy disposed him to cause the favor asked of Pharaoh in the first instance to be so moderate, that he could easily have granted it, had he chosen to do so and thus have disciplined himself to accede to the request for the release of the whole nation, a request which, if made at first, would

---

5 Keil and Delitzsch, *Commentary on the Pentateuch,* Vol. I, p. 446.

have been too much for him. On the other hand, the purpose to manifest his justice disposed God to cause the favor asked of Pharaoh to be so reasonable that his obduracy might appear so much the more glaring, and might have no excuse in the greatness of the requirement. In short, God's foreknowledge resolves the difficulty that we are considering. The whole narrative is based on it. Moses was directed to make his request with the divine assurance that it would not be granted. He was aware from the first that it was designed to furnish a just occasion for the plagues, "the mighty hand" by which at last they were to be delivered.

(2) The ethical difficulty presented by the wars of extermination is a more comprehensive, if not more serious one. It proceeds, not only from the acts of the Children of Israel as a nation commissioned by God to drive out and destroy the original inhabitants of the land of promise, but also all acts of individuals in more or less conscious furtherance of the divinely revealed policy of extermination, as, for example, the killing of Sisera by Jael.

The solution of this difficulty requires us to consider:

(a) The intrinsic rightfulness of God's policy of extermination. This may be vindicated on the following grounds:

(i) God, because God, has the right to destroy both nations and individuals; and it is a right which he is constantly exercising. As God, he is the author of life and of death. Even the king of Israel asked, "Am I God, to kill and to make alive?" (2 Kings 5:7). As life is an absolutely free gift from him, it is his to recall it whenever he pleases and in whatever way he pleases consistently with righteousness.

Moreover, the constant exercise of this right by God demonstrates it. By the natural instrumentality of pestilence and famine or by men as his agents of destruction God, throughout all history, has been wiping communities and even nations out of existence. This is a fact which no believer in providence can deny. It is a fact, too, which proves the point at issue. Surely God, who must do right, has the right to adopt as his policy and even formally to command what he is continually doing. This is only another form of the self-evident truth, that the right to do involves the right to do deliberately and avowedly.

(ii) The justice of God's exercise of this right in adopting a policy of extermination in the case of the Canaanites is fully *manifested* (in the case under consideration) by:

(*a*) The uniquely gross wickedness of the nations to be exterminated. This was such that they deserved destruction. So abominable were many even of their everyday vices that they may not be named, much less described, in public.

When, therefore, we are disposed to question the intrinsic rightfulness of God's policy respecting these nations, let us remember how wicked they were; and that, as we read in Deuteronomy 9:4 and 5, "Not for thy righteousness or for the uprightness of thine heart dost thou go in to possess their land; but for the wickedness of these nations Jehovah thy God doth drive them out before thee, and that he may establish the word which Jehovah sware unto thy fathers, to Abraham, to Isaac, and to Jacob." It was then because of the wickedness of these nations that the Lord dealt with them as he did.

(*b*) This appears more clearly in view of the warning that they had. They were not cut off without notice. On the contrary, abundant opportunity for repentance was afforded. When the day of vengeance came, "Forty years had passed since the news of the passage of the Red Sea, and of the wonders in Egypt, had proclaimed the greatness of Jehovah above all gods. The recent conquest of the kings of Gilead and Bashan had no less vividly shown that a mighty invincible Power fought on the side of Israel, and rightfully claimed universal homage. Rahab in Jericho had heard of these judgments, and, doubtless, the conviction of the people at large through the land, however they may have stifled reflection, was the same as hers, that 'Jehovah, the God of Israel, was God in heaven above and in earth beneath.' "[6] If, therefore, because of the enormity of their sins they deserved the punishment which they received how much more must this have been the case in view of the warning which they had!

(iii) The mercifulness, in addition to the justice of God's policy of exterminating the inhabitants of Canaan appears:

---

6 Geikie, *Hours with the Bible* II, p. 398.

(*a*) In the fact that their iniquity, had it been rebuked less sharply, would have ruined the surrounding nations. In an important sense the inhabitants of Canaan were cut off that the rest of the world might not be corrupted. That is, they were treated justly that a far greater number might be treated mercifully. As regarded the world as a whole, it was a very merciful policy.

(*b*) This appears more clearly in view of the relation of this policy of extermination to the development of the divine plan of salvation. The nation out of which the Messiah was to arise, through which the highest manifestation of God on earth was to be made known among men, must not only have a local abiding place, but must in it be kept pure and distinct from all others as "the chosen people." Hence, it was that, in addition to being given the land of promise, they were commanded to destroy its inhabitants. Had they been permitted merely to subjugate the Canaanites, contact with them would still have corrupted them. Objection to the fate of these nations, therefore, is really an objection to the highest manifestation of the grace of God. He commanded the Canaanites to be destroyed that the Saviour of the world might be revealed.

(iv) Nor may it be replied that in spite of all this, the divine policy of extermination involved doing evil that good might come. We do not so reason in like cases. It is rather doing good in spite of certain necessary evil consequences. It is analogous to the action of the surgeon who does not refrain from amputating the gangrened limb, though he cannot do this without cutting off much healthy flesh. But this is not all. Not only, as we have just seen, would we not condemn in our own case a policy in kind, if not in degree, like the divine policy of extermination, but certain principles that we have already established should justify it for us on God's part. One of these is that we may not object to God's doing immediately and personally what we do not object to his doing mediately, through providence. The other is that in all that is above reason we should judge of what God ought to do, not by our opinion in the matter, but by what he is observed to do in providence. Now nothing is more certain than that providence is administered on the principle that individuals share in the life of the family and of the nation, to which they belong; and that, consequently, it is right that they should participate in its punishments as in its rewards. Hence, God's policy of exterminating the Canaanites does not lay him open to the charge of doing evil that good may come. Though many innocent persons could not but suffer, it was *right,* because of the relation in which they stood to the guilty, that this should be. So much for the intrinsic rightfulness of the divine policy.

These wars of extermination they were never allowed to regard as precedents. Even with the command to drive out and exterminate the Canaanites, they were given for their permanent rule: "If a stranger sojourn with thee in your land, ye shall not vex him. But the stranger that dwelleth with you shall be unto you as one born among you, and thou shalt love him as thyself; for ye were strangers in the land of Egypt: I am the Lord your God" (Lev. 19:33-34). Thus were they taught the extraordinary nature of their commission. They were not to expect that even God would call on them again for this strange work of judgment. Once more, in the performance of it they were limited, and the danger of it was subsequently as well as at the time clearly implied. Thus, aggressive war was permitted only at certain specified points and for certain specified objects. Otherwise, war was to be merely defensive. Under no circumstances was war for war's sake encouraged. Because he had been a man of war, David was denied the honor of building the temple. In these and in other ways were the people guarded against the indulgence of a fierce spirit and even against the development of a warlike disposition. It was kept impressed on them that always and in all respects they were to be the executors of the will of the Lord.

e. A fifth objection to the ethics of the Old Testament is found in its sanctions. It is claimed that the sanctions by which it commends and enforces what it requires, are mercenary and, therefore, inferior, if not immoral. Thus, Bolingbroke says that God purchased the obedience of His people; the book of Proverbs is charged with motives of prudence rather than of love; the human agent, affirms Munscher, is taught to regard the present rather than the future; and in general it is insisted that sanctions like these, which embody good and ill and do not demand virtue simply for its own sake, are

THE ETHICS OF THE OLD TESTAMENT
223

inferior and demoralizing. They could not result in a high type of character, and so they are unworthy of a God of high character.

The solution of this difficulty, at first sight serious, is to be sought along the following lines:

(1) In order to the vindication of a sanction it must be shown: (*a*) that the sanction is right in itself; that is, that it binds men to duty and deters them from sin by means in themselves right; (*b*) that in addition to being right in itself, the sanction is adapted to those to whom it is given; (*c*) that besides this, the sanction, if inferior, is so related to the higher as to prepare for the appreciation of them.

For example, we may at once admit that if a father were to expect his children to do right simply for right's sake, he would be using a higher sanction than if he were now and then to promise a half-holiday as the reward of obedience or to threaten the loss of a half-holiday as the punishment of disobedience. Nevertheless, we should have no difficulty in justifying his procedure. A half-holiday is good in itself. It may be a very trifling good as compared with many others, but still it is a good. Neither is it wrong that it should be a reward of virtuous action. On the contrary, we instinctively feel it to be right that the sum of good things and not merely the highest good things, should follow virtue; and if so, then that the lesser good things should do this as well as the greater. Indeed, one of the strong arguments for a future life is based on the fact that such a life is felt to be demanded that the glaring inequality between virtue and the few good things which in many cases it enjoys in this life may be evened up. In using, therefore, the half-holiday as a sanction in the training of his children a father would be doing only what was in itself right.

He would be employing, too, a sanction adapted to those whom he would train. Abstract considerations, such as right for right's sake, though the highest, would probably not appeal to little children. While they might feel, they could not appreciate the full claim of the right simply as such. They would not be sufficiently developed morally to do this. A half-holiday, however, if made a reward of virtue in their case would commend to them most

strikingly the excellence, if not the uniqueness of virtue. That must
be good, they would feel, which secures to us such a good as a
half-holiday. Thus this sanction, in addition to being right in itself,
would be effective; it would prompt that right action which a
higher, though more spiritual, sanction would be powerless in the
case of children to secure.

Nor would it be open to the objection that the action which it
would prompt, while virtuous in matter, would not be so in motive;
that the children, because they would do right only for the sake of
reward, would not really do right. The unexpressed premise in this
reasoning is not necessarily true. Lower motives are not incompatible with higher ones. Because a child eagerly anticipates the promised half-holiday, it does not follow that his obedience is not
determined chiefly, or even solely, by love for his parents. Many a
child would obey just as fully if no half-holiday were promised. In
his case, therefore, it encourages him to obedience without necessarily taking the place of the right motive to obedience. Instead of
destroying that motive, it makes it easier for it to operate. Of
course, in the case of a child who had no affection for his parents it
would not be so, but it is not the case of such a child that we are
considering.

Nor is this all. Not only does the half-holiday make it easier for
the child who loves his parents to obey them from love to them;
but developing in this way true obedience, it develops the child's
whole moral nature.

f. A sixth objection to the ethics of the Old Testament is that in
it the principle of human brotherhood receives only very partial and
inconsistent treatment. Thus Bolingbroke declares that the particularism by which the Jews were taught to regard themselves as God's
"peculiar people" made them selfish and took them out of obligation to the rest of mankind.

To this we would reply:

(1) It is not the fact that the brotherhood of man is not clearly
taught in the Old Testament. If we compare it with other contemporaneous writings, nothing is more significant than the emphasis
which it lays on this principle. Thus in Exodus 23:9 the Israelites
were forbidden to oppress strangers. In Leviticus 19:33 they were

instructed to treat them kindly. The doors of the Jewish sanctuary were kept guardedly open to proselytes. Numbers 15:15 declares, "As ye are, so shall the stranger be before the Lord." Deuteronomy 10:18 represents God as loving the stranger.

The Prophets lay even more stress on this principle. Micah 4:2 predicts that many nations shall come and say, "Come and let us go up to the mountain of the Lord, and to the house of the God of Jacob." Isaiah 56:7 foretells how "God's house shall be a house of prayer for all people." Isaiah 66:19 prophesies the declaration of God's "glory among the Gentiles," and the whole sixtieth chapter is given to describing the access that the gospel shall have to all the nations of the earth. Indeed, the injustice of the objection that we are considering should be apparent when we remember, as has been remarked, that it is in the Hebrew Prophets that we find the first philosophy of universal history and that the "Chosen People" were the only one in all antiquity that had any, even the least conception of a redemption for the world.

(2) The objection mistakes the nature, ground, and aim of the particularism of the Hebrew system and, indeed, of the particularism in the divine administration in general. The Hebrews are represented in the Old Testament as brothers in one human race, and as made to differ for a time largely that good may result to all. Such is the nature of the particularism objected to.

This closer relation of the Hebrews to God is not a meritorious one. It is not the consequence of what they are in themselves, but of what God in the exercise of his sovereign grace would make of them. Such is the ground of the particularism in question.

Its aim is twofold:

(a) Defensive: that they may be kept from contamination as being the sons of his love and so his special agents on earth.

(b) Thus the objection under consideration falls. Indeed, it and the objections to the doctrine of election in general proceed on three glaringly false principles: first, that God may not favor some that they may be agents of blessing to all; second, that God cannot love all, unless he shows his love in the same way to all; and third and fundamental that God is bound to treat all sinners, we do not say justly, but alike.

g. The seventh and final objection to the ethics of the Old Testament is that it contains positive precepts and indirect requirements and sanctions that are in conflict with the teachings, and implications of the New Testament and so with high morality. To be more specific, the objection is that under the Old Testament loose divorce and polygamy were sanctioned, also slavery and also retaliation. How, then, it is asked, can the moral system of the Old Testament be from God? We would answer:

That we may appreciate this, let us put ourselves, if we can, in the age in which the precepts that we would vindicate were given. We should then find polygamy and divorce in general use or rather abuse. We should meet a hardhearted and rebellious people who not only did not regard the marriage relation as supremely sacred, but who were even disposed to act as if it were not sacred at all. In this deplorable state of things we should scarcely deem it prudent, it would seem, to forbid altogether a practice so common as divorce, especially in view of the disposition to dissolve marriage without divorce and even to do away with marriage altogether. Might not divorce, however, be regulated? and if so, would it not be better to regulate it than to prohibit it? So radical a measure as prohibition would be likely to be utterly disregarded. A law regulating divorce, however, would probably be heeded. Through such a law, the husband might be prevented from casting off his wife without ceremony. He might be restrained even from putting her away in a passion. He might be required to take time to consider the matter, to bring it before some scribe or learned man, to go through the long and slow formalities in order to a legal divorce. In this way much more opportunity might be given for the reconciliation of husband and wife. In this way the regulation of divorce would lessen the number of divorces, while the absolute prohibition of it would, doubtless in that rude age result in utter disregard of the marriage relation. In this way a regulative enactment would do all that could be done then to guard its sacredness.

Take slavery. Were we to go back to the time of the Pentateuch, we should find it well-nigh universal. We should discover, too, that, with scarcely an exception, it was horribly cruel. Egyptian bondage would seem to be the type rather than the exception. Certainly it was no more oppressive than the slavery with which, hundreds of years later, we meet in Greece and even in Rome. Nor is this all. In that rude age of which we are speaking slavery, while it need not have been as rigorous as it was, could scarcely have been other than universal. Indeed, it is difficult to see how it can be dispensed with in certain phases of society without, at all events, entailing severer evils than it produces. When, for example, war is carried on for conquest or revenge, there are but two ways of dealing with the captives, namely, putting them to death or reducing them to slavery; and slavery is the milder of the two. Thus in this and in many other cases slavery was the better of the alternatives that offered, and may hence be regarded as in such an age a blessing rather than a curse.

Under these circumstances, therefore, it would scarcely seem possible to prohibit slavery altogether. If it were done, there would be no likelihood that any would heed the prohibition. Moreover, though it should be possible, it would not appear to be wise. The better of two necessary alternatives, it would be an evil to do away with it. It could, however, be regulated. While sanctioned, it might be rendered less oppressive. With considerable prospect of being regarded, we might admonish the master to treat his slave, "not as a bond servant, but as an hired servant and a sojourner," and again, "not to rule over him with rigor." We might even, with some hope of carrying our point, provide for a termination of servitude in the case of individual slaves and enjoin masters when that time should in any case arrive "not to let the slave go away empty, but to remunerate him liberally out of his flock, his floor and his wine-press." We might thus, as the Mosaic law did, while sanctioning slavery, regulate and restrain it in very many directions. In this way we should both render it less oppressive and should foster a sentiment which would tend toward the abolition of slavery. Thus, while we should not eradicate it at once, we should do all that, under the circumstances, could be done towards its extinction.

(1) Nor may it be objected that God's conduct in these cases is like that, for example, of municipalities which license the admittedly evil saloon, hoping by thus regulating it to work toward its entire prohibiton. The objection overlooks what is essential; viz.,

the difference between man's relation to the present constitution of things and God's relation to it. That difference, as has already been often pointed out, is this. Man, because included in the present constitution of things, is bound by the laws which it implies; and he is thus bound just so long as the present constitution of things continues. Hence, for him of himself to license the saloon even with a view to at length prohibiting it, or for him of himself to sanction unscriptural divorce even for the purpose of finally abolishing it, would be to do evil that good might come. Inasmuch as the present constitution of things, in which he is included and by which he is bound, is such as to render both intemperance and loose divorce contrary to it, man has no right of himself to license or tolerate either for any purpose for even a moment.

God's relation, however, to the constitution of things is radically different. Because He is the author of the present constitution of things and so independent of it, he is not bound by it as is man, but is bound only by the righteousness of his own essential nature. Hence, for righteous reasons, God may modify or repeal for the time being the implications of the constitution of things though that constitution continues. Thus he may declare that divorce under certain limitations shall not be wrong; and if *he* does so in the interest of righteousness as *he* will and must, then it will neither be wrong for men to use divorce within those limitations, nor for him to provide that they may. In a word, while man, if he were of himself to license loose divorce, would be doing evil though he were to act out of regard for righteousness; God, when he licenses it, is simply doing what he as God has the right to do and what thus in his case is right, that good may come. Of course, it would be otherwise in the case of precepts such as that requiring truthfulness which are founded on his immutable nature. These even he may not and cannot change on any account. God never relaxes in the interest of idolatry or because of idolatry. This is because idolatry is against his nature. Laws, however, like those which we have been considering and which are rooted only in the order of things which he himself has freely appointed he may modify when the "hardness of men's hearts" or other abnormal reasons, as the changes wrought by sin, render such a course in the interest of morality.

(2) Nor may it be objected either that God's policy in regulating the evils under consideration instead of prohibiting them seems to be a recognition of the false principle that ability limits obligation. His concession is not to inability, but to incapacity; not to a lack of moral power growing out of a sinful disposition, but to a weak because undeveloped moral nature. Now for this latter, which we call incapacity, men may not be held responsible. It is self-evident that one may not be required to be or to do what he has not the faculties to be or to do, or what he has not the opportunity to be or to do. The standard of right is the same for a child as for a man, but the child may not be expected to realize the standard as the man is expected to. He is too little.

Nor may it be replied that the incapacity of the Israelites was in part the result of sin; that their wickedness both retarded their moral development and weakened their moral perceptions. This is true. It does not, however, alter the case. As A. A. Hodge says, "this irresponsibility arises solely from the bare fact of the inability (incapacity). It matters not at all in *this respect* whether the inability (incapacity) be self-induced or not, if only it be a real incapacity. A man, for instance, who has put out his own eyes in order to avoid the draft, may be justly held responsible for *that act,* but he can nevermore be held responsible for seeing, i.e., for using eyes which he does not any longer possess."[7] In like manner, God might not have made concessions to any inability of the Israelites that consisted in the want of proper desires and affections, that, in a word, was voluntary and so sinful; but he might, and he did, make numerous concessions to lack of capacity or of opportunity; and he might as he did do so when this lack of capacity or of opportunity was in large part the result of sin. This would not be to affirm the false principle that ability limits obligation; it would be to affirm the true principle that the nature and not the origin of a human condition determines the relation of its consequences to responsibility. For the consequences of what is voluntary and so moral, however caused, we are responsible; and so God may not make ·concessions to these consequences: but for the consequences of

---

7 *Outlines of Theology,* p. 344.

what is not moral, for what is incapacity rather than inability, however caused, even though the result of sin, we are not responsible, and so, God may, and often should as he does make concessions to these.

(3) The difference between the Old Testament and the New in the respects under review is formal rather than real; of degree only, and not of kind. The inconsistency alleged and objected to is one of appearance merely. True identity does not reside in looks or even in sameness of material, but in unity of organizing principle. The plant in full flower appears altogether unlike the little blade which first makes its way above the ground, and its elements are constantly being destroyed and renewed and increased and modified. Nevertheless, the plant in full flower is the same with the little blade; there is the most beautiful and wonderful consistency between them; the organizing principle of both is identical.

2. In what, then, will the complete vindication of Old Testament ethics consist?

a. As has just been shown, it is not required of us to relieve the ethical system of the Old Testament of the charge of inferiority to that of the New. Indeed, were it not inferior to it, that would be a decided objection. It would then be out of relation to and so unfitted for its own stage in God's scheme of ethical progress.

b. What, however, is required of us, if we would vindicate the ethics of the Old Testament, is:

(1) To evince, as has been done, that this inferiority consists in incompleteness only and so involves no imperfection and thus no immorality. The inferiority is that of the seed to the blade, that of the blade to the budding plant, that of the bud to the flower, that of the flower to the fruit. Though inferior to the flower in development and so failing to manifest not a few of its beauties, the bud is just as perfect as the flower, if we consider it in relation to its function in the expanding life of the plant. While it is a very incomplete exhibition of the life of the plant, there is in it nothing out of harmony with the life principle of the plant. Indeed, were it more nearly complete, it would be out of harmony with the general development of the plant. Both in itself, therefore, and in its

adaptation to the growth which it expresses and forwards it is perfect.

The vindication of the ethics of the Old Testament calls on us first of all, to establish that, while less nearly complete than and so inferior to New Testament ethics, both in itself and with reference to the moral life that it expresses and would forward, it is *perfect*.

(2) We must show, that, with all its incompleteness and consequent inferiority to New Testament ethics, Old Testament ethics is so different from and so superior to the ethics of all contemporaneous religions as to be most evidently divinely unique. Not only is it all that it should be in itself: but in the respects in which it is most manifestly this, it is conspicuously out of analogy with the other ethical systems of that day; it is so evidently not of earth that it must be from heaven. Its characteristic features are clearly of unearthly origin. These features, these elements of unique superiority over the ethics of that age, are as follows:

(a) The emphasis put on the personality of God. As we saw, this is *the* characteristic of the ethics of the Old Testament. It refers everything to the will of God. Duty is what he bids us do; virtuous is what he would have us be; the supreme good is his voluntary and gracious favor.

(b) The emphasis put on the holiness of God. Among the ethnic religions no such doctrine was inculcated. In a word, the conception of Jehovah as the Holy One, as the Righteous Ruler, was original. It was a unique excellence of Old Testament ethics.

(c) The emphasis laid on the personality of man. In striking contrast with all heathen views, according to which man is either subject to nature or has nature constantly before him as a cramping and never wholly to be overcome power, the Old Testament teaches, that man is made in the image of the divine Person; that, like him, he is a free and ought to be a holy being; that dominion over nature has been given to him; and that he will be held strictly accountable for the use which he may make of his freedom.

(d) The resulting practical conception of evil. Heathen ethics relegated it almost exclusively to the purely ideal sphere. It conceived of evil as a mere possibility, or as an exceptional and isolated reality, or as a natural necessity which underlay all human guilt and in which, consequently, guilt lost its distinctive character as guilt. The Old Testament, on the contrary, and as might have been expected from its unique discernment of divine and human personality, looks evil earnestly and squarely in the face, and regards it as a sad all-prevalent reality, the guilt of which lies in the free act of man, and is participated in without exception. "Hence, it is not the power of fate, but the law of righteousness to which he gives prominence in the intricate fabric of human affairs."

(e) The spirituality of the ethical life. This results from the Old Testament's vivid conception of both sin and personality. Righteousness attaches fundamentally to the will, to the heart, to the personality; and it is not only the sinful act, but equally the disposition to evil that is condemned.

(f) The Old Testament makes faith the root of true obedience. As it points to the will of God as the sole standard of duty, so it points to the grace of God as the only adequate power for duty.

(g) The hope for the future that pervades the Old Testament. From the protevangelium to the last word of the latest prophet its look is ever forward, nor is there ever a doubt that that look will be rewarded.

(h) This moral regeneration and the redemption of which it was part were conceived of by the Old Testament as of the world. The "peculiar people" of God, the Hebrews alone of all antiquity were taught to regard Him as the Saviour of *all* men. In almost no respect does Old Testament ethics show its superiority to all other systems so conspicuously as in this, its universalism.

(i) The already and frequently implied progressive character of Old Testament ethics. Nowhere does this appear so clearly as in relation to the particularism and the universalism which we have just been considering. The first conception of charity, for example, was that it should not extend outside the nation of Israel. The stranger who had not become a citizen was to be beyond its reach. This limitation, however, is one that tends to pass away. In the book of Ruth a Moabite woman is taken into a Hebrew family and becomes famous as the ancestress of King David. The beautiful prayer of Solomon at the dedication of the Temple does not fail to include "the stranger that cometh out of a far country." In the Prophets the universal spirit of love begins to breathe out hopes of a time when of Egypt and Assyria it shall be said by God, "Blessed be Egypt my people, Assyria the work of my hands, and Israel mine inheritance" (Isa. 19:25). As another has written, "All this shows that while the moral codes of other nations either remain where they began, or else grow narrower and less pure with the progress of years, that of Israel tends to purify itself, and to widen out into a stream that shall carry cleansing and blessing to all mankind." A law with such inherent power of working out to wider accomplishment, and with such force of self-purification, was the product of no mere human legislation.

(j) The unique and inferentially supernatural superiority of the ethics of the Old Testament appears finally and yet more significantly in the humane spirit that pervades it. Not only does it prohibit, as we have seen, all unneccessary harshness; it is characteristically and positively kind. A law that exacts strict justice, for which reason it is often objected to as harsh, it is also a law whose spirit, as truly if not so conspicuously as in that of the New Testament, is love.

The Mosaic code did, it is true, employ the death penalty more frequently than we do, yet it never employed or allowed cruelty in punishment. Its criminal legislation was vastly more humane than that of England only 150 years ago. This, particularly in that barbarous age, is worthy of notice.

We may not, however, content ourselves with negative proofs, when positive ones are so numerous that we can mention only a few of them.

For example, the provision made for the poor, "When ye reap the harvest of your land, thou shalt not wholly reap the corners of thy field, neither shalt thou gather the gleanings of thy harvest. And thou shalt not glean thy vineyard, neither shalt thou gather every grape of thy vineyeard; thou shalt leave them for the poor and the stranger. I am the Lord your God" (Lev. 19:9, 10). To this add other provisions for the poor. It was said that the poor were never to cease out of the land (Deut. 15:11). Therefore, "Thou shalt open thine hand wide unto thy brother, to thy poor, and to thy needy, in thy land" (Deut. 15:11). Every man was to have a care for his neighbor, and if he saw him "waxing poor and falling into decay"— getting behind-hand, we should say—he was by law to relieve him (Lev. 25:35-37), even though he was a foreigner. No interest was to be taken of such an one, nor any increase; i.e., no payment in any kind over and above the amount loaned. In this and in other respects the law of the Old Testament was much more humane than the best legislation of today. A law of Massachusetts, for example, allows pawn-brokerage. It sets no limit, and makes no provision with regard to it, except a fine for carrying it on without a license. The poor man who is compelled to pawn his watch or his furniture is at the mercy of the broker for the best bargains that he can make; and it generally turns out that the article is lost for a tithe of its value. Our system of pledges is by attachments, mortgages, and bonds, under which, in failure of redemption, the law knows no mercy, and is always in favor of the creditor—never of the debtor.

Set now in contrast with this the Mosaic law. Pledges might be taken; but certain articles, for instance the upper and nether mill-stones and the widow's raiment might not be taken. But when pledges were taken of the poor they were not to be kept over night. When it was raiment especially it was to be returned before sundown. It was a law in favor of the poor. Still further, with reference to the poor, the fatherless, and the stranger, as if the provision noticed were not enough, every third year there was to be a tithing of the increase for them. The stranger also was not to be vexed or oppressed, as was the custom among the surrounding and barbarous nations, the remains of which custom are to be found in modern legislation in the form of passports, imposts, prohibitions and disabilities laid upon the foreigner and his traffic.

But enough. In the words of one who has made the institutions of the Old Testament the subject of special study, "The Mosaic, so far from being a barbarous or bloody code, surpasses beyond comparison every other code of the world ever known, for delicate, thoughtful, and beneficent humaneness. . . . No one, I suppose, will accuse Professor Huxley of prejudice in favor of the Old Testament, yet he says: 'There is no code of legislation, ancient or modern, at once so just and so merciful, so tender to the weak and poor, as the Jewish law.' "[8]

BIBLIOGRAPHY

Bruce, W. S. *The Ethics of the Old Testament.* 2nd. ed., Edinburg: T. & T. Clark, 1909. (Excellent coverage of subject, but use with care.)

Geisler, Norman L. *Ethics: Alternatives and Issues.* Grand Rapids: Zondervan Publishing House, 1971. (A superb evangelical treatment which adopts the position of ethical hierarchicalism. See especially pp. 139-259 for discussion of Biblical issues and passages.)

Henry, Carl F. H. "The Biblical Particularization of the Moral Life: The Old Testament" in *Christian Personal Ethics.* Grand Rapids: Wm. B. Eerdmans, 1957, pp. 246-77. (Temporal vs. the eternal aspect of the law.)

Murray, John. *Principles of Conduct: Aspects of Biblical Ethics,* Grand Rapids: Wm. B. Eerdmans, 1957. (Excellent for exegesis of several O.T. passages.)

Smith, B. L. "The Bible and Morality". *Themelios,* VI (1969) pp. 44-52. (A very thought-provoking article marking out much new ground.)

---

[8] *Agnosticism and Religion,* p. 200.

XIII

THE NEW COVENANT

by E. W. Hengstenberg

Editor's Introduction

How is the old covenant to be related to the new covenant? The Old Testament to the New Testament? Law to Grace? Many have quickly decided that they just can't be related now. Their favorite word is "BUT" (according to the English perversion of John 1:17).

Hengstenberg has given us one of the best essays ever written on this subject and his Scriptural evidences should bring a return of fresh air to all true evangelicals.

"Behold, days come, saith the Lord, and I make a new covenant with the house of Israel, and with the house of Judah."
—Jeremiah 31:31

"Not as the covenant that I made with their fathers, in the day that I took them by the hand to bring them out of the land of Egypt, which my covenant they brake; but I marry them to me, saith the Lord."—Jeremiah 31:32

What is to be understood by the making of a covenant? We cannot here think of a formal transaction, of a mutual contract, such as the covenant made on Sinai. This appears from verse 32, according to which the old covenant was concluded on the day when the Lord took Israel by the hand, in order to bring them out of Egypt; but at that time a covenant-transaction proper was not yet mentioned. Most interpreters erroneously suppose that by the words: "In the day," etc., the abode at Sinai is designated. But since the *day* of the deliverance from Egypt is commonly thus spoken of (comp. Exod. 12:51ff.); since this *day* was, as such, marked out by the annually returning feast of the Passover, we must, here also, take "day," in its proper sense. And there is the less reason for abandoning this most obvious sense that, in Exodus 6:4; Ezekiel 16:8; Haggai 2:5, a covenant with Israel is spoken of, which was not first concluded on Sinai, but was already concluded when they went out from Egypt. *Farther*—No obligation is spoken of in reference to the new covenant; blessing and gifts are mentioned, and nothing but these.

But the question is, whether the making of a covenant cannot be spoken of in passages, where there is no mention of transactions of a mutual agreement between two parties. The substance of the covenant evidently precedes the outward conclusion of the covenant, and forms the foundation of it. The conclusion of the covenant does not first form the relation, but is merely a solemn acknowledgment of the relation already existing. Thus it is ever in human relations; the contract, as a rule, only fixes and settles outwardly, a relation already existing. And that is still more the case in the relation between God and man. By every benefit from God, an obligation is imposed upon him who receives it, whether it may, in express words, have been stated by God, and have been outwardly acknowledged by the recipient or not. This is clearly seen in the case under consideration. At the giving of the Law on Sinai, the obligatory power of the commandments of God is founded upon the fact, that God brought Israel out of the land of Egypt, the house of bondage. Hence, it appears that the Sinaitic covenant existed, in substance, from the moment that the Lord led Israel out of Egypt. By apostatizing from the Lord, the people would have broken the covenant, even if it had not been solemnly confirmed on Sinai; just as their apostacy, in the time between their going out and the transactions on Sinai, was treated as a violation of the covenant. It would have been a breach of the covenant, if the people had answered, in the negative, the solemn questions of God, whether they would enter into a covenant with him. This appears so much the more clearly, when we keep in mind, that the New Covenant was not at all sanctioned by such an external solemn act. But if, nevertheless, it is a covenant in the strictest sense; if, here, the relation is independent upon its acknowledgment, then, under the Old Testament too, this acknowledgment must be a secondary element.

The same is the case with all the other passages commonly quoted in proof, that "to make a covenant" may also be used of mere blessings and promises. Thus, e.g., Genesis 9:9: "Behold, I establish my covenant with you, and with your seed after you." That which is here designated as a covenant is not the promise *per se,* that in future the course of nature should, on the whole, remain undisturbed, but in so far only, as it imposes upon them who receive it, the obligation to glorify, by their walk, the Lord of the order of nature. In part, this obligation is afterwards outwardly fixed in the commandments concerning murder, eating of blood, etc. Genesis 15:18: "In the same day God made a covenant with Abraham, saying: Unto thy seed I give this land." In what precedes, a promise only is contained; but this promise itself is, at the same time, an obligation; and this obligation existed even then, although it was at a later period only, solemnly undertaken by receiving the sign of the covenant, circumcision. Exodus 34:10: "And he said: Behold I make a covenant; before all thy people I will do marvels such as have not been done in all the earth, nor in any nation; and all the people among whom thou art, shall see the work of the Lord; for it is a terrible thing that I will do with thee." The covenant on Sinai is here already made; the making of the new covenant here spoken of consists in the mercies by which God will manifest himself to his people as their God. Every one of these mercies involves a new obligation for the people; every one is a question in deeds: This I do to thee, what doest thou to me?—It will now be possible to determine in what sense the Old Covenant is here contrasted with the New. The point in question cannot be a new and more perfect revelation of the Law of God; for that is common to both the dispensations. No jot or tittle of it can be lost under the New Testament, and as little can a jot or tittle be added. God's law is based on his nature, and that is eternal and unchangeable, compare Malachi 3:22 (4:4). The revelation of the Law does not belong to the going out from Egypt, to which the making of the former covenant is here attributed, but to Sinai. As little can the discourse be of the introduction of an entirely new relation, which is not founded at all upon the former one. On this subject, *David Kimchi's* remark is quite pertinent: "It will not be the newness of the covenant, but its stability." The covenant with Israel is an everlasting covenant. Jehovah would not be Jehovah, if an entirely new commencement could take place—so the Apostle writes in Romans 15:8.

The sending of Christ with his gifts and blessings, the making of the New Covenant, is thus the consequence of the covenant-faithfulness of God. If then the Old and New Covenants are here contrasted, the former cannot designate the relation of God to Israel *per se,* and in its whole extent, but it must rather designate the former mode only, in which this relation was manifested—that whereby the Lord had, up to the time of the Prophet, manifested himself as the God of Israel. With this former imperfect form the future more perfect form is here contrasted, under the name of the New Covenant. The New Covenant which is to take the place of the Old, when looking to the form (comp. Heb. 8:13), is in substance, the realization of the Old. These remarks are in perfect harmony with that which was formerly said concerning the meaning of *make a covenant.* We saw that this expression does not designate an act only once done, by which a covenant is solemnly sanctioned, but rather that it is used of every action, by which a covenant-relation is instituted or confirmed. If, then, the Old Covenant is the former form of the covenant with Israel; and the New Covenant the future form of it, another question is: Which among the manifold differences of those two forms are here specially regarded by the Prophet? The answer to this question is supplied by that which the Prophet declares concerning the New Covenant. For since it is *not* to be like the former covenant, the excellences of the New must be as many defects of the Old. These excellences, however, are all of a spiritual nature, first, the forgiveness of sins, and then the writing of the Law in the heart. It follows from this, that the blessings of the Old Covenant were *pre-eminently* (for we shall afterwards see that an entire absence of these spiritual blessings cannot be spoken of, and that the difference between the Old and the New Covenant is, in this respect, a relative one only, not an absolute one) of an external nature; and this is also suggested by the circumstance, that it is represented as being concluded when the people were led out of Egypt; in which fact, all the later similar deliverances and blessings are comprehended. The Prophet, if any one, had learned that, in the way hitherto pursued, they could not successfully continue. The sinfulness of the people had, at this time, manifested itself in such fearful outbreaks, that, even when looking at the matter from a human point of view, he could not but feel most deeply that, with outward blessings and gifts, with an outward deliverance from servitude, the people were very little benefited. What is the use of a mercy which, according to divine necessity, must be immediately followed by a punishment so much the more severe? The necessary condition for the true and lasting bestowal of outward salvation, is the bestowal of the internal salvation; without the latter the former is only a mockery. It is this internal salvation, therefore, which is the highest aim of the Prophet's longings; to it he here points as the highest blessing of the Future; compare also 32:40: "And I make an everlasting covenant with them, and I will no more turn away from them to do them good, and I will put my fear in their hearts that they shall not depart from me."

The reason why a better covenant was required (Heb. 8:6), appears sufficiently from that which, in verses 33, 34, is said of this new covenant in contrast to the old. Here, however, it is rather the infinite love of God, the greatness of His covenant-faithfulness which are pointed out; and this thought is, from among all others, best suited to the context. "They" and "I" form an emphatic contrast. *They,* in wicked ingratitude, have broken the former covenant, have shaken off the obligations which God's former mercies imposed upon them. God too—so it might be expected—ought now to annul the old covenant, and forever withdraw from them the old mercies. But, instead of doing so, He grants the new covenant, the greater mercy. He anew takes in marriage apostate Israel, and in such a manner that now the bond of love becomes firm and indestructible. *Bleek* objects to our interpretation: "The object is not the city of Jerusalem, or even the Congregation of Israel, but the single Israelites, who may indeed be designated as the children of Jehovah, but not as His spouse." But, in such personifications, it is quite a common thing that the real plurality should take the place of the ideal unity. In Exodus 34:15, for instance, it is said: "And they go a whoring after their gods," instead of the congregation, to which the *whoring* properly belongs, (comp. Isa. 57:7), the individual members are mentioned (comp. Hos. 2:1, 2) (1:10; 2:19).

"For this is the covenant that I will make with the house of Israel after these days, saith the Lord: I give my law in their inward parts, and will write it in their hearts; and I will be their God, and they shall be my people."—Jeremiah 31:33

"For" is, by some interpreters, here supposed to mean "but"; so much, only however, is correct that "but" might *also* have been put; *for* is here quite in its place. The words: "Not as the covenant . . . ," in the preceding verse, are here vindicated, and expanded by a positive definition of the nature and substance of the New Covenant. It is just because it is of such a nature, that it is not like the former covenant.

"These days," on the contrary, are a designation of the Present; "after these days," equivalent to "at the end of days." The Prophet so repeatedly and emphatically points to the Future, because unbelief and weak faith imagined that, with the Present, the history of the covenant-people was finished, and that no Future was in store for them. *Calvin* pertinently remarks: "It is just as if the Prophet had said, that the grace of which he was prophesying could not be apprehended, unless they, believers, kept their minds composed, and patiently waited until the time of the promised salvation had come."

As regards the following enumeration of the blessings, in and by the bestowal of which the new covenant-relation is to be established, *Venema* very correctly remarks: "The blessings are distinguished into radical or causal ones, and subsequent or derived ones."

The second "for," in verse 34: "*For* I will forgive their sin," proves the correctness of this division.

Torah never means "doctrine," but always "law"; and the fact that it is only *the* law of God, the eternal expression of his nature, and common, therefore, to both the Old and New Covenants, which can be here spoken of, and not a new constitution for the latter, is seen from the reference in which the giving in the inward parts and the writing on the heart (the tables of the heart, 2 Cor. 3:3), stand to the outward communication and the writing on the tables of stone on Sinai. The law is the same; the relation only is different in which God places it to man.

One might easily infer from the passage before us a confirmation of the error, that the law under the Old Covenant was *only* an outward dead letter. Against this error *Buddeus* already contended, who (p. 117) acknowledges that it is a relative difference and contrast only, which are here spoken of. He says: "This, of course, was the case with the Old Testament believers also; here, however, God promises a richer fulness and higher degree of this blessing." *Calvin* declares the opinion that, under the Old Testament dispensation, there did not exist any regeneration, to be absurd, and says: "we know that, under the Law, the grace of God was rare and dark; but that, under the Gospel, the gifts of the Spirit were *poured* out, and that God dealt much more liberally with His Church."

The idea of a purely outward giving of the Law is indeed one which is quite inconceivable. God would, in that case, have done nothing else towards Israel than he did to the traitor Judas, in whose conscience he proclaimed his holy Law, without communicating to him strength for repentance. But such a proceeding can be conceived of, only where there is a subjective impossibility of "renewing unto repentance." Every outward manifestation of God *must,* according to the constitution of human nature, be accompanied by the inward manifestation, since it is inconceivable that He who knows our nature, should mock us by the semblance of a blessing. As soon as we know the outward fact of the deliverance from Egypt, we know, at the same time, that God has then powerfully touched the heart of Israel. As soon as it is established that the Law on Sinai was written on tables of stone by the finger of God, it is also established that he, at the same time, wrote it on the tables of Israel's heart. But that which is thus implied in the matter itself, is confirmed by the testimony of history.

In the Law itself, circumcision is designated as the pledge and seal of the bestowal, not merely of outward blessings, but of the circumcision of the heart, of the removal of sin attaching to every one by birth: so that man can love God with all his heart, all his soul, and all his powers (Deut. 30:6). This circumcision of the heart which, in the outward circumcision, was at the same time *required* and promised by God (comp. Deut. 30:6 with 10:16), is not substantially different from the writing of the Law on the heart.

Farther—If the Law of the Lord had, for Israel, been a mere outward letter, how could the animated praise of it in the Holy Scriptures, e.g., in Psalm 19, be accounted for? Surely, a bridge must already have been formed between the Law and him who can speak of it as rejoicing the heart, as enlightening the eyes, as converting the soul, as sweeter than honey and the honeycomb. That is no more the Law in its isolation which worketh wrath, but it is the Law in its connection with the Spirit, whose commandments are not grievous (comp. my commentary on Ps. 19:8ff).

A *new* heart was created under the Old Testament also (Ps. 51:12); and not to know the nature of this creation was, for a teacher in Israel, the highest disgrace (John 3:10). Yea, that which is here promised for the Future, a pious member of the Old Covenant expresses in Psalm 40:9, *in the same form,* as being already granted to him as his present spiritual condition: I delight to do thy will, O my God, and thy Law is in the midst of my bowels, words which imply the same contrast to the Law as outward letter, as being written on tables of stone, compare Proverbs 3:1-3: "My son, forget not my law, and let thine heart keep my commandments . . . . bind them about thy neck, write them upon the table of thine heart." (Compare my commentary on Psalms, Vol. iii., p. lxvii.)

But how is it to be explained that the contrariety which, in itself, is relative, appears here under the form of the absolute contrariety, the difference in degree, as a difference in kind? Evidently in the same manner as the same phenomenon must be explained elsewhere also, e.g., John 1:17, where it is said that the Law was given by Moses, but mercy and truth by Christ. By overlooking this fact, so many errors have been called forth. The blessings of the Old Covenant which, when considered in themselves, are so important and rich, appear, when compared with the much fuller and more important blessings of the New Covenant, to be so trifling that they vanish entirely out of sight. It is quite similar when, in Jeremiah 3:16, the Prophet represents the highest sanctuary of the Old Covenant, the Ark of the Covenant, as sinking into entire oblivion in future; when, in 23:7, 8, he describes the deliverance from Egypt as no longer worthy of being mentioned. Parallel to the passage under consideration is the promise of Joel of the pouring out of the Spirit (3:1, 2 [2:28, 29]); so that that which we remarked on that passage, is applicable here also. But, in that passage, the relative nature of the promise appears more clearly than it does here, just because, in general, under the New Covenant, in its relation to the Old, there is nowhere an absolutely new beginning, but always a completion only (just in the same manner as, on the other hand, under the New Covenant itself, it is in the relation of the *regnum gloriae* to the *regnum gratiae*). Joel, in reference to the communication of the Spirit, puts the abundance in the place of the scarcity; the many in the place of the few.

Compare, moreover, 24:7: "And I give them a heart to know me, that I am the Lord; and they shall be my people, and I will be their God"; 32:39: "And I give them one heart and one way, that they may fear me for ever, for the good of them and of their children after them"; but especially Ezekiel 11:19, 20; 36:26, 27.—It is not without meaning, that the words: "And I will be their God . . ." follow upon: "And I give my Law in their inward parts. . . ." The Law is the expression of God's nature; it is only by the Law being written in the heart that man can become a partaker of God's nature; that his name can be sanctified in him. And it is this participation in the nature of God, this sanctification of God's name, which forms the foundation of: "I will be their God, and they shall be my people." Without this, the relation cannot exist at all, as truly as God is not an idol, but the True and Holy One. These words express, as *Buddeus* (p. 94) rightly remarks: "That he will impart himself altogether to them."

But how were it possible that God, with his blessings and gifts, should impart himself entirely and unconditionally to them who are not of his nature? Of all unnatural things, this would be the most unnatural. Here, however, likewise the relative character of the promise most clearly appears. As early as to Abraham, God had promised that he would be a God to *him,* and to his seed after him; and this promise he had afterwards repeated to the whole people (Lev. 26:12; comp. Exod. 29:45); "And I dwell in the midst of the children of Israel and will be their God." In the consciousness that this promise was fulfilled in the time then present, David exclaims in Psalm 33:12: "Blessed is the nation whose God is Jehovah, the generation whom he hath chosen for his inheritance."

Hence, here too, there is nothing absolutely new. If such were the subject of discourse, then the whole Kingdom of God under the Old Testament dispensation would be changed into a mere semblance and illusion. But the small measure of the condition—with which even God himself cannot dispense, but of which he may vouchsafe a larger measure, viz., the writing of the Law in the heart, whereby man becomes a copy of God, the personal Law—was necessarily accompanied by the small measure of the consequence. The perfect fulfilment of God's promise to Abraham and Israel, to which the prophet here alludes, could, therefore, be expected from the future only.

"And they shall teach no more a man his neighbor, and a man his brother, saying: Know the Lord; for they all shall know me, small and great, saith the Lord; for I will forgive their iniquity, and I will remember their sin no more."—Jeremiah 31:34

Even from ancient times, the first hemistich of the verse has created great embarrassment to interpreters, from which very few of them, not excepting even *Calvin,* manage to extricate themselves skilfully. The declaration that, because all will be taught by God, human instruction in things divine is to cease, has, at first sight, something fanatical in it, and, indeed, was made use of by Anabaptists and other enthusiasts in vindication of their delusion. Many interpreters attempt an evasion, by referring the words to the future life.

But the matter is, indeed, not at all difficult. All that is necessary is to keep in mind that human instruction is here excluded, in so far only as it is opposed to divine instruction concerning God himself; that hence, that which is here spoken of, is *mere* human instruction, by which men are trained and drilled in religion, just as in every other branch of common knowledge, a result of which is, that they may learn forever without ever coming to the knowledge of the truth. Such an instruction may be productive of historical faith, of belief in human authority; but it is just by this, that the nature of religion will be altogether destroyed. Even the true God becomes an idol when he is not known through himself, when he himself does not prepare the heart as a place to dwell in. He is, and remains a mere idea that can impart no strength in the struggle against sin which is a real power, and no comfort in affliction.

Now, such a condition was very frequent under the Old Testament dispensation. The mass of the people possessed only a knowledge of God, which was chiefly, although not exclusively, obtained through human instrumentality. By the New Covenant, richer gifts of the Spirit were to be bestowed, and along with them, the number of those was to be increased who were to partake in them, just as Isaiah (7:16) represents believers under the Old Testament as being taught by the Lord, while in 54:13, in reference to the Messianic time, he announces: "And all thy children shall be taught of the Lord." Under the New Covenant, the antithesis of teaching by God, and teaching by man, is to cease. The teachers do not teach in their own strength, but as servants and instruments of the Lord. It is not they who speak, but the Holy Spirit in them. Those who are taught by them hear the word that comes to them through men, not as man's word, but as God's word; and they receive it, not because it satisfies their limited human reason, but because the Spirit testifies that the Spirit is truth. How this antithesis is done away with, and reconciled in a higher unity, is, among other passages, shown by 2 Corinthians 3:3: "You are an epistle of Christ ministered by us, written not with ink, but with the Spirit of the living God." They are "God-taught," but through the ministry of the Apostle who, in so far as he performs this service, is not different from God, but only a conductor of his power, a channel through which the oil of the Holy Spirit flows to the Church of God (comp. remarks on Zech.

4). The same is taught in 1 John 2:20, 27. The teaching here signifies the human teaching in contrast to that which is divine, such an one as undertakes by its own power to work knowledge in him who is taught. Such a teaching cannot take place under the new covenant. A fundamental knowledge is already imparted to all its members; the Holy Ghost, alone teaches them (John 14:26); He leads them into all truth (John 16:13).

But, just because this is the case, the teaching by means of those whom God has given, in his Church, as apostles, prophets, evangelists, teachers (Eph. 4:11), to whom he has communicated his charisma, is quite in its place. The apostle writes just *because* they know the truth. If it were otherwise, his efforts would be altogether in vain. Of what use is it to give instruction about colors to him who is blind? In things divine, the truth becomes truth to the single individual, only because his knowledge of God is founded on his being in God; and that can be accomplished only by his being connected to God through God. Being, life, and hence, also, real living knowledge, can proceed only from the fountain of all being and life. But in the case of those who are in God, who possess the fundamental knowledge, this knowledge must be developed, carried on, and brought to full consciousness through the instrumentality of those to whom God has granted the gifts for it. A glance into the deep meaning of our passage was obtained by the author of the book *Jelammedenu,* which is quoted by *Abarbanel* (in *Frischmuth,* p. 863); he says: "Under the present dispensation, Israel learns the Law from mortal men, and therefore forgets it; for as flesh and blood pass away (comp. Matt. 16:17, where the antithesis existing between a knowledge of divine things which rests on human ground, and that which rests on divine ground, is brought before us in its strictest form), so also its instruction passes away. But a time shall come when a man shall not learn from the mouth of a man, but from the mouth of the blessed God, for it is written: 'All thy children shall be taught by God.' In these words, it is implied that hitherto the knowledge of the Law was an artificial one obtained by mortal men. But for that reason, it cannot stand long, for the effect stands in proportion to its cause. At the time of the deliverance, however, the knowledge of the law will be obtained in a miraculous manner."

It is, however, quite obvious that this promise, too, must be understood relatively only. All the pious men of the Old Covenant were "God-taught"; and under the New Covenant, the number of those is infinitely great who, through their own guilt, stand to truth in a relation which is entirely or pre-eminently mediate. Instead of the "small," by way of individualization, servants and handmaids are mentioned in Joel 3:2 (2:29; compare remarks on Rev. 11:18).

We have already seen that in the last words of the verse, the fundamental blessing is promised. But whether "for" be referred only to that which immediately precedes, or to everything which goes before amounts to nearly the same thing; for that which immediately precedes includes all the rest. We have before us nothing but designations of the same thing from various aspects; everything depends upon the richer bestowal of the gifts of the Spirit. This has the forgiveness of sins for its necessary foundation; for, before God can give, he must first take. The sins which separate the people and their God from one another, must first be taken away; it is then only that the inward means can be bestowed, so that the people may become truly God's people, and God's name may be sanctified in them.

It is obvious that, here too, a relative difference only between the Old and New Covenant can be spoken of. A covenant-people without forgiveness of sins is no covenant-people; a God with whom there is not forgiveness, in order that he may be feared, who does not heal the bones which he has broken, who in this respect gives promises for the future only, is no God, and no blessing. For if he does not grant this, he cannot grant anything else, inasmuch as everything else implies this, and is of no value without it.

Forgiveness of sins is the essence of the Passover as the feast of the Covenant. On the Ark of the Covenant, it was represented by the Mercy Seat (see *Genuineness of the Pentateuch*, Vol. ii., p. 525f.). Without it the sin-offerings appointed by God are a lie; without it, all that is untrue which God says of himself as the covenant-God, that he is gracious and merciful (Exod. 34:6). The holy Psalmists often acknowledge with praise and thanks that God *has* forgiven sins; compare e.g. Psalm 85:3: "Thou hast taken away the iniquities of thy people, thou hast covered all their sins." In the same manner they are loud in praising the high blessing bestowed upon the individual by the forgiveness of sins; compare Psalm 32:5. The consciousness that their sins are forgiven, forms the foundation of the disposition of heart which we perceive in the Psalmists (see *Commentary on the Psalms,* Vol. iii. p. lxv.f.). "What a confidence, what a joy of tranquil and quiet conscience shines forth in the psalms and prayers of David!"

We have thus before us merely a difference in degree. To the believers of that time, the sin of the covenant-people appeared to be too great to admit of its being forgiven. Driven away from the face of the Lord, so they imagined, it would close its miserable existence in the land of Nod. But, in opposition to such fears, the Prophet declares, in the name of the Lord, that they would not only return, but come, for the first time, in the true and full sense; that where they imagined to behold the end to the forgiveness of sins, there would be its real beginning; that where sin abounded, the grace of God should there so much the more abound. Only, they should not despair, and thus place a barrier in the way of God's mercy. Your God is not a mere hard task-master; he himself will sow and then reap, as surely as He is God, the gracious and merciful One.

BIBLIOGRAPHY

Anderson, Bernard W. "The New Covenant and The Old" in *The Old Testament and Christian Faith* (Bernard W. Anderson, ed.) New York: Harper and Row, 1963, pp. 225-42.

Berkouwer, G. C. "Promise and Fulfillment," in *The Person of Christ,* Grand Rapids: Wm. B. Eerdmans, 1954, pp. 113-52.

Grogan, Geoffrey. "The Experience of Salvation in the Old and New Testaments," *Vox Evangelica* (ed. Donald Guthrie) 1967, 4-26. (A beautiful solution to a key problem in relating the two testaments.)

Kaiser, Walter C. Jr. "The Old Promise and the New Covenant," *Journal of Evangelical Theological Society,* XV (1972).

Verhoef, Pieter A. "The Relationship between the Old and the New Testaments" in *New Perspectives on the Old Testament.* (J. B. Payne, ed.), Waco, Texas: Word Books, 1970, pp. 280-303. (A good survey of the problem.)

Wallis, Wilber B. "Irony in Jeremiah's Prophecy of a New Covenant," *Journal of Evangelical Theological Society,* XII (1969), pp. 107-110. (An interesting suggestion. Note the O.T. passages cited for each of the new covenant's provisions.)

XIV

IMMORTALITY

IN THE OLD TESTAMENT

by James Orr

Editor's Introduction

Were the Hebrews totally in the dark about any sort of future life? Did they live for God in this present life only to face the grim reality of the chilling prospect of the grave as the summation of all their living? Or to use Job's form of the question: if an Old Testament man dies, will he live again?

James Orr, a household name among evangelicals, answered with a solid, "Yes!"

The statement is often made that the Old Testament, especially in the older books, has no distinct doctrine of Immortality. Many explanations have been offered of this difficulty, but I would humbly suggest that the real explanation may be that we have been looking for evidence of that doctrine in a wrong direction. We have been looking for a doctrine of "the immortality of the soul" in the sense of the schools, whereas the real hope of patriarchs and saints, so far as they had one, was, in accordance with the Biblical doctrine already explained, that of restored life in the body.[1]

The early Hebrews had no manner of doubt, any more than we have, that the soul, or spiritual part of man, survived the body.[2] It would be strange if they had, for every other ancient people is known to have had this belief. The Egyptians, e.g., taught that the

---

[1] The view defended in this chapter will be found indicated in Hofmann's *Schriftbeweis*, iii. pp. 461-477; and Dr. P. Fairbairn's *Typology of Scripture*, 3rd ed. i. pp. 343-359.

[2] Cf. Max Muller, *Anthropological Religion*, on "Belief on Immortality in the Old Testament," pp. 367, 377.

dead descended to an under-world, where they were judged by Osiris and his forty-two assessors.[3] The Babylonians and Assyrians conceived of the abode of the dead as a great city having seven encircling walls, and a river flowing round or through it.[4] A name they gave to this city is believed by some to have been *"Sualu,"*[5] the same word as the Hebrew Sheol, which is the name in the Old Testament for the place of departed spirits. It is one of the merits of the Revised Version that it has in many places (why not in all?) printed this word in the text, and tells the reader in the preface that "Sheol," sometimes in the Old Version translated "grave," sometimes "pit," sometimes "hell," means definitely "the abode of departed spirits, and corresponds to the Greek 'Hades,' or the underworld," and does *not* signify "the place of burial." But the thought of going to "Sheol" was no comfort to the good man. The gloomy associations of death hung over this abode; it was figured as a land of silence and forgetfulness; the warm and rich light of the upper-world was excluded from it;[6] no ray of gospel light had as yet been given to chase away its gloom. The idea of "Sheol" was thus not one which attracted, but one which repelled, the mind. Men shrank from it as we do from the breath and cool shades of the charnel-house. The saint, strong in his hope in God, might believe that God would not desert him even in "Sheol"; that his presence and fellowship would be given him even there; but it would only be in moments of strong faith he could thus triumph, and in hours of despondency the gloomiest thoughts were apt to come back on him. His real trust, so far as he was able to cherish one, was that God would not leave his soul in "Sheol," but would redeem him

---

[3] Cf. Renouf, Hibbert Lectures, pp. 195, 196; Budge, *Dwellers on the Nile* ("By-Paths of Bible Knowledge" Series), chap. ix.; Vigouroux's *La Bible et les Découvertes modernes,* iii. pp. 133-141.

[4] Cf. the *Descent of Ishtar,* in Sayce's Hibbert Lectures, Lecture IV.; Budge's *Babylonian Life and History* ("By-Paths of Bible Knowledge" Series), pp. 140-142; Vigouroux, *La Bible et les Découvertes modernes,* iii. pp. 123-132.

[5] Thus F. Delitzsch, and Boscawen in British Museum Lecture on *Sheol, Death, the Grave, and Immortality.* But the identification is held by others to be conjectural (Schrader, *Keilinschriften,* ii. p. 80 [Eng. trans.]; Budge, *Babylonian Life and History,* p. 140, etc.; Vigouroux, iii. p. 125). The Assyrian gives the name as Aralu.

[6] Thus also in the Babylonian and Greek conceptions. Cf. Sayce, Hibbert Lectures, p. 364; Fairbairn, *Studies,* "The Belief in Immortality," pp. 190, 191.

from that state, and restore him to life in the body.[7] His hope was for resurrection.

To illustrate this state of feeling and belief, in regard to the state of the separate existence of the soul, it may be well to cite one or two passages bearing on the subject. An indication of a belief in a future state of the soul is found in an expression several times met with in Genesis—"gathered to his people"—where, in every instance, the gathering to the people (in "Sheol") is definitely distinguished from the act of burial (Gen. 25:8, 9; 35:29; 49:29, 31, 33). Other evidences are afforded by the belief in necromancy, the narratives of resurrection, etc. What kind of place "Sheol" was to the popular imagination is well represented in the words of Job:

> I go whence I shall not return,
> Even to the land of darkness and the shadow of death,
> A land of thick darkness, as darkness itself,
> A land of the shadow of death, without any order,
> And where light is as darkness (Job. 10:21, 22).[8]

There was not much cheer in looking forward to an abode like this, and it is therefore not surprising that even good men, in moments of despondency, when it seemed as if God's presence and favor were taken from them, should moan, as David did:

> Return, O Lord, deliver my soul;
> Save me for Thy loving kindness' sake,
> For in death there is no remembrance of Thee,
> In Sheol who shall give Thee thanks? (Ps. 6:4, 5).

or with Hezekiah:

> Sheol cannot praise Thee, death cannot celebrate Thee:
> They that go down into the pit cannot hope for Thy truth.
> The living, the living, he shall praise Thee, as I do this day
> (Isa. 38:18, 19).

It is not, therefore, in this direction that we are to look for the positive and cheering side of the Old Testament hope of immortality, but in quite another. It is said we have no doctrine of Immortality in the Old Testament. But I reply, we *have* immortality at the very commencement—for man, as he came from the hands of

---

[7] See passages discussed below.

[8] Cf. description in *Descent of Ishtar,* Hibbert Lectures.

his Creator, was made for immortal life. Man in Eden was immortal. He was intended to live, not to die. Then came sin, and with it death. Adam called his son Seth, and Seth called his son Enoch, which means "frail, mortal man." Seth himself died, his son died, his son's son died, and so the line of death goes on. Then comes an interruption, the intervention, as it were, of a higher law, a new inbreaking of immortality into a line of death. "Enoch walked with God, and he was not; for God took him" (Gen. 5:24). Enoch did not die. Every other life in that record ends with the statement, "and he died"; but Enoch's is given as an exception. He did not die, but God "took" him, i.e., without death. He simply "was not" on earth, but he "was" with God in another and invisible state of existence.[9] His case is thus in some respects the true type of all immortality, for it is an immortality of the true personality, in which the body has as real a share as the soul. It agrees with what I have advanced in the Lecture, that it is not an immortality of the soul only that the Bible speaks of—that is left for the philoso-phers—but an immortality of the whole person, body and soul together. Such is the Christian hope, and such, as I shall now try to show, was the Hebrew hope also.

It is a current view that the doctrine of the Resurrection of the dead was a very late doctrine among the Hebrews, borrowed, as many think, from the Persians, during, or subsequent to, the Baby-lonian exile. Dr. Cheyne sees in it an effect of Zoroastrian influence on the religion of Israel.[10] My opinion, on the contrary, is that it is one of the very oldest doctrines in the Bible, the form, in fact, in which the hope of immortality was held, so far as it was held, from the days of the patriarchs downward.[11] In any case, it was a doctrine of very remote antiquity. We find traces of it in many

---

[9] So, later, Elijah.

[10] *Origin of Psalter*, Lecture VIII.; and papers in *The Expository Times* (July and August 1891) on "Possible Zoroastrian Influences on the Religion of Israel."

[11] Thus also Hofmann: "Nothing can be more erroneous than the opinion that the resurrection from the dead is a late idea, first entering through human reflection, the earliest traces of which, if not first given by the Parsees to the Jews, are to be met with in Isaiah and Ezekiel."—*Schriftbeweis*, iii. p. 461. Cf. on this theory of Parsic influence, Pusey's *Daniel*, pp. 512-517.

ancient religions outside the Hebrew, an instructive testimony to the truth of the idea on which it rested. The Egyptians believed, e.g., that the reanimation of the body was essential to perfected existence; and this, according to some, was the thought that underlay the practice of embalming.[12] The ancient Babylonians and Assyrians also had the idea of resurrection. One of their hymns to Merodach celebrates him as the

> Merciful one among the gods,
> Merciful one, who restores the dead to life.[13]

The belief was probably also held by the Persians, though it is still a disputed question whether it is found in the older portions of the Zend-Avesta. That question is not so easily settled as Dr. Cheyne thinks;[14] but in any case the older references are few and ambiguous, and are totally inadequate to explain the remarkable prominence which this doctrine assumed in the Old Testament. [15] The Bible has a coherent and consistent doctrine of its own upon the subject, and is not dependent on doubtful allusions in Zoroastrain texts for its clear and bold statements of the final swallowing up of death in victory. Let me briefly review some of the lines of evidence.

I have referred already to the case of Enoch in the beginning of

---

12 "There is a chapter with a vignette representing the soul uniting itself to the body, and the text promises that they shall never again be separated."—Renouf, Hibbert Lectures, p. 188. "They believed," says Budge, "that the soul would revisit the body after a number of years, and therefore it was absolutely necessary that the body should be preserved, if its owner wished to live for ever with the gods."—Dwellers on the Nile, p. 156.

13 Cf. Boscawen, British Museum Lecture, pp. 23, 24; Sayce, pp. 98-100; Cheyne, Origin of Psalter, p. 392. There is no evidence, however, of a general hope of resurrection.

14 Cf. Pusey, pp. 512-517; and Cheyne's own citations from recent scholars, Origin of Psalter, pp. 425, 451. M. Montet formerly held that the germs of the doctrine came from Zoroastrianism, but "in 1890, in deference, it would seem, to M. Harlez, and in opposition not less to Spiegel than to Gelder, he pronounces the antiquity of the resurrection doctrine in Zoroastrianism as yet unproven."—Cheyne, p. 451. Cf. Schultz, Alttest. Theol. p. 762.

15 Anyone can satisfy himself on this head by consulting the passages for himself in the Zend-Avesta, in Sacred Books of the East. The indices to the three volumes give only one reference to the subject, and that to one of a few undated "Miscellaneous Fragments" at the end. Professor Cheyne himself can say no more than that "Mills even thinks that there is a trace of the doctrine of the Resurrection in the Gathas. . . . He (Zoraster) may have had a vague conception of the revival of bodies, but not a theory."—Origin of Psalter, p. 438.

the history, as illustrative of the Biblical idea of immortality. As respects the patriarchs, the references to their beliefs and hopes are necessarily few and inferential, a fact which speaks strongly for the early date and genuineness of the tradition. The New Testament signalizes them as men of "faith," and certainly their conduct is that of men who accounting themselves "strangers and pilgrims" on the earth, look for a future fulfilment of the promises as of something in which they have a personal interest (Heb. 11:13). Not improbably it was some hope of resurrection which inspired (as with the Egyptians) their great care for their dead, and prompted the injunctions left by Jacob and Joseph regarding the interment of their "bones" in the land of promise (Gen. 1:5, 25; Exod. 13:19; Heb. 11:22). It is significant that the Epistle to the Hebrews connects Abraham's sacrifice of Isaac with his faith in a resurrection. "By faith Abraham, being tried, offered up Isaac . . . accounting that God is able to raise up, even from the dead; from whence also he did in a parable receive him back."[16] The Rabbis drew a curious inference from God's word to Abraham, "I will give *to thee,* and to thy seed after thee, the land wherein thou art a stranger" (Gen. 17:8). "But it appears," they argued, "that Abraham and the other patriarchs did not possess that land; therefore it is of necessity that they should be raised up to enjoy the good promises, else the promises of God should be vain and false. So that here we have a proof, not only of the immortality of the soul, but also of the foundation of the law—namely, the resurrection of the dead."[17] If this be thought fanciful, I would refer to the teaching of a greater than the Rabbis. Reasoning with the Sadducees, Jesus quotes that saying of God to Moses, "I am the God of Abraham, and the God of Isaac, and the God of Jacob," adding, "God is not the God of the dead, but of the living" (Matt. 22:23). The point to be observed is that Jesus quotes this passage, not simply in proof of the continued subsistence of the patriarchs in some state of being, but in proof of the resurrection of the dead. And how does it prove that? Only on the ground, which Jesus assumes, that the relation of

---

[16] Heb. 11:17-19; cf. Hofmann, pp. 461, 462.

[17] Quoted in Fairbairn, i. p. 353.

the believer to God carries with it a *whole* immortality, and this, as we have seen, implies life in the body. If God is the God of Abraham and Isaac and Jacob, this covenant relation pledges to these patriarchs not only continuance of existence, but Redemption from the power of death, i.e., resurrection.

It is, however, when we come to the later books—the book of Job, the Psalms, the Prophets—that we get clearer light on the form which the hope of immortality assumed in the minds of Old Testament believers; and it may be affirmed with considerable confidence that this light is all, or nearly all, in favor of the identification of this hope with the hope of resurrection. I take first the book of Job, because, whenever written, it relates to patriarchal times, or at least moves in patriarchal conditions. The first remarkable passage in this book is in Chapter 14. This chapter raises the very question we are now dealing with, and it is noteworthy that the form in which it does so is the possibility of bodily revival. First, Job enumerates the appearances which seem hostile to man's living again (vv. 7-12). Then faith, rising in her very extremity, reasserts herself against doubt and fear:

> Oh that Thou wouldest hide me in Sheol,
> That Thou wouldest keep me secret, till Thy wrath be past,
> That Thou wouldest appoint me a set time, and remember me!
> If a man die, shall he live again?
> All the days of my warfare would I wait,
> Till my release should come.
> Thou shouldest call, and I would answer Thee,
> Thou wouldest have a desire to the work of Thy hands.[18]

There seems no reasonable room for question that what is before Job's mind here is the thought of resurrection. A. B. Davidson explains: "On this side death he has no hope of a return to God's favor. Hence, contemplating that he shall die under God's anger, his thought is that he might remain in Sheol till God's wrath be past, for He keepeth not His anger forever; that God would appoint him

---

18 Job 14:13-15 (R.V.). The margin translates as in A.V., "Thou shalt call," etc. As remarked, the form in which the question is put in this passage is as significant as the answer to it. It implies that revived existence in the body is the only form in which the patriarch contemplated immortality. Life and even sensation in Sheol are presupposed in v. 22.

a period to remain in death, and then remember him with returning mercy, and call him back again to His fellowship. But to his mind this involves a complete return to life again of the whole man (v. 14), for in death there is no fellowship with God (Ps. 6:5). Thus his solution, though it appears to his mind only as a momentary gleam of light, is broader than that of the Psalmist, and corresponds to that made known in subsequent revelation."[19]

The second passage in Job is the well-known one in Chapter 19, translated in the Revised Version thus:

> But I know that my Redeemer liveth,
> And that He shall stand up at the last upon the earth [Heb. *dust*].
> And after my skin hath been thus destroyed,
> Yet from my flesh shall I see God:
> Whom I shall see for myself,
> And mine eyes shall behold and not another (Job. 19:25-27).

I do not enter into the many difficulties of this passage, but refer only to the crucial line, "Yet from my flesh shall I see God." The margin gives as another rendering, "without my flesh," but this is arrived at only as an interpretation of the word "from," which is literally the one used. The natural meaning would therefore seem to be, "Yet from [or out of] my flesh shall I see God," which implies that he will be clothed with flesh.[20] Dr. Davidson allows the admissibility of this rendering, and says: "If therefore we understand the words 'from my flesh' in the sense of *in* my flesh, we must suppose that Job anticipated being clothed in a new body after death. Something may be said for this view. Undoubtedly, in 14:13 *seq.*, Job clearly conceived the idea of being delivered from Sheol and living again, and fervently prayed that such a thing might be. And what he there ventured to long for, he might here speak of as a thing of which he was assured. No violence would be done to the line of thought in the book by this supposition." Yet he thinks "it is highly improbable that the great thought of the resurrection of the body could be referred to in a way so brief," and so prefers

---

[19] *Com. on Job, in loc.* (Cambridge Series). I can scarcely agree that Job's solution is broader than that of the Psalmist's. See below.

[20] Cf. Pusey, p. 508, and Vigouroux, iii. pp. 172-180.

the rendering "without."[21] I think, however, this is hardly a sufficient reason to outweigh the tremendously strong fact that we have already this thought of resurrection conceded in Chapter 14, and, further, that the thought of living again in the body seemed the only way in which Job there could conceive the idea of immortality. If that is so, it may explain why more stress is not laid upon resurrection here. The hope which absorbs all Job's thought is that of "seeing God," and the fact that, if he does so at all, he must do it "in" or "from" the flesh, is taken for granted as a thing of course.[22]

The question of the testimony of the Psalms is greatly simplified by the large concessions which writers like Dr. Cheyne are now ready to make, in the belief that in the references to resurrection doctrine they have a proof of "Zoroastrian influences." The passages, however, are happily of an order that speak for themselves, and need no forcing to yield us their meaning. A conspicuous example is Psalm 16:8-11, cited in the New Testament as a prophecy of the resurrection of Christ:

> I have set the Lord always before me:
> Because He is at my right hand, I shall not be moved.
> Therefore my heart is glad, and my glory rejoiceth;
> My flesh also shall dwell in safety [or *confidently*],
> For Thou wilt not leave my soul to Sheol;
> Neither wilt Thou suffer Thine Holy One to see corruption [or *the pit*].
> Thou wilt show me the path of life:
> In Thy presence is fulness of joy;
> In Thy right hand there are pleasures for evermore.[23]

Another passage is in Psalm 17:15, where, after describing the apparent prosperity of the wicked, the Psalmist says:

> As for me, I shall behold Thy face in righteousness:
> I shall be satisfied, when I awake, with Thy likeness.

---

21 *Commentary on Job,* Appendix on chap. 19:23-27, p. 292.

22 Dr. Davidson's remark, "On Old Testament ground, and in the situation of Job, such a matter-of-course kind of reference is almost inconceivable" (p. 292), involves the very point at issue.

23 See Acts 2:24-31. Cf. Delitzsch, *in loc.;* and Cheyne, *Origin of the Psalter,* p. 431.

The "awakening" here, as Delitzsch says, can only be that from the sleep of death.[24] Yet more distinct is Psalm 49:14, 15:

> They [the wicked] are appointed as a flock for Sheol:
> Death shall be their shepherd:
> And the upright shall have dominion over them in the morning;
> And their beauty shall be for Sheol to consume, that there be no habitation for it.
> But God will redeem my soul from the power [hand] of Sheol:
> For He shall receive me.

There is here again, it is believed, clear reference to the "morning" of the resurrection. The passage is the more significant that in the last words, as well as in Psalm 73:24, there is direct allusion to the case of Enoch. " 'God,' says the Psalmist, 'shall redeem my soul from the hand of Hades, for He shall take me,' as He took Enoch, and as He took Elijah, to Himself."[25] Psalm 73:24 reads thus:

> Nevertheless I am continually with Thee:
> Thou hast holden my right hand.
> Thou shalt guide me with Thy counsel,
> And afterward receive me to glory.
> Whom have I in heaven but Thee?
> And there is none on the earth that I desire beside Thee.
> My flesh and my heart faileth:
> But God is the strength of my heart and my portion for ever.

These, and a few others, are the passages usually cited in favor of the doctrine of Immortality in the book of Psalms, and it will be seen that in all of them this hope is clothed in a form which implies a resurrection.[26]

I need not delay on the passages in the prophetic books, for here

---

[24] *Com., in loc.* Thus also Pusey, Perowne, Cheyne, Hofmann, etc. "The awakening," says Cheyne, "probably means the passing of the soul into a resurrection body."—*Origin of Psalter,* p. 406.

[25] Perowne, *in loc.* Thus also Pusey, Delitzsch, Cheyne, etc. "The 'dawn,' " says Cheyne, "is that of the resurrection day."—*Expository Times,* ii. p. 249; cf. *Origin of Psalter,* pp. 382, 406, 407. Delitzsch, in note of Ps. 16:8-11, says: "Nor is the awakening in 49:15 some morning or other that will very soon follow upon the night, but the final morning, which brings deliverance to the upright, and enables them to obtain dominion."

[26] Or if not resurrection, then immortality in the body without tasting of death, as Enoch. But this is a hope the Old Testament believer could hardly have cherished for himself. The view of deliverance *from* death seems therefore the more probable in Ps. 49:15, etc. A very different view is taken by Schultz in his *Alttestamentliche Theologie,*

it is usually granted that the idea of resurrection is familiar. Not only is the restoration of the Jewish people frequently presented under this figure, but a time is coming when, for the Church as a whole, including the individuals in it, death shall be swallowed up in victory. We have a passage already in Hosea, which is beyond suspicion of Zoroastrian influence:

> After two days will He revive us:
> On the third day He will raise us up, and we shall live
> before Him.

And again:

> I will ransom them from the power of Sheol;
> I will redeem them from death:
> O death, where are thy plagues?
> O grave, where is thy destruction?[27]

The climax of this class of passages is reached in Isaiah 25:6-8; 26:19. (Cf. also Ezek. 37:1-10, the vision of the dry bones.)[28]

The last Old Testament passage I will quote is an undisputed one, and has the special feature of interest that in it for the first time mention is made of the resurrection of the wicked as well as of the just. It is that in Daniel 12:2: "And many of them that sleep in the dust of the earth shall awake, some to everlasting life, and some to shame and everlasting contempt." This needs no comment.

From the whole survey I think it will be evident that I was entitled to say that from the first the manner in which the hope of immortality was conceived by holy men in Israel was that of a resurrection. Yet, when all is said, we cannot but feel that it was

---

pp. 753-758. Schultz not only sees no proof of the resurrection in the passages we have quoted, but will not even allow that they have any reference to a future life. So extreme a view surely refutes itself. It is at least certain that if these passages teach a future life, it is a life in connection with the body.

27 Hos. 6:2, 13:14. Cf. Cheyne, p. 383.

28 On the passages in Isaiah, Cheyne remarks: "Instead of swallowing up, Sheol in the Messianic period shall itself be swallowed up. And this prospect concerns not merely the church-nation, but all of its believing members, and indeed all, whether Jews or not, who submit to the true King, Jehovah."—*Origin of Psalter,* p. 402. Cf. *Expository Times,* ii. p. 226. In Ezekiel, the subject is national resurrection, but "that the power of God *can,* against all human thought and hope, reanimate the dead, is the general idea of the passage, from which consequently the hope of a literal resurrection of the dead may naturally be inferred."—Oehler, *Theology of Old Testament,* ii. p. 395 (Eng. trans.). Oehler does more justice to these passages than Schultz.

but a *hope*—not resting on express revelation, but springing out of the consciousness of the indissoluble relation between God and the believing soul, and the conviction that God's Redemption will be a complete one. Life and immortality were not yet brought to light as they are now by Christ in his gospel (2 Tim. 1:10). The matter is unexceptionably stated by A. B. Davidson in the following words, with which I conclude: "The human spirit is conscious of fellowship with God; and this fellowship, from the nature of God, is a thing imperishable, and, in spite of obscurations, it must yet be fully manifested by God. This principle, grasped with convulsive earnestness in the prospect of death, became the Hebrew doctrine of Immortality. This doctrine was but the necessary corollary of religion. In this life the true relations of men to God were felt to be realized; and the Hebrew faith of immortality—never a belief in the mere existence of the soul after death, for the lowest superstition assumed this—was a faith that the dark and mysterious event of death would not interrupt the life of the person with God, enjoyed in this world. . . . The doctrine of Immortality in the Book (of Job) is the same as that of other parts of the Old Testament. Immortality is the corollary of religion. If there be religion—that is, if God be—there is immortality, not of the soul, but of the whole personal being of man (Ps. 16:9). This teaching of the whole Old Testament is expressed by our Lord with a surprising incisiveness in two sentences—'I am the *God* of Abraham. God is not the God of the dead but of the *living.*' "

BIBLIOGRAPHY

Dahood, Mitchell, "Death, Resurrection, and Immortality," in *The Anchor Bible: Psalm III: 101-150.* Garden City: Doubleday & Company, 1970, xli-lii. (This material will be much maligned and greatly debated for years to come, but never forgotten.)

Davis, John D. "The Future Life in Hebrew Thought," *Princeton Theological Review,* VI (1908), pp. 246-68. (Great article for Ancient Near Eastern comparisons.)

Honsey, Ralph E. "Exegetical Paper on Job 19:23-27," *Wisconsin Lutheran Quarterly* (1970), pp. 153-206.

Schep, J. A. *The Nature of the Resurrection Body.* Grand Rapids: Wm. B. Eerdmans, 1964, pp. 17-63. (Superb on "flesh" and "body" in O.T. There is also an analysis of a dozen texts in the O.T.)

Smick, Elmer, "The Bearing of the New Philological Data on the Subject of Resurrection and Immortality in the Old Testament," *Westminster Theological Journal* XXXI (1968), 12-21.